WENSLEY CLARSKON is one of Britain's most knowledgeable writers when it comes to the criminal underworld. His books – published in more than thirty countries – have sold almost two million copies. He has also written movie screenplays and made numerous TV documentaries in the UK, US and Spain.

www.wensleyclarkson.com

Also by Wensley Clarkson

THE CURSE OF BRINK'S-MAT
HASH
COCAINE CONFIDENTIAL
LEGAL HIGHS

SEXY BEASTS

THE REAL INSIDE STORY OF
THE HATTON GARDEN MOB

WENSLEY CLARKSON

Quercus

First published in Great Britain in 2016 by Quercus Editions Ltd
This paperback edition published in Great Britain in 2016 by

Quercus Editions Ltd
Carmelite House
50 Victoria Embankment
London EC4Y 0DZ
An Hachette UK company

A CIP catalogue record for this book is available
from the British Library

PB ISBN 978 1 78429 816 6
Ebook ISBN 978 1 78429 815 9

Every effort has been made to contact copyright holders.
However, the publishers will be glad to rectify in future editions
any inadvertent omissions brought to their attention.

Diagram of

'*We was the original Sexy Beasts. We pulled every bird in sight. We blew every penny we had. We lived it up. There was this aura of invincibility around us. We was untouchable. Mind you, there was no DNA, computers, or even mobile fuckin' phones back then.*'

Billy, retired South London robber

To 'Billy'

Without him this story could not have been told.
Just a shame I can't use his real name to thank him!

THE SEXY BEASTS

'When you think about it we must have been crackers, we got to be stone crackers.'
Terry Perkins, Hatton Garden gang member

The Guv'nor

Sharp as a razor but feeling his age

The Fixer

Old man on a mission

The Muscles

The Big I Am who wanted to conquer the world

The Lookout

Not the brightest old tool in the box

The Ghost

Coolest customer you'll ever meet

The Sidekick

Lost his bottle when it really mattered

The Fish

Out of his depth and paid the price

The Friendly Face

Charming Irishman with a gift of the gab

CONTENTS

PART THREE

THE JUSTICE

Hatton Garden heist: how it happened

The building where the theft took place was made up of a number of businesses, with a communal entrance. The safety deposit business was in the basement.

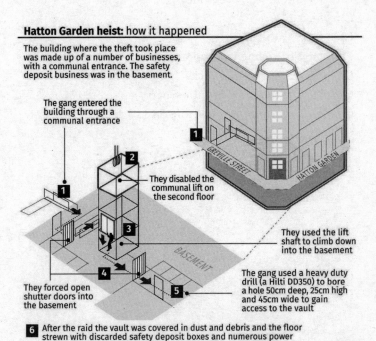

The gang entered the building through a communal entrance

1

2 They disabled the communal lift on the second floor

3

They used the lift shaft to climb down into the basement

4 They forced open shutter doors into the basement

5 The gang used a heavy duty drill (a Hilti DD350) to bore a hole 50cm deep, 25cm high and 45cm wide to gain access to the vault

GREVILLE STREET

HATTON GARDEN

BASEMENT

6 After the raid the vault was covered in dust and debris and the floor strewn with discarded safety deposit boxes and numerous power tools, including an angle grinder, concrete drills and crowbars

Source: Metropolitan Police PA

PROLOGUE

JULY 2015

A yellowy, elderly bald man wearing spectacles – with an over-dyed auburn *Paul McCartney-rinse* and covered in liver spots – pumped away desperately on a cycling machine in his baggy shorts and sleeveless string vest like a sagging tortoise without it's shell, seemingly oblivious to all around him.

In another corner of the same gym, a slightly younger, fitter looking man with streaked blonde hair, orange spray-on tan and Rod Stewart mullet danced nonchalantly up and down. He threw a few casual air punches in the direction of a flaccid brown leather punch bag, hanging by a thick link chain from the ceiling. Then he fired up with a surprisingly vicious flurry of left-hand jabs, followed by a straight right, which made the bag swing forward and almost hit him.

That brought a knowing smile to the face of a blubbery giant of an old man with a crew cut and a crumpled triple chin in an orange T-shirt lying flat on his back struggling to perform a bench press. He looked exhausted; as if he might be having second thoughts and was about to collapse on the settee in the far corner of the gym, which had been put there for precisely that purpose.

The man in the orange T-shirt puffed up his cheeks and

blew out a big, noisy mouthful of rancid breath, slammed his weights noisily down on the ground, struggled to his feet and stomped out of the gym without saying a word to the others, who looked across at him while rolling their eyes at each other and shaking their heads.

I watched them all from the lobby while waiting to meet that same old boy in the orange T-shirt. He'd contacted me through an armed robber from South East London, who'd helped me with another book I wrote a few years back.

My man – we'll call him Billy in order to protect his identity – was well above average height and now changed out of his gym gear, he wore a black tracksuit with a white stripe down either side of the trouser legs, rounded off with black trainers. Billy later told me some of his fellow residents complained that this outfit made him look like a cat burglar, which most of them would know all about.

Billy made me promise on my family's life that I would never reveal his true identity because he didn't want anyone to think he was a snitch. For that reason I can't even give away the location of the old folks home where he now lives, except to say it gets less all-year-round sunshine than almost anywhere else in Europe. I heard it was discretely financed by a 'collective' of London gangsters. They wanted a final destination for themselves and exactly the sort of elderly villains who pulled off the Hatton Garden job in such spectaclar fashion in April 2015.

Despite Billy's bulky frame – to which frequent nocturnal excursions into alcohol, gourmet food and a wide variety of illegal substances had no doubt contributed – his vice-like handshake clearly proved he'd retained considerable power and strength for a man approaching his 79th year.

PROLOGUE

Billy's chin jutted out just far enough to usually point in the direction he was moving. His thin top lip was covered by part of a goatee he'd worn since growing out his moustache in the summer of 1977, when he'd been a member of one of South London's most notorious armed robbery gangs. Billy had needed an instant new look because his photofit was circulating the capital's police stations at the time.

Billy's life of crime had taken off back in the so-called Swinging Sixties. In those days, London and the South East of England was still evolving into what it has become today, the Wild West of Europe; a frontier zone full of deadly mavericks from all four corners of the globe; one of the fastest growing countries in the world, where black money still rules, thanks mainly to the latest mishmash of foreigners, who've haemorraged into the Garden of England, aka Kent, via the ports of Dover and Folkestone. Those famous white cliffs now mark the entry point for everyone from dodgy Russian billionaires to Moldovan pimps.

'First of all,' Billy told me breathlessly as we settled down on a sofa in the tiny sitting room of his apartment. 'I want to go through the history of it all because then the readers of your book will really appreciate the professionalism that went into this job.'

Billy told me the blatant greed of the foreign gangsters who now invaded our shores had helped convince his mates it was now or never to pull off the Hatton Garden Job. Two of those involved had blown their approaching old age to smithereens on golf courses and in tatty bars on Spain's so-called Costa del Crime, only to return brasso broke to Blighty.

But then these sort of old-fashioned, postwar crooks that London and South East England is still famous for didn't exactly qualify for state pensions. They hadn't signed up on the social

3

like most others because their annual income had always been derived from robbing banks, holding up security vans, and, sometimes, even boatloads of drugs.

Billy told me he and his associates had grown tired of those moments when they'd wake up and wish they'd pulled off that one last *Big Job*. These characters knew all about skeletons in the closet because they had a whole graveyard filled with them.

'Yeah. I was gonna be on that team,' explained Billy, in a gruff, deadpan voice. 'Then I got sick.'

It turned out Billy's life had altered drastically – virtually overnight – like the flick of a switchblade when he got a blood clot on his lung. He'd had no choice but to pull out of joining his pals on what was going to be the Hatton Garden Job.

Now – not long after it was carried out in such spectacular circumstances – Billy felt able to tell me the real story behind the raid. His contribution to this book has turned out to be invaluable because it helps give it another dimension, by opening up the story in so many different directions.

As Billy told me: 'This job had been waiting more than 30 years to be done. We all knew about that vault. And of course we'd all talked about it when we was locked up together. That's what happens in prisons. You work out yer next crimes. But this one was a bleedin' long time coming!'

Billy stopped in mid-sentence, got up from the sofa and walked across the floor of his apartment, opened the draw of a sideboard and pulled out a big leather bound album, which contained hundreds of carefully cut and pasted newspaper cuttings.

'I've followed every moment of it. I s'pose you could say I've lived that job through the lads themselves, even though I didn't go on it in the end.'

I was about to hear how a bunch of old men planned and executed a criminal enterprise that would overshadow everything from the Great Train Robbery to the Brinks-Mat gold bullion heist.

As the memories of what might have been began flooding through his mind, Billy's eyes lit up and he smiled whistfully.

Then his voice crackled as he quietly said: 'Lookin' back on it, the lads must have been fuckin' mad to try and pull it off. But there was no stoppin' 'em'.'

Billy is just one of many professional criminals I've met over the past 25 years. In the main, they're reasonable men to deal with, despite their fearsome reputations. However that's not to say there haven't been a few tricky moments. By a strange twist of fate, one of those occasions was a meeting with the so-called mastermind of the Hatton Garden Mob, Brian Reader.

My connection to Reader goes back almost 20 years to the early summer of 1997 in the most unlikely of places; the deserted hinterlands of North Cyprus. A strange unwelcoming Turkish-run bolthole in the Mediterranean, where there is no extradition treaty with the UK. This makes it the perfect destination of choice for professional criminals from London, who need to lie low for a while. It's said that there are now more British villains on the north side of this partitioned island than anywhere else in the world, apart from Spain's so-called Costa del Crime and Thailand.

Little wonder that Brian Reader – then an old time South London safe cracker and stolen gold bullion handler – chose to flee to North Cyprus in the violent aftermath of the Brink's-Mat robbery in the early 1990s. He had other criminals on his tail and had left London 'in a hurry' after his release from prison.

I'd flown to North Cyprus in pursuit of Reader's old friend

and criminal associate Kenneth Noye – who was at that time the subject of a book I was writing and a TV documentary. Perhaps not so surprisingly, Reader and his associates were less than welcoming when I turned up in the dusty driveway of a vast building development site on a swelteringly hot morning in May, 1997.

'Fuck off,' were the only words Reader uttered in response when I introduced myself. When I pressed him further, another man from his entourage grabbed an iron bar out from behind a bush and said: 'You got ten seconds mate, then I'm gonna turn you into mincemeat.'

Another of Brian Reader's associates then gave me what can only be described as a 'death stare', so I immediately retreated. Later I learned that a timeshare holiday development he was building at the time eventually ground to a halt and was sold unfinished to a local businessman. Reader apparently lost a fortune on that business, as did a bunch of his associates. Going straight had cost Reader a lot of cash, it seemed.

So by the time 2012 came along, Brian Reader was just another old age pensioner with a dodgy past and an even dodgier ticker, struggling to make ends meet and rattling around in a big house in the drab town of Dartford, close to the border between Reader's beloved South East London and Kent. His friends say he was desperately lonely after the death from cancer of Lyn, his wife of forty-five years.

Reader had tried to deal with his isolation by joining a local 'Monday Club' for widowed pensioners. He must have found it a strange experience talking to other elderly people about the more mundane things in life.

Reader even tried to raise some money by building two houses in the large back garden of that big house in Dartford. But that project went way over budget and the houses were never properly completed. So, in his mid-seventies, widower Brian Reader decided to push ahead with having one last crack at what he did best. That meant utilizing the skills he'd honed for more than 50 years on the streets of London and the South East of England.

Reader had been obsessed for more than thirty years with breaking into a vault in the heart of an area of London closely connected to many of his most lucrative criminal enterprises. So he joined forces with another legendary criminal 'face' from the same 'profession' and they set out to hand-pick a team to pull off the crime of the century.

And that is how *The Hatton Garden Job* was born.

SKY-NEWS REPORT – APRIL 8, 2015

Gems stolen in one of the largest and most daring jewellery heists ever will already be out of the country, a former Flying Squad chief believes.

Jewellery and precious stones, which could be worth millions of pounds, were snatched by thieves from a vault in Hatton Garden, London, over the weekend.

The audacious villains are believed to have broken into the building through the roof and abseiled down a lift shaft to access the vault.

A statement from the Metropolitan Police said heavy cutting equipment was then used to get into a vault at the premises, where sixty to seventy safe boxes were raided.

The vault is believed to be reinforced with thick metal and concrete protection doors, up to two feet thick.

Speaking to Sky News earlier, former Flying Squad chief Barry Phillips described the heist as 'sophisticated' and 'highly organised'.

He said the robbery will have been carried out by a 'professional team'.

'This has all the hallmarks of a TV or Hollywood film production,' Mr Phillips said.

'It's highly likely that any gems or jewellery will have already been sourced and out of the country.

'That takes a high degree of organization on behalf of the villains.'

Neil Duttson, a diamond dealer who buys stones for pri-

vate clients, said tracing any gems stolen in the heist would be nearly impossible.

He said: 'Once diamonds have been recut and polished there is no geological map. I imagine they will be sat on for six months. You can expect some cheap diamonds will be coming on the market soon.'

Police have not put a value on the goods stolen, but estimates vary widely from hundreds of thousands of pounds to £200 million.

Sky's Crime Correspondent Martin Brunt said: 'The suspects have had perhaps several days [over the Easter weekend] in which to get in. One report, I'm told, suggested that they used a lift shaft at some stage to get into the centre, which must be pretty heavily protected.'

Hatton Garden is known as London's jewellery quarter and the safe deposit boxes are mainly used by local jewellers to store loose diamonds in packets.

Other boxes – around 10 per cent of them – are rented by private individuals and so the true value of the heist may never be known.

Sky News' veteran crime correspondent Martin Brunt instantly realized the Hatton Garden Job had all the ingredients of a great story. A classic old-fashioned criminal enterprise. No one hurt. And a massive payday for the team of villains who'd pulled it off. This one was going to run and run.

But not even Brunt could have predicted that the Hatton Garden Job would end up being hailed as the Crime of the Century.

PART
ONE

THE
HISTORY

The bandit is an outsider and a rebel, a poor man who refuses to accept the normal rules of poverty and establishes his freedom by means of the only resources within the reach of the poor, strength, bravery, cunning and determination. This draws him close to the poor; he is one of them. It sets him in opposition to the hierarchy of power, wealth and influence: he is not one of them.

E.J. Hobsbawm, author of *Bandits*

CHAPTER ONE

CRIME'S LABYRINTH

In the middle of a road on the boundary between London's Clerkenwell and Hatton Garden – in the place once known as Little Italy – is a manhole cover through which you can hear the sound of the River Fleet, which still flows beneath this part of the city. Warrior monks once had a wharf upon the Fleet where they moored their ships, returning weary from distant lands to tend verdant estates upon the hillsides descending to the river valley. In time, these religious communities gave way to Renaissance palaces, superseded by prisons for the unacceptable people and fine brick terraces for the artisans, all surrounded by squalor and thievery, as this fast expanding area overcame plagues and fires while the river delved through its midst.

This spider's web of subterranean streets and tunnels fifty feet beneath what today is Hatton Garden have provided criminals with an escape route for at least the past 500 years. Traders who work in the area often say they're amazed the whole place hasn't caved in from the weight of the gold and heavy metal above all these ancient, watery passageways honeycombing the ground beneath their feet.

Walk through the streets of Hatton Garden at any time of the day or night and you cannot fail to notice the history of this ancient district of London. Down the narrow alleyways and cobbled streets winding between the tall buildings strode many names from English history, including the most famous crime writer of all, Charles Dickens.

Round the corner from Hatton Garden itself is number 48 Doughty Street – once the London home of Dickens. His two eldest children were born here and it's where he wrote many of his most famous books, inspired by his real-life experiences in Hatton Garden, Bloomsbury and Holborn.

Fagin's Kitchen in *Oliver Twist* was located at number 8 Saffron Hill and owned in real-life by De Beers, until it was demolished to make way for an office block in the late 1980s. Dickens based the notorious Fagin on a man called Ikey Soloman, a well-known fence and criminal who ran a gang of pickpocketing children stealing for food, clothing and shelter.

Number 54 Hatton Garden was the police court house featured in *Oliver Twist* and presided over by lawmaker Mr Fang, who in real life was the cold and calculating magistrate, Mr A. S. Laing. Dickens used some clever subterfuge in order to meet the hated magistrate, which provoked such a violent outburst of anger from Laing that he was subsequently removed from his post. Dickens also frequently visited The One Tun pub in Saffron Hill and 'converted' many of those real-life regulars into characters for his books.

But you have to step back another 300 years to find out why this area was called Hatton Garden in the first place. Just off Ely Place is a narrow alleyway leading through to Hatton Garden known as Mitre Alley. Midway along this alley is a pub called the The Olde Mitre Tavern, built by Bishop Goodrich of Ely in 1546 to entertain his servants. It was constructed around a cherry tree and it's where Elizabeth I had secret trysts with her lover Sir Christopher Hatton before she gave him the land now known as Hatton Garden.

Hatton was a bit of a celebrity landowner back in those days, thanks in part to sponsoring Sir Francis Drake's round-the-world voyage. After his death and following the Great Fire of London in the 1660s, Hatton's family began building houses on what was then still known as Hatton Street. It would only be renamed Hatton Garden 200 years later.

But crime has always been in the heart and soul of Hatton Garden . . .

On a Sunday evening in December 1678, a Hatton Garden-based carpenter called Wartton, opened his front door to six armed men. They said they were looking for Catholics, but when he asked to see their warrant, one of them said there was no time to show him as 'the Traytors might escape'. After searching every room in the house, the gang of men declared: 'It was money we came for, and money we will have.' Then they opened Wartton's front door to 'about half a score' of their accomplices, and warned the household there was no point making any fuss because others in the gang were outside watching the streets.

Wartton and his family were locked in a room while the thieves ripped through the house. The gang eventually made off with his daughter's rings (valued at £100) and 380 ounces of plate.

The following Tuesday a woman offered to sell 'a considerable parcel of Plate' to a Hatton Garden trader and took him to a house in nearby Shoe Lane. But the trader had informed the authorities, who raided the house, arrested five men and found the stolen plate in the cellar. The thieves were dispatched to Newgate prison where one managed to escape dressed in woman's clothes, despite being weighed down with sixty-pound irons. The others were executed at Tyburn Gate.

Late in the eighteenth century, a Bedfordshire labourer called William Smith (just over five feet tall, with grey eyes and a 'fresh complexion', according to the criminal register) was tried for a 'singular and daring' robbery committed on a banker's clerk in Hatton Garden. By this time robberies in the area were so commonplace that the police virtually gave up patrolling the streets.

In November 1881, the Hatton Garden post office was robbed of a mailbag containing registered letters and packets, including a large consignment of diamonds destined for the continent. The value of goods stolen was estimated at £80,000, which is more than £60 million in today's currency.

At the end of the nineteenth century, De Beers chose to sell all its diamonds through Hatton Garden, creating a culture of related trades that persists to this day. As a result, it attracted a tight-knit community of Hasidic Jews, who were the master-craftsmen able to produce a wide range of jewellery.

Then in 1913 came the Hatton Garden pearl robbery. It set the scene for a century of hard-hitting crimes – high-profile thefts of large sums and valuables that required detailed planning and a team to carry them out. On this occasion, the target was 'the most famous necklace of pearls in the world', valued by Lloyd's at £150,000. It had been sent from Paris to a Hatton Garden trader called Max Mayer, but when he opened the registered package, he found it contained eleven sugar lumps. The mastermind of this cunning plot was diamond merchant Joseph 'Cammi' Grizzard, who was caught after a sting operation and given seven years penal servitude; shorter sentences in those days, but harsher regimes.

Until the Second World War, business in Hatton Garden was

often conducted on the street, or in one of several local kosher cafes. Prices were usually agreed with a handshake and a cry of 'Mazel'. It wasn't until after the war that a plethora of jewellery shops opened in Hatton Garden, shifting the business away from manufacturing for the wholesale market towards the retail trade, especially for engagement and wedding rings. In all, at least 300 separate companies and sixty shops – many of them run by Orthodox Jews – emerged by the 1950s.

Back then, Hatton Garden's reputation was built around its dealers in precious stones, which were nearly always diamonds. So not surprisingly, security became of paramount importance to all local traders.

At the start of holidays such as Easter and Passover, many of those with workshops and offices perched above the jewellers that lined Hatton Garden itself made the short walk to 88–90 Hatton Garden, where a well-respected local company called the Hatton Garden Safe Deposit Limited ran an underground vault from 1954. It had been specially constructed ten years earlier and provided metal boxes for traders to store their valuables in.

The company who owned the vault even persuaded BBC TV to film a news item after they took it over since it was the biggest and most unique vault in the country at that time. That black-and-white footage shows fashionable furniture in an office that led to the vault, which helped make the location look glamorous and, even more importantly, safe.

The vault soon proved extremely popular as many dealers preferred to keep their diamonds under lock and key when they were not around. The local underworld also got to hear about the vault. So it wasn't such a big surprise when – three years after that opening in 1954 – a gang of three men attempted to break open the Hatton Garden vault. They failed and fled the building before anyone could catch them and the incident further reassured locals that the vault was the safest place to keep their valuables.

By this time, depositors regularly darted anxiously in through the back door of 88–90 Hatton Garden and down to the vault to make their deposits as discreetly as possible. Few declared even to the vault's owners what they put in the small brick-sized metal safety deposit boxes on the basis that *loose lips sink ships*.

But it was an open secret that not all the boxes in the underground vault of the Hatton Garden Safe Deposit Limited contained '100 per cent legal goods'.

Clients paid a relatively small annual fee of less than £100 for a medium-sized box inside the vault. They had to give their name, address and identification. But there never has been any requirement to state what was in the box. Private rooms without CCTV cameras were provided for clients to open their property, giving rise to speculation that box owners were storing anything from piles of cash to firearms.

Customers later described going down into the vault in Hatton Garden as being like entering the secret world of a James Bond baddie. Some private diamond dealers would walk into the building with their own bodyguards while carrying expensive gems. And no one questioned the security of the vault.

One customer later explained: 'It is a secure steel vault – a room lined with hundreds of boxes. People can keep absolutely anything there: it could be a new Rolex, it could be a family heirloom, but for most around here it will be the tools of their trade – diamonds.'

Business was booming for the Hatton Garden Safe Deposit company in the 1950s. Clients were given a personalised fob and code to gain access through two doors to a reception where staff behind bulletproof glass identified clients as they gave their biometric data to enter the vault.

'Even if you penetrated the outer wall, which you couldn't, there were laser beams, motion sensors – if anyone tried to break in, an armed response was supposed to arrive within minutes,' explained another former staff member.

In the dingy fluorescent light of the Hatton Garden Safe Deposit company offices, an attendant waited behind a barred window to deal with each customer, blissfully unaware that the vault continued to be of great interest to the *wrong* sort of people.

For only a short distance from this picturesque Olde Worlde corner of London and just across the nearby River Thames, was a veritable breeding ground for criminals, many of whom had always kept a close eye on Hatton Garden.

CHAPTER TWO

LONDON'S BADLANDS

Brian Henry Reader – who would later be dubbed the mastermind of the Hatton Garden Job – was born in the riverside tenements of Deptford, in June 1939, just three months before the outbreak of the Second World War. He was the eldest child of Doris and Henry Reader, who'd married nine months earlier and went on to have another son Colin and daughters Doreen and Sharon. It's often been said Reader got his first lessons in crime from his father, a renowned 'ducker and diver' who dealt in stolen goods.

Reader picked up twisted values as a young child during those war years, when few men were around and even less police, resulting in what can be described as a moral vacuum. Many associates and friends of some of the men who later became famous for the Hatton Garden Job said their childhoods were empty of family values because there simply were no complete families during the war.

In the nearby docklands, stealing was accepted – virtually encouraged – because it helped impoverished people survive. Most were still imbued in the ethos of thievery, which had been instilled in them by those communities where they'd been born. Being honest didn't help you survive in a slum like Deptford or any of the other rundown Thames-side tenements.

At the end of the war, Reader's spiv father abandoned the family leaving Reader – aged just seven – as the oldest male in the household. It was a heavy burden to carry for one so young.

Deptford never really shook off the stench of Victorian poverty until the combined efforts of Hitler's bombing raids and the economic realities of life in post-war Britain effectively flattened much of its slums into submission. After the Second World War, the descendants of many of those disease-ridden ghetto victims finally turned their backs on the cobbled streets and were encouraged to start afresh in the suburbs that were sprouting up in the cleaner air and wider fields where South East London met the so-called Garden of England, Kent. These suburbs were supposed to represent the acceptable new face of Middle England, with many appealing features but few of the old inner city's bad habits.

It has to be said that most of the suburbs with names like Bromley and Bexleyheath on the border between South London and Kent were a bit dull. Compared with the harsh, dilapidated streets of Deptford, Bermondsey, Walworth, Rotherhithe and Waterloo, however, they must have seemed like heaven. These new suburbs even retained a few traditional reminders of London life like a fine range of pubs, chippies and pie and eel shops, and enough memories of the capital and its history to make sure these new residents felt at home.

Reader was brought up in these new post-war suburban wastelands that were supposed to bring stability and happiness for all their inhabitants. But as one old South East London resident pointed out: 'You could take Brian Reader out of Deptford but you could never take Deptford out of Brian Reader.'

No wonder that in the newly developed South London suburbs, corner sweetshops became fair game for kids who'd loiter outside them after school most afternoons. They'd steal empty bottles of Tizer by slipping through the side gates to the back yard where all the empties were stored. Then they'd walk brazenly in through the front of the shop and claim the penny deposit per bottle, buying sweets with the money. These so-called 'Cheeky Charlies' were perceptive and streetwise characters from a young age. And their remarkably sharp powers of observation would be put to good use in later years.

Back then Brian Reader and his mates looked up to the old criminal 'faces' who emerged immediately after the war. These were larger than life characters dubbed by newspapers with outlandish names such as the 'King of the Underworld' and the 'King of the Dog Dopers'.

Back in the suburbs, long before they left school Reader and his contemporaries would earn extra pocket money working part-time jobs such as early-morning newspaper rounds . This would help fuel their obsession with earning much larger sums of cash when they grew up. Children like Brian Reader soon 'graduated' to stolen bicycle parts, nicking radios out of cars and even shoplifting. Everything was fair game but cigarettes, spirits and clothing were the 'big earners'. Railway containers were raided at night and their contents would end up on local street markets the following day.

The details are sketchy but Reader later admitted to some of his associates that his first conviction came at the age of eleven when he was caught breaking into five shops. That most probably made him a hero in the eyes of many of his friends.

As ex-robber Billy later explained: 'Being nicked at that age helped elevate the young crooks to a position of great influence among their mates.'

When talking to those who in later life committed some of

the biggest robberies in British criminal history, they all agreed that from an early age they'd boast to anyone who'd listen what they wanted to do when they grew up. 'Earn a big fat wedge of cash,' was always the reply.

Brian Reader and his friends formed gangs and dodged train and bus fares to get up to central London to steal wallets and people's belongings from tourist coaches parked in places like Constitution Hill, near Buckingham Palace. So-called scally-wags like Reader made as much as five pounds a day by selling everything onto a 'fence', an older man who handled stolen goods.

Fences were Dickensian-type characters renowned as good organizers and greatly respected in these post-war working class communities. Such a 'career' was considered a very profitable and crafty way to make good money out of crime without getting your hands dirty.

Meanwhile Brian Reader and his mates also nicked lead off roofs and collected scrap to sell down at the riverside yards that sprung up where Hitler's bombs had flattened buildings during the Blitz. But characters like Reader and his chums preferred to be out and about on the streets of South London, looking for opportunities, rather than scrabbling precariously around on rooftops. One of his school friends later explained: 'Brian had these sharp, beady little eyes that darted around in all directions, scanning the streets on the lookout for trouble or a chance to get up to a bit of mischief.'

By the early 1950s, dockworkers on both sides of the Thames – east and south – started losing their jobs as the post-war recession dragged the country downwards. Wages plummeted and even more people turned to crime in order to survive. Soon London's new heroes were the 'pavement artists' – robbers – who'd scoop a few hundred pounds from a Post Office stick-up and then buy everyone a round of celebratory drinks in the local pub.

True, they'd sometimes get caught by police, stand trial at places like the Old Bailey and go down for a stretch. But, as ex-robber Billy later recalled: 'At least they lived in style. We was quite in awe of those types of villains back then. They had guts and courage.' Many in the community were furious about the lengthy sentences handed down to such criminals, who were in many ways considered latter-day Robin Hoods.

At the age of fifteen, Brian Reader left school and became a butcher's boy but it wouldn't turn out to be a long-term career for him. He was more interested in getting out and about with his mates and making some real cash.

In the 1950s, the relationship between the police and petty criminals was a civilized one, at least on the surface. A lot of coppers and villains had been brought up in the same neighbourhoods and many went to the same schools. They'd often bump into each other in the local pub and exchange pleasantries, despite often being 'nicked' the previous week.

There were no professional security companies to protect money back in those days. More often than not, two or three trusted workers in a company would be given a few extra bob to pick up the cash from a nearby bank. If they were lucky they were armed with a cosh. Workers often informed their criminal associates about the transportation of large sums of money in exchange 'for a drink'.

And in the middle of this heady criminal environment, prison became a breeding ground for even bigger robberies as villains linked up with new partners-in-crime while serving time.

The most legendary 'job' of this era was the one old-time

professional London villains call, even to this day, 'the Mother of all robberies'. It was a lorry hijack committed in September 1954, outside the KLM Airline offices in Holborn, just around the corner from Hatton Garden. It was to become the precursor for some of the UK's most notorious hold-ups. Brian Reader lapped up all the details reported on the front pages of every newspaper at the time.

Raiders got away with two boxes containing £45,500 in gold bullion, a haul that would have been worth millions today. The sheer audacity of the KLM job left the great British public gasping, amid cries of how London's underworld was ruling the streets at this time.

The long arm of the law eventually located the van used in the KLM raid plus a couple of sets of false number plates, but nothing else. When Scotland's Yard's illustrious Flying Squad rounded up all the usual suspects they discovered every one of them had a cast-iron alibi and no trace of the gold was ever discovered. No wonder many in the London underworld proclaimed it to be the perfect crime.

One of Brian Reader's favourite hobbies at this time was attending the local greyhound track (known as 'going to the dogs'), where he and his associates liked to gamble. Dog tracks back then were a hotbed for local villains. Ever-observant and perceptive youths like him loved to watch these tough, edgy older characters in their sheepskin coats, who seemed to carry endless bundles of five pound notes around in their pockets.

Then, in the middle of this colourful existence, Brian Reader was called up by the armed forces as conscription still existed in the UK. He twice tried to fail his medical but the army didn't fall for it and so, in early 1955, Reader was faced with at least eighteen months away from his favourite South London haunts.

Reader was outraged by the very notion of conscription. He'd come from a family whose numbers had been seriously depleted in the trenches of the so-called Great War of 1914–18. He had no desire to serve Queen and country. He'd already had a taste of earning decent money as a criminal and also feared that someone else might move in on his 'patch' while he was away in the army.

Reader was put in a unit for troublesome recruits. Typically, Reader finally accepted his fate and decided to keep his head down and try to learn a few new skills while he was in the army. He was particularly interested in explosives and weaponry and 'cutting' through metal and the equipment needed for such activities. It had dawned on Reader that he could pick up some invaluable experience, which might help him when he got back to London at the end of his national service.

It was said back then that many youths would be 'knocked into shape' by their experiences in the services. But in the case of Brian Reader and many of his South London associates, nothing could be further from the truth. They didn't become conformist after suffering at the hands of brutal sergeant majors. Instead, they became even more insubordinate and resentful when they returned to the civilian world.

By the time he was back on his manor, Reader only had one thing on his mind; to earn a living 'ducking and diving' through the mean streets of South East London. Back in the civilian world he was soon on the lookout for more recruits to his cause. It was clear Reader already had an intense work ethic. He and his contemporaries were all opportunists, determined not to live within the 'normal' world where salaries were rock bottom and people struggled to survive.

Naturally, as Reader's circle of acquaintances grew, so did his dodgy habits. When one classmate from his school days got a job in a garage he started supplying Reader with stolen car parts. But few in the community frowned upon such activities at this time.

Reader often recruited other bright, quick-witted youths with an eye for the main chance. In some ways, he was a bit of a Fagin-type character back in those days, working with teams of younger criminals out on the streets of London.

Back then most men under the age of 25 had an obsession with owning a motor car and Brian Reader was no exception. His father hadn't been able to afford one, which made Reader doubly determined to own 'a good pair of wheels'. But characters like Reader tended not to bother visiting the local car showroom. Instead, they'd look around for a car that took their fancy and 'nick it'. Reader himself became well known for driving around in a different car virtually every week.

And in the middle of all this, Reader and his friends retained an unhealthy disregard for anyone in authority. As far as Reader was concerned, policemen, judges and Home Office officials were all 'the enemy'. They were all out to stop him and his mates from doing what they did best – thieving.

Brian Reader may have been the consummate young opportunist criminal from an early age, but all that was watered down when he had his head turned by a pretty girl from Dulwich called Lyn. She worked in a local turf accountants where Reader was a daily punter. When they first began 'courting', Lyn's family tried to put her off Reader 'the scallywag'. It wasn't surprising that this drove Brian and Lyn further into each other's arms.

With a girlfriend and sometimes his own mother to impress, Brian Reader must have felt a lot of pressure to bring home a 'decent salary'. It's no wonder, then, that Reader had to delve even deeper into the underworld to earn the money he required to keep his dependants afloat.

No doubt Brian Reader's sweetheart Lyn craved a 'normal' life. She must have known her boyfriend was up to no good but he always brought home a 'decent wedge', so she would have found it hard to criticize him. To be fair, Reader's number one priority was Lyn and he saw himself as the hard-working breadwinner in their relationship for almost the next fifty years.

At one stage, Reader even agreed to have another go at making a living in a 'straight profession'. This time it was as an apprentice jeweller in Hatton Garden, of all places. But Reader objected to what he considered to be slave labour wages of £3 a week and walked away from the job after a couple of weeks. He felt he had been badly treated and held a grudge against Hatton Garden as a result.

CHAPTER THREE

WATCHING AND LISTENING

By 1962, Brian Reader had become a regular at the Chop House restaurant in Clerkenwell, where London's gangsters would congregate, including the Kray twins. It was a short distance from Hatton Garden, which the villains often talked about. Reader already knew from his brief career in the jewellery trade that great riches were just waiting to be stolen from there.

The Chop House had its own unique, heady environment although the shy, almost reclusive Reader must have seemed a very small 'player' in the eyes of the notorious villains who assembled there most days. However, Reader treated this venue very much like he did when he went to the dogs as a teenager. Reader enjoyed listening, watching and learning. He was absorbing the rules of the game, the people in the know.

The criminal ascendancy of the Brian Readers of that world owed much to the transitional period that Britain had been going through at that time. People – especially the poor – were still struggling despite a newly introduced welfare state. That forced characters like Reader to go out on the streets and look for new challenges – and that's when banks started to become extremely popular targets for the South East London underworld.

Bank raids back then were usually carried out in the dead of night, with a 'master cutter' – as Brian Reader was later described by a Flying Squad detective who once arrested him – pitting his wits against whatever security precautions happened to be in place at the time.

But as lock design and other security improved, tackling a safe became a much tougher challenge. Even the use of the bank robber's 'best friend' – gelignite – was no longer considered a sound bet thanks to a device that when triggered by the force of an explosion would throw extra bolts across the safe door.

Professional robbers then began using oxyacetylene torches to get around this problem. But these proved slow and cumbersome and, on occasion, would actually reduce the safe's contents to charred paper before the door could even be ripped open.

As a result, criminals started carrying out more daring across-the-counter bank raids. Breaking open safes hadn't required any confrontation on the part of the robbers. But going into a bank in broad daylight meant it was essential for the robbers to be in control – and that's when firearms began appearing with more regularity on the streets of London.

Banks responded by installing reinforced glass screens to protect their cashiers. London villains soon noted that armed raids in banks were higher risk, even though the rewards were generally lower. That's when the capital's so-called professional criminals began looking for new, more lucrative targets. Cash in transit seemed the perfect answer.

Post Office vans were considered a soft target because they often had just one driver, and he usually didn't even know how much cash he was carrying. The 'blaggers' usually had a 'snitch' inside the main Post Office, who'd be able to tell them which days there was a lot of cash on board the vans. A popular target was the pension run to Post Offices, although the pickings were still not usually much more than a few hundred pounds.

But besides the cash there was another much longer-term reward for a career as a robber – underworld notoriety. Picking up the evening paper from a street vendor and seeing a screaming headline POST OFFICE VAN HIJACK meant that locals would often be full of admiration for the villains who'd pulled off this sort of daring job.

However, a bunch of South London criminals well known to Brian Reader were about to put all those van hold-ups in the shade with a robbery that would capture the nation's imagination more than any other crime before it.

Brian Reader was 24 years old when the Great Train Robbery occurred in August 1963. No doubt he and many other young villains would have loved nothing more than to be involved in the heist. Reader had met many of the gang at pubs and clubs in and around the Old Kent Road, in the heart of South East London.

Despite the police eventually rounding up the entire mob, the Great Train Robbery was still considered the most successful and glamorous heist in British criminal history.

The lengthy sentences eventually handed down to the robbers were supposed to send out a message to the London underworld that such outrageous crimes would not be tolerated. But instead they spurred characters like Brian Reader on, making them even more determined to follow in the footsteps of their heroes.

But despite his underworld career, Brian Reader still wanted to lead a normal, traditional life at home with Lyn, to whom he was engaged to marry by this time. Reader enjoyed his home comforts and deeply disapproved of some of the habits of London's thriving post-war underworld. Many younger criminals back then had started taking purple hearts (a mixture of amphetamine and barbiturates) but Reader looked on all drugs as 'the devil's candy'. It was all about 'control' and Reader couldn't see the point of putting yourself in such a vulnerable, weakened state, especially in the dark alleyways and powder-keg pubs frequented by him and his contemporaries.

Around this time in the mid-1960s, Brian Reader was arrested and charged with handling stolen goods. Few details of the case are known, except that Reader received a suspended sentence and his arrest by all accounts did little to put him off his chosen life of crime.

It seemed that the Great Train Robbery had single-handedly helped heists take on a romantic hue all of their own and even made the underworld seem positively glamorous. Many people looked on the train robbers as modern-day Robin Hoods striking blows against the traditional enemy: the coppers, the filth, the cozzers and all the other derogatory names the police were called.

In 1964, Reader married childhood sweetheart Lyn and by all accounts he was a loyal, faithful husband who went home most nights. It seems he rarely went to the sort of nightclubs so often frequented by his friends in the underworld. 'He was a quiet family man and he did everything for them,' said one old friend. Reader's son Paul was born some months after their wedding and their daughter, a year later.

Around this time, new specialized security firms began taking on the responsibility of transferring money in transit. Armoured vans replaced vulnerable clerks carrying briefcases or driving burnt-out old jalopies. These new security vans and their guards were to become primary targets for professional criminals.

Soon a bunch of South East London 'firms' were dominating the 'business' in the capital. Wealthy, older criminals often financed these hold-ups but they would never dare tell the experts how to go about their work. These 'blaggers' were consisted consummate professionals.

Such characters were celebrated and referred to in the underworld as heroes because many saw them as getting one back on the Establishment. South East London pubs like The Frog and Nightgown, The Connoisseur, The Prince of Wales and The Beehive in Peckham all became notorious haunts for villains like Brian Reader and his associates. In some lesser known pubs, guns could be obtained virtually over the counter. Many of those same taverns were also considered virtual no-go areas by the police.

And in the middle of this urban 'war' lived South London's most legendary crime family of all, the Richardsons. They were treated like royalty south of the Thames. During the 1960s, the Richardsons ran a hugely profitable empire stretching from South London scrapyards and West End drinking clubs to gold mines in South Africa. Their leader Charlie Richardson was known as the hardest man in South London. Even the East London-based Kray twins were wary about venturing onto his turf.

But when, in the late 1960s, Charlie and his brother Eddie got themselves sent down for a long stretch, a lot of younger hoods known to Brian Reader saw an opportunity to move up the underworld ladder. As one senior Flying Squad officer from that era explained: 'The whole place opened up. Tight-lipped younger villains with strong personalities decided to move in.'

And this new breed of professional criminal didn't play by the same rules, either. Many of them were not afraid to start running feuds with certain police officers, who were forever trying to arrest them for a variety of petty offences. The police of this era were often accused of resorting to framing these younger villains to ensure they took the would-be gangsters off the streets.

Other up-and-coming criminals took a more pragmatic approach. They wanted to keep certain policemen on their side so they won over 'friendly coppers' by tipping them off on certain minor crimes they'd heard about. These artful crooks reckoned they would then be left to their own devices on other, bigger jobs. It was nothing more than cynical back-scratching. But it left many criminals known to Brian Reader open to accusations that they were 'grasses'. Later in life this would come back to haunt Reader and some of his associates.

Professional gangs of robbers – carefully selected and constantly on the lookout for lucrative targets – were undoubtedly taking over the underworld inhabited by Brian Reader and his contemporaries during the late 1960s. These characters didn't run nightclubs in Soho or protection rackets or pimp women. They treated robbing banks and security vans as their chosen career path.

Crime in the UK at this time was approaching epidemic proportions, especially in London. Tens of millions of pounds worth of stolen property changed hands virtually every week. Violent offences were up by more than 10 per cent each year from 1965, and the number of drug convictions was gradually beginning to rise, although it was not yet the popular 'earner' it would eventually become.

Better-organized criminal networks emerged, often run by outsiders, rather than blood relatives. They were prepared to finance every aspect of major crimes such as robbery. Hijacked goods lorries carrying items such as cigarettes and alcohol were another popular source of income at the time. Usually the driver would be bunged a few bob in advance to ensure a successful raid.

Many in the South East London underworld were not afraid of going to prison if they were caught 'bang to rights', either. They often shrugged their shoulders and accepted that jail was inevitable and when it happened, they'd take their 'bird' (sentence) and deal with it. But British prisons in the late sixties were much more dangerous places than they are today.

On 24 October 1969 a massive disturbance erupted after inmates in Parkhurst, on the Isle of Wight, began protesting about conditions. For forty terrifying minutes, seven members of staff were held captive by riot-crazed inmates. One prisoner came within a whisker of slitting the throat of an officer. Nine inmates – including a bunch of London 'faces' known to Brian Reader – eventually surrendered. Accounts of their 'daring' behaviour spread like wildfire through the pubs and drinking clubs of the Old Kent Road.

Many professional villains in prison at this time believed the authorities were trying to break their spirit in a bid to prevent them planning new crimes with other inmates. No wonder many criminals other main preoccupation inside prison was keeping fit. Every time they did a press-up they saw it as a mark of defiance against the system.

By 1970, Brian Reader was known to Scotland Yard and in underworld circles as an ambitious character on the up and up. That year he took wife Lyn to Paris one weekend because he did not want to be implicated in a job planned by a rival mob. A photograph of the glamorous coupled enjoying dinner at a top restaurant, plus passport stamps, provided him with an airtight alibi when the police came calling.

Out on the streets of London the latest breed of clinical, well-organized professional robber didn't hesitate to strike fear and trepidation into their victims. Often they did that confident that they had some London police officer 'in their pockets', just in case they were in need of any 'help'.

By this time, security company guards were always equipped with batons and truncheons when escorting large quantities of cash. So the blaggers stepped up the level of threats and actual violence in order to continue robbing with impunity on the streets of London. That meant firing guns if and when required.

Britain's Swinging Sixties must have seemed like a distant dream by this time. New Conservative Prime Minister Edward Heath was struggling with the country's economy as the UK veered from one crisis to the next with alarming regularity. Striking miners and others taking industrial action were accused of crippling the nation.

When Heath participated in the British victory in the Admiral's Cup yacht race in the summer of 1971, it outraged many working folk, who believed he should have been glued to his desk at Number Ten with unemployment threatening to top the one million mark for the first time in Britain's history.

In the second week of September 1971, the troubles in Northern Ireland escalated following the death of fourteen-year-old Annette McGavigan, fatally wounded by a gunshot in crossfire between British soldiers and the IRA.

In that same September week, a team of professional London 'blaggers' pulled off what was to be hailed as the heist of the decade. Their target was the Lloyds Bank in Baker Street, central London. Many believe Brian Reader played a role in this robbery but he denies it categorically. However, since it was probably the robbery that most closely resembles the Hatton Garden Job forty-four years later, it still deserves a big mention here. Baker Street was less than a mile from Hatton Garden and renowned as the home of Britain's most famous fictional detective, Sherlock Holmes.

The bank robbers had rented a leather goods shop called Le Sac, located just two doors down from Lloyds Bank and then tunnelled a distance of approximately 50 feet under the fried chicken restaurant between them and the bank. They'd deliberately decided to dig over the weekend to avoid anyone hearing the noise of their equipment.

Then, using something called a thermic lance, they began 'burning' through the three feet of reinforced concrete, which formed the floor of the vault. But when this high-tech piece of equipment didn't create a big enough hole, the gang had to use explosives to get through instead. This produced eight tons of rubble, which had to be excavated and left behind in the shop.

The gang had no idea an amateur radio ham living in nearby Wimpole Street, had stumbled upon their walkie-talkie frequencies and was listening to a live commentary of the robbery. The man phoned the police but they ignored his call. He was so outraged, he started recording the voices coming through on his radio transmitter.

The radio ham again alerted the police and this time two officers came to his house and listened to the robbers but couldn't work out which bank was being robbed. When two beat constables eventually stumbled on the actual bank in question they saw nothing suspicious and gave the premises the all-clear. The raiders – who'd been just 12 inches away from them still inside the bank vault – escaped a few hours later with their loot and disappeared into the London underworld.

On the following Monday morning, scores of empty safety

deposit boxes were found broken open and lying all over the floor of the vault. It would be a scene almost identically replicated in 2015 on the floor of a vault in Hatton Garden.

A sign daubed on the wall of the bank vault after the robbery said it all:

Let Sherlock Holmes solve this one

A number of the gang, it later emerged, had become ardent readers of the Sherlock Holmes stories during earlier spells in prison.

An embarrassed Scotland Yard soon had to admit the robbers had planned the heist with military precision and extreme professionalism; they'd stolen the contents of 268 deposit boxes, worth in excess of £3 million, which, in 1971, made it the largest ever bank robbery on British soil. That £3 million would probably be worth at least £20 million today.

However – also like Hatton Garden all those years later – Scotland Yard's humiliation acted as a spur for the Flying Squad, who went into a state of manic overdrive knocking down doors, dragging villains out of bed and turning over properties until they eventually rounded up most of the robbers.

Four men pleaded guilty at the Old Bailey and each received twelve-year sentences. Another pleaded not guilty but was subsequently convicted and received eight years. He was the man who signed the lease on the shop used by the robbers. Two other men accused of handling banknotes from the robbery were never prosecuted. It was later claimed the mastermind of the robbery was a well-known London car dealer, who was never brought to justice.

The Flying Squad's eventual success in rounding up the

Lloyd's Bank gang reminded the London public that the city was also filled with sharp-eyed young detectives determined to rid the streets of these highly professional teams of villains.

The Flying Squad single-mindedly pledged to take on the London robbery gangs. Among those names on their list of 'interesting people' was Brian Reader the so-called 'master cutter.' This was to mark the beginning of a series of cat-and-mouse games between Reader and Flying Squad detectives that would go on for decades and be peppered with accusations of everything from police bribery to the alleged participation of certain officers in actual robberies.

CHAPTER FOUR

KNOCKING DOWN DOORS

Scotland Yard's Flying Squad had been in existence for so long in London that the squad's nickname in rhyming slang, The Sweeney (from Flying Squad/Sweeney Todd, the notorious Fleet Street barber who turned his customers into meat pies) was already regarded as a cliché. The squad had been initially set up as a special police unit at the end of the First World War, when London experienced a crime wave as large numbers of men recently released from the armed forces emerged onto the streets of the capital, many of them hardened to violence after the carnage of the Western Front.

This specially formed police unit enjoyed rapid crime-busting success back then, and in 1920 was provided with two motor tenders, capable of a top speed of 35mph. (The speed limit at the time was just 20mph.) Then a *Daily Mail* journalist referred to them as 'a flying squad of picked detectives' and the name stuck. Their exploits went on to figure in a number of British films, and in the mid-1970s the squad would be immortalized in a TV series, *The Sweeney*, starring John Thaw and Dennis Waterman.

Thaw's character Detective Inspector Jack Regan told one gang after a shootout: '*We're The Sweeney! We kill you – nothing! You kill us – thirty years!*'

But the glamorous, hard-nosed image of the Flying Squad in the 1970s was leaving officers wide open to accusations of corruption. It was alleged that a strategically placed officer could, for a fee, ensure bail was granted for a criminal, hold back evidence and details about past convictions from a court, or pass on to a person under investigation details of a case being made against him or warnings about police operations in which he could become compromised.

In the mid-1970s – with up-and-coming characters like Brian Reader and others making a name for themselves in the South London underworld – Scotland Yard's newly appointed Deputy Assistant Commissioner David Powis ordered a crackdown to stop corrupt Flying Squad officers from creaming off reward money meant for informants. Powis insisted on meeting all police informants as part of a vetting process and pledged that all payments of more than £500 would be handed over only by himself.

The relationship between the Flying Squad and the blaggers (robbers) was further complicated by so-called 'supergrasses', who were to become the key to the squad's success. These characters were a cut above the usual 'grasses' and 'snouts' who'd always helped the police with their enquiries in exchange for a free pint or a fiver. Now the stakes were much higher, and often that meant immunity from prosecution in exchange for the inside track on major robberies.

Flying Squad detectives began to actively persuade some members of close-knit gangs to inform on robberies in advance. Perhaps the most notorious of all supergrass deals was the controversial 'chit-to-freedom' that bank robber Bertie Smalls negotiated from the Flying Squad. Smalls' gambling chips were times, places, hauls and Christian names. Smalls became a hated figure in the London underworld after he 'joined the other side'. Many villains said they'd 'gladly kill that bastard for nothing. He's vermin and should be wiped off the face of this earth.'

Brian Reader witnessed all these changes in the underworld with great trepidation, even though he was not averse to some 'back scratching' with the Flying Squad. But he would never stoop as low as Bertie Smalls. However, some of Reader's associates in South London clearly had other ideas. They reckoned being a supergrass had certain advantages, especially if you wanted to get a rival criminal off the streets.

At this time, Brian Reader was regularly being hauled in by the police and accused of being connected to particular crimes, though detectives never seemed to have any genuine, substantial proof. At the same time, some of Reader's associates were being approached by crime bosses trying to frame certain high-ranking police officers, just before they were due to give evidence in major trials. The aim was to smear the officers' names to such an extent that their evidence would be seriously questioned in court.

And then there was jury nobbling; some of Brian Reader's known associates saw it as their duty to try and beat the justice system any way they could. If that meant greasing the palms of a few innocent jury members then so be it. And if that didn't work then a bit of old-fashioned intimidation was always worth a try.

By the end of the 1970s, it's estimated there were at least half a dozen armed robberies every week in London and South East England. In the pubs and clubs of the capital, the stories of these heists helped popularize a new four-letter word – the 'buzz'. As 1970s East London robber Bernie Khan later explained: 'The buzz on those jobs was better than any drugs. All that adrenalin pumping through you was fuckin' incredible and the feelin' of elation once you'd snatched that cash was out of this world. It drove us all to commit bigger and bigger crimes. We were addicted to that buzz.'

On TV, the violent, booze-sodden adventures of Inspector Regan on *The Sweeney* frequently continued to mirror real life crimes. One of Brian Reader's favourite episodes involved a gem robbery in Hatton Garden.

Reader himself sported a longer hairstyle not dissimilar from the actors on *The Sweeney*. He also had a penchant for flared trousers, jackets with wide lapels that flapped in the wind and kipper ties. Even the cars criminals stole to use as getaway vehicles tended to be Rovers or Jaguars, which were very popular with the fictional police detectives on British television at the time.

As ex-robber Billy later recalled: 'Real life was like an episode from *The Sweeney* back then. The cozzers would resort to violence and intimidation to nick the villains and the villains were not afraid to shoot back if they had to.'

And then along came a robbery so lucrative and beautifully executed that it made Brian Reader and the entire London underworld sit up and take notice. In 1976, raiders stole £8 million from the Bank of America in Mayfair, in the heart of London's West End.

But – as was so often the case – the inside man was to prove the gang's undoing. He crumbled under police interrogation and agreed to turn informant to help the police arrest the gang who'd carried out the raid.

Seven men were eventually found guilty of the Bank of America job and sentenced to a combined 100 years in jail. The gang's alleged leader, however, escaped the UK and went to live in Spain. Only £500,000 of the money stolen was ever recovered.

Meanwhile, back on the streets of London, blaggers were resorting even more to firearms. Most professional criminals back then would swear blind that they never intended to injure anyone but they were not shy about using the obvious 'fear factor' of firing a gun to scare their victims into surrendering their money. As a result, people often got hurt and in some cases killed.

Scotland Yard's Flying Squad saw this as the villains openly declaring war on the streets of London. The Sweeney became particularly obsessed with catching robbers preying on security vans. On payday – which back then was usually on Thursdays – many detectives were simply sent onto the streets of London to look for robbers.

Shortly after the Bank of America job, Reader joined a group of older well-respected criminals in a pub in South East London to set up a new gang to carry out 'high end' burglaries only. The gang's total haul would eventually exceed the £2 million mark, making them one of the UK's most successful ever team of burglars. And Reader was very happy that the targets were 'soft'. That meant the gang would avoid encountering any people during a job. Reader much preferred it that way. He didn't like guns and even claimed his eyesight wasn't good enough to use one. Reader also knew his prison sentence would be doubled if he was ever caught 'tooled up'.

Brian Reader had a reputation as a very accomplished 'technician' at this time. One Flying Squad officer from this era told me recently: 'We knew all about Brian Reader. He was good at slicing holes in things. We'd heard his name in connection to a lot of burglaries and he was on our "to watch" list.'

Reader was, according to his associates, fascinated by cutting equipment and especially the argon arc gun, a high-powered electric torch that could cut its way through metal. It wasn't available in shops, and could only be ordered, which should have made it easier for the police to trace back to the legitimate owners. So Reader's associates found a factory in West London that stored argon guns, broke in and stole six of them.

The burglary gang Reader allegedly worked for went on to burgle premises across most of the southern half of England. Reader wasn't always on the team, but when he was, he was renowned for finding his way through any impregnable surfaces such as metal and concrete.

On the streets of London, blaggers armed themselves with weapons through gun shop break-ins and shady criminal gun dealers, including one notorious character who – even though he had once been a policeman – would eventually become South London's most infamous 'merchant of death'.

And in the middle of all this, Scotland Yard's Flying Squad issued a chilling message to the mainstream robbers of London: 'You'll be shot dead if you carry arms.' To some criminals at this time, the police had become judge, jury and executioner all rolled into one. Reader told others this was the precise reason why he wouldn't carry a gun like most of his associates and preferred to stick to burglaries.

Brian Reader liked to think he was above all the violence and mayhem out on the streets of London. But he was certainly not averse to using some very manipulative methods to ensure the boys in blue left him alone.

In the late 1970s, a number of South East London's most notorious professional villains, including Brian Reader, joined a Freemasons' lodge following an introduction from a well-known Kent criminal, who had big 'connections' inside the Freemasons.

It's since been alleged that membership applications by these criminals ended up being proposed and seconded by serving police officers, who wanted to keep certain highly influential villains 'onside'.

Other Masons at the lodge which Reader and his associates joined included gold bullion dealers from Hatton Garden, as well as the more traditional members such as policemen, judges and lawyers.

Though the Freemasons are looked upon by outsiders as a mysterious and secretive organization, most members insist it is a society of men concerned with moral and spiritual values. Members are said to be taught its principles through a series of ritual dramas in the form of two-part plays, which are learnt by heart and performed by members within each lodge. These plays follow ancient forms, using stonemasons' customs and tools as allegorical guides.

But membership of a Freemasons' lodge was also a natural step for ambitious London criminals in the late 1970s. They wanted to infiltrate a circle of acquaintances that crossed all social divides and often included senior members of the judiciary and police.

Villains relished mastering the art of the Freemasons' handshake, which involved putting the thumb between the first and second finger and pressing the knuckle on the middle finger. This would indicate that the person in question was on the third degree – Mason-speak for being a member. When such criminals met a policeman they thought was a Mason, they'd make a point of using that handshake very carefully to ascertain his or her membership.

A number of Freemason police officers were even alleged to have lied for criminals who were members because they genuinely believed that their membership put these characters above the law.

As one police officer later explained: 'Many criminals cynically manipulated themselves into Freemasonry as if it was the right pub for them to be seen at. While some police officer members were outraged by the presence of known criminals in their ranks, others saw it as an ideal opportunity to pick up new informants.'

Another police source later recounted to me the day he arrested a notorious South East London criminal well known to Brian Reader.

'He's on the square,' a Mason detective told the arresting officer at the Kent police station, where the man had been brought. Within minutes the prisoner was released without charge.

A lot of the Freemasons Reader encountered were involved with the gem business in the centre of London's diamond trade, the district of Hatton Garden. Reader knew it reasonably well because he'd fenced quite a lot of the proceeds from his burglary gang in Hatton Garden. He'd long since recognized it as a prime area for making money from crime, but he decided it was time to build up even more contacts in Hatton Garden, which might prove very useful in the future.

CHAPTER FIVE

IN THE MONEY

By the late 1970s, Brian Reader was doing so well he'd managed to buy with cash a large detached house in Blackheath, one of South East London's most sought after areas. But Reader the consummate professional villain remained as 'hungry' as ever; still constantly on the lookout for any potential new targets for crime. Sometimes he'd take Lyn and the children out for a drive on a Sunday afternoon and use them as cover while he was 'casing' places to break into. Reader believed the police wouldn't take much notice of a car occupied by a young family, even if it was circling around factories, stately homes and sometimes even banks.

Reader's Sunday afternoon family outings in his car summed up his own split personality, typical of the type of characters defining the London underworld at this time. He was a hardened villain and yet out with his wife and kids on the vast, grassy heath near his home, he was a genuinely loving family man. However, Reader steadfastly refused to discuss his 'work' at home. If Lyn ever asked her husband about a TV news item on a robbery, his reply would always be the same: 'Good luck to 'em.'

It was vital in London's so-called professional underworld

never to directly admit your crimes to anyone, not even your nearest and dearest. If Lyn asked Reader where he was going as he left the house, he'd take a deep breath and reply along the lines of: 'Darlin', don't worry. I won't let you down. Just don't ask questions.'

In many ways characters like Brian Reader thrived on leading this double life. As one old friend later explained: 'Brian was essentially a loner. He rarely got too close to people. But he did try his hardest to be a good family man.'

Reader greatly appreciated returning to the security of a stable home after days and nights of 'heavy work'. Maybe he recognized how hard the struggle to survive in the 'bad' world was if he didn't at least have a 'good' world to return to.

By all accounts though, Reader was a fairly easy-going character, the antithesis of the criminal wide boy, who'd even stayed in touch with his old pals from school. Every now and again he'd try to go 'straight' to please Lyn. He got a job working in a haulage business run by an old school friend but that didn't last long. Another time he even worked briefly for a jewellery dealer in Hatton Garden through another contact. But neither job earned him enough cash and he always went back to what he knew best.

The London underworld of 1980 was dominated by young villains and equally youthful Flying Squad detectives. Few of them were over 40 years of age. Brian Reader, then aged 41, was on the verge of being considered a bit of an 'old codger'.

Robbery was a young man's game, or so the London underworld presumed, until a team of relatively old villains carried out a daring robbery right in the heart of Reader's favourite area of London, Hatton Garden. The gang's *modus operandi* was hardly sophisticated but it was still highly effective. One of the gang initially knocked on the door of a jeweller's pretending to be a postman. The owner then looked through the spyhole, saw a doddery old boy and opened the door only to be 'greeted' by two masked men with sawn-off shotguns, who barged straight past him and announced their intentions by waving their weapons in the air.

One member of staff later recalled that all the gang members huffed and puffed so much under their ski masks that staff in the jeweller's had no doubt they were elderly. There was genuine surprise that a bunch of old men would even try to pull off such an 'energetic' crime.

Shortly after this, Hatton Garden was the scene of another robbery. This again exposed the 'vulnerability' of the area, which had always intrigued Brian Reader. A pair of so-called Hatton Garden jewel traders recruited two professional robbers to steal £778,000 worth of gems in a 'fake robbery'. The pretend thieves would then return the gems and share an insurance payout with the jewellers. But a notorious police informant had met the two robbers at the home of one of the Hatton Garden traders and then informed the Flying Squad about the scam. Later it emerged that one of the 'fake robbers' had even kept back some of the jewels and put them in the safety deposit box vault at 88–90 Hatton Garden.

It was clear back then that informants were playing a huge role in helping the Flying Squad retake the streets, or so it seemed to the London underworld. And the supergrass phenomenon was about to bite Brian Reader very hard on the backside and turn him into the alleged suspect in a major criminal investigation.

*

THE HISTORY

On 25 March 1980, ten tons of silver bullion was hijacked on its way to the docks at Tilbury on the Thames Estuary. In the space of one well-planned minute, a gang of blaggers held up a reinforced security lorry when one of them – dressed as a policeman – flagged down the vehicle and its security escort in a busy high street.

A blue van then pulled up behind the truck and six men with shotguns leapt out and forced the driver and two guards into their van at gunpoint. The truck then roared off with one of the robbers at the wheel. The three captives were driven to a garage, tied up and dumped. They managed to contact police three hours later.

The daring daylight robbery gang got away with 321 ingots of silver worth £4 million, which were being transferred from a City of London bank called Samuel Montagu & Co. to East Germany.

Leader of the gang was a well-known villain called Michael 'Skinny' Gervaise. But after his capture by the Flying Squad, Gervaise offered to turn supergrass and on 4 June 1980 he led police to most of the stolen silver ingots.

Gervaise was someone equally loathed and admired, especially by Brian Reader and his associates. Reader and Gervaise had first met when Gervaise was still working as a burglar alarm engineer. He was an unimpressive looking character, said to be balding 'with the mild air of a retail tobacconist'. He had earlier received eighteen months in prison for a small role in the Bank of America job but had no other criminal record of note.

So when he was caught 'bang to rights' for the silver bullion job he decided to risk the hate and revenge of the London underworld by becoming the most talkative supergrass since the infamous Bertie Smalls.

Gervaise not only grassed up the silver bullion gang but also his involvement with the same nationwide burglary team as Brian Reader. He even implied to detectives that Reader had been on the silver bullion job. But then he would say that, wouldn't he?

As one flying squad detective said many years later: 'We'd heard of Reader before but this was quite a breakthrough because we wanted to nail him and his mates. It eventually turned into a massive investigation.'

Gervaise eventually brought the entire burglary team down after telling Operation Jenny detectives all about the numerous raids they'd carried out. The police were delighted to have rounded up such a successful gang of villains with relatively little effort. One senior Flying Squad officer later described them as 'top grade criminals and safe-blowers. We'd got the big boys.'

Gervaise claimed to detectives that Brian Reader had cut open dozens of safes and vaults across the country and he was eventually among thirty suspects arrested for their alleged involvement in the burglary gang. Reader and others were soon being marched in and out of a specially convened court in central London, which operated through the night to process the charges against the numerous burglary gang suspects.

Flying Squad detectives also recovered weapons and even police uniforms, which had been used by the gang. Those arrested were held at police stations all over North and East London.

When the Flying Squad raided a lock-up garage in South London connected to the burglaries they found it full of equipment including thermic lances, petrochemical lances, radios tuned to police wavelengths. The owner of the garage admitted his involvement and was eventually persuaded to become another informant.

THE HISTORY

No one knows if Brian Reader himself was asked to become a supergrass. But there is no doubt he and his associates were fuming about Gervaise.

Reader had been arrested initially alongside his friend and criminal associate John Goodwin, an old fashioned East End villain with a big reputation. Goodwin was the ultimate professional. He openly admitted he would do anything to get one over on his sworn enemies the police.

Thirty-five years later, Goodwin's name even came into the frame when detectives first tried to work out who might have been involved in the Hatton Garden Job in 2015. 'I was convinced he had his fingerprints on the Hatton Garden Job but then I found he'd died just before it happened,' one retired Flying Squad officer later told me.

Reader and Goodwin felt very hard done by because they'd only been arrested on the word of Gervaise the supergrass and in the underworld that was not considered a 'fair cop'. It left them with a feeling of overwhelming injustice and both men decided to do everything in their power to avoid prosecution.

Brian Reader was astonished but delighted a few days later when he was granted bail after standing before a magistrate on charges associated to those multimillion-pound burglaries. Most of his fellow gang members had much longer criminal records and were refused bail.

Some later speculated that Reader must have 'done a deal' with the Flying Squad but there is no concrete evidence to back up those claims.

A few days after he was bailed, Reader received a phone call from someone threatening to kill him and his family. The police were unsympathetic to his plight as they were still annoyed that he'd even been granted bail in the first place.

So Brian Reader took a life-changing decision and went on the run. He headed to the only safe place that could offer his old-fashioned home comforts like fish and chip shops and draught beer – Spain, where there was then no extradition treaty with the UK.

Back in the UK, Brian Reader's close friend John Goodwin was about to face an Old Bailey jury on the same burglary charges as Reader. He'd remained in custody throughout. During Goodwin's first trial, the jury couldn't agree a verdict and it was eventually abandoned by the judge. The second trial was also abandoned when Goodwin claimed he'd suffered a heart attack.

Then in Goodwin's third trial in February 1982, he was acquitted after producing a tape-recording of a detective accepting money from him. Goodwin had bugged his meeting with the officer by hiding a microphone in a Christmas tree.

Two months later, Goodwin turned up yet again at the Old Bailey to face new charges relating to the burglary gang. This time the main witness was supergrass Mickey Gervaise. But Gervaise then withdrew his evidence, claiming robbery squad officers had ordered him to falsely implicate Reader and Goodwin in burglaries they were not involved with.

However Goodwin, then aged 41, was eventually found guilty of perverting the course of justice by allegedly bribing jurors at one of his previous trials. Reader remained on the run in Spain. Eight other people, including a juror, were sentenced for their part in what the prosecuting counsel described as a 'determined attempt to poison the fountain of British justice'.

The court was told that four jurors – and possibly four more – had been offered bribes of £1,000 each to bring in not guilty verdicts against Goodwin and the absent Reader. It was alleged that others who were never identified had accepted the bribes. But the plot was said to have failed because one member of the jury panel – a waitress from South East London – had reported to the court that an approach had been made to her. Goodwin was eventually jailed for seven years for supposedly trying to nobble the jury. However the case against him was later quashed by the Court of Appeal.

So while Brian Reader soaked up the sun and sangria on the Mediterranean, Operation Jenny detectives secured convictions on seventeen men for their part in a total of 107 burglaries. involving the theft of goods worth more than £3 million.

Shortly after John Goodwin went to jail, his wife Shirley was kidnapped by a gang of London criminals who were furious with Goodwin for not giving them their share of the loot from various crimes. Three men were eventually caught by police and jailed. Shirley Goodwin survived unhurt but the incident proved to the Flying Squad that professional criminals still thought they owned the streets and were prepared to do anything to stay in control.

Brian Reader remained on the run with Lyn and their two children and by all accounts enjoyed a life far removed from his war-ravaged boyhood. The family spent some time in a villa on Spain's Costa Blanca. Reader had a yachting licence and chartered boats around the world, taking his family with him. They also took winter skiing holidays in the glitzy French resort of Meribel.

Reader had clearly developed a taste for the finer things in life like sunshine holidays, fine wine and gourmet food. But Lyn later told one friend that their life on the run was far from glamorous. She hated having to move house all the time and complained about how she'd no sooner made them homely then they'd be off to another location.

Then in late 1982, Reader had no choice but to take the family back to the UK after Lyn's mother became sick. Reader kept a low profile and somehow managed to stay out of the criminal 'limelight'. He tried to sound out the police through his contacts to see if they would come after him now he was back in England, but was given no cast-iron guarantees. His point had always been that his friend John Goodwin had been acquitted so surely the same would happen to him if he faced a trial.

In any case, Brian Reader looked a lot different from when he'd 'gone on the lam' after his arrest on the burglary charges. He'd picked up a certain style of dressing while he'd been living it up in Europe. Now he sported a droopy Zapata-style moustache and had a penchant for tight-fitting sweaters. As one of his oldest friends later said: 'He was almost unrecognizable from a couple of years earlier. He looked more like a smooth Mexican bandit than a south-east London villain. No wonder the police didn't notice he was back. The boy did good. He'd survived a scare and had managed to slide quietly back into the London underworld.'

CHAPTER SIX

AS GOOD AS GOLD

By early 1983, Brian Reader had become a bit of an enigma as far the Kent and South East London underworld was concerned. He was known as this shadowy figure supposedly still on the run but doing relatively little to hide himself away from the law. Some criminals believed Reader might have become an informant and that the police were ignoring the fact he was back in Britain, encouraging him to feed them information. But there is no actual evidence to support this theory. However, during this time Reader did definitely reconnect with an old criminal acquaintance called Kenneth Noye, who lived in an isolated detached house near the sleepy village of West Kingsdown, in Kent.

Many other villains claimed that Noye himself had become a police informant to ensure that detectives gave his own criminal lifestyle a wide birth in exchange for a few tit-bits about his underworld rivals.

Reader and Noye teamed up to launch a criminal enterprise they believed would earn them more money than all the bank robberies committed in London over the previous twenty years.

Prime Minister Margaret Thatcher – who'd come to power in 1979 – had inadvertently created a unique opportunity for fraudsters by scrapping VAT on gold coins such as krugerrands. Reader had heard all about this from his 'friends' in Hatton Garden. They'd buy the krugerrands from banks, melt them down and sell the ingots back to the banks as gold bullion, charging 15 per cent VAT in the process – having avoided paying it out in the first place.

Customs and Excise eventually got wise to the scam and legislation was passed to plug the loophole. The only problem was that by this time financially savvy characters like Reader and Noye had simply sourced their gold sovereigns from the continent, where VAT was low or non-existent, and carried on as before.

Back on the streets of London, robberies still remained the crime of choice for more traditional villains than Reader and his friend Noye. And then in 1983, two gangs of professional London criminals pulled off probably the two most daring heists in UK criminal history. And they both involved villains who'd later team up to pull off the Hatton Garden Job.

In the early months of 1983, East End-born Terry Perkins joined forces with a gang of professional criminals including actress Barbara Windsor's then husband Ronnie Knight, his brother John, Ronnie Everett and one-time Krays associate Freddie Foreman. They'd earmarked the Security Express money depot in Shoreditch, on the edge of London's financial district.

Terry Perkins was a close friend of John Knight and had a solid reputation as a good, reliable professional. He'd had a few runs-ins with the Flying Squad but had never actually been prosecuted for anything apart from drink driving.

Perkins was an opportunist. Some might call him an entrepreneur. He owned various businesses, including a sweet shop in the City of London. He prided himself on investing all his cash into 'straight' businesses. He artfully sold the sweet shop shortly before the Security Express raid because, he later claimed, he wanted to free up his money to invest in more property.

After months of careful, detailed reconnaissance work, the gang had specifically chosen the long four-day Easter Bank Holiday weekend of 1983 to hit their target. They believed those two extra days and the deserted surrounding streets would be crucial to their success. They'd even spent months watching the depot from a nearby derelict office block. During that reconnaissance, it became clear to all the robbers, including Terry Perkins, that they could also steal much more if they allowed themselves plenty of time and showed patience and professionalism.

One of the robbers later summed up the driving force behind the job perfectly: 'It was all about the planning. You didn't just pick a place and rob it. You watch it and wait for the right moment. You clock all the activity. You know who is going in and out. Even down to when the fuckin' milkman comes.'

The gang had calculated that on this particular Bank Holiday weekend in 1983, the vaults at the depot would be overflowing with *five tons* of paper money, worth many millions of pounds.

The day of the robbery happened to be Terry Perkins' 35th birthday. His wife later said she remembered it well because Perkins had got up so early that morning he missed his children's birthday greetings.

And so it was that on Good Friday, April 1983, a gang of hardened middle-aged professional robbers found themselves hiding inside a giant dustbin in the yard of the Security Express depot as snowflakes fluttered all around them.

The heavily fortified red-brick complex had 12-foot-high walls and steel shuttered doors plus alarms and CCTV cameras placed around the entire perimeter wall. The gang had carefully pin-pointed a section that was a blind spot to those overhanging cameras.

At almost 4 a.m., the gang broke their self-imposed silence to exchange a few words. The floor beneath them was ice-cold and, as on every public holiday weekend, the City of London was deserted. Only the noise of distant goods trains rumbling along the track at nearby Liverpool Street station broke the dead, snow-buffered silence.

A further three hours later – at 7 a.m. – the door to the building opened and a new guard took over from the duty nightshift man. Inside the main office of the depot, the same guard poured some hot water from a kettle into a cup before realizing that he had to go outside to get the milk.

As the gang heard the heavy bolt slide open on the outside door, they struck. The guard instantly came face to face with a masked man brandishing a sawn-off shotgun. Terry Perkins and the rest of the gang raced into the building through the open entrance. Two wore monkey masks and the others were in balaclavas. All had on boiler suits and gloves and were armed. Then the gang opened the glass door to the main reception area and swept further inside the building.

The gang even adopted faux-Irish accents and called themselves Paddy One, Paddy Two and Paddy Three. They waited patiently for a further six hours while the rest of the staff drifted in because these were the employees who had the keys and relevant codes to open three of the main underground vaults.

The first captured security guard was forced to open the doors for each of his workmates as they arrived. One by one they were wrapped up in women's stockings and a plaster put over their mouths. One 'troublesome' guard, 61-year-old James Alcock, was doused in petrol and a box of matches rattled by his ear with the threat that he would be 'incinerated' if he failed to hand over the keys needed to gain access to the vaults. The gang knew only too well that one incorrect turn of a key or a code put in wrongly and bells and sirens would ring in the building's alarm system.

With the vault doors open, Terry Perkins and the others transferred the cash onto trolleys and sent them up on a lift to the loading bays, where a 7-ton truck was waiting. Each sack of cash they moved along a human chain contained £100,000.

After more than six hours on the premises, Perkins and the rest of the gang had packed bundles of bank notes in denominations of £50 downwards totalling £5,961,097 into their van. As the robbers exited, they warned the staff: 'We've got a man upstairs. He's going to be there for twenty minutes just watching out for you. He's got a shooter and he's as fucking mad as they come.'

The driver then fired up his vehicle and headed across the yard towards the narrow entrance gate. The rest of the gang followed on foot, dispersing casually as if they were depot workers. They headed to their getaway vehicles parked in the surrounding streets.

As one of Terry Perkins' fellow robbers later told me: 'It went as smooth as butter and the final scene with all the fellas peeling off in their own directions was magic. We'd proved ourselves to be a brilliant team. No doubt about it.'

The extremely unseasonal freezing temperatures guaranteed that there was even less traffic than normal for a Bank Holiday weekend. So the gang – in all their separate vehicles – slipped through the empty London streets with ease.

Job done.

It was later said that Terry Perkins had performed all his tasks with great efficiency and precision. One of his former associates told me: 'Terry is a complete pro. He doesn't get worked up. He is steely determined and he always does exactly what he is supposed to do.'

Perkins and the rest of the gang said later they'd never felt such a buzz as they did during the Security Express job. It undoubtedly fuelled their addiction to crime, something that probably had a huge influence on Perkins' decision to pull off an even bigger job thirty-two years later.

The Security Express gang intended to disperse the millions of pounds in used notes very gradually, so as not to alert the authorities. But laundering tons of stolen banknotes would be no easy task. It might have taken a criminal genius to plan and commit the robbery but, as usual, the hardest part would be getting away with it.

So Perkins and the rest of the gang kept a low profile in the days and weeks following the raid. Perkins remained with his wife Jacqueline and family at his semi-detached home in the North London suburb of Enfield. But – as is so often the case – those millions of pounds in cash were burning a hole in all the gang's pockets.

Over the next few months Perkins flew to the Channel Islands many times, where he deposited much of the cash in bank accounts. The gang believed these could not be touched by the authorities. Perkins' own accountant later said that Perkins turned up one day at his office after the Security Express job and gave him £50,000 in cash and asked him to 'look after it'.

Perkins' wife Jacqueline later said she knew Perkins had been up to something. But it wasn't until he started giving her vast wads of cash that she realized he must have been on the Security Express team. Perkins was a walking contradiction. He was smart and savvy one moment and incredibly clumsy the next. It was the story of his life.

Perkins was eventually arrested at his house in Enfield, where £5,000 in cash from the robbery was discovered by detectives. It then emerged that Perkins had used some of his share of the Security Express cash to buy a number of London properties. At the time of his arrest, detectives calculated he'd already earned £250,000 profit on property transactions he made following the robbery.

But it was the cash payments Perkins made into his elderly mother's bank account that provided the most blatant evidence of all to police. The large amounts of money couldn't be explained away easily as the elderly Mrs Perkins was a lavatory cleaner. Once again, investigators were amazed at how sloppy Perkins had been.

Then Jacqueline Perkins virtually implicated herself in her husband's crimes by talking openly about her husband's involvement in the raid. This certainly wasn't supposed to happen to the wife of a professional criminal. Detectives investigating the robbery decided to charge her with handling the stolen cash.

Meanwhile, some of Perkins' fellow gang members fled to Spain's Costa del Crime before they could be arrested. Perkins had a villa in another part of Spain. One visitor to this area – the so-called Costa Blanca – had been Brian Reader. Both men had been introduced to each other through a mutual acquaintance just before the Security Express job, according to sources who have spoken to this author.

Back in London in February 1985, Perkins and his wife Jacqueline went on trial alongside some of the other members of the Security Express gang. Perkins told the court he'd made all his money out of property deals and had not committed the robbery. He appeared very nervous during the trial and claimed he had a long-standing heart problem.

Perkins was found guilty of the robbery and sentenced to twenty-two years. The judge called him and co-defendant John Knight 'two evil, ruthless men'.

Jacqueline was acquitted, kissed her husband on the lips and wished him 'good luck' when she left the dock. Perkins always believed his sentence was unfairly long and he held a grudge against the Establishment from that moment onwards. Later, he appealed against his sentence but then didn't bother turning up in court because he didn't believe he would get a fair hearing.

Perkins' biggest gripe with his sentence was that he'd reached the age of 37 yet never been in any trouble before. Sure, he'd spent much of his adult life frequenting scrapyards, pubs and nightclubs used by the London underworld but that didn't make him guilty of any crimes in the eyes of the law.

One of Perkins' oldest friends later said: 'Terry wasn't happy about the length of the sentence but he prided himself on his professionalism so he got his head down and let it be known that he was prepared to do his "bird". That's the sign of a true professional.'

Back in the late summer of 1983 – with the public still captivated by the daring, headline-grabbing Security Express heist – a group of South London robbers were about to pull off a heist that would put Terry Perkins and his Security Express mates in the shade. Their target was the Brink's-Mat security warehouse near Heathrow airport.

The BBC TV news bulletin on Saturday, 26 November 1983 summed it up perfectly:

THE HISTORY

An armed gang has carried out Britain's largest ever robbery at London's Heathrow airport.

Over £25m worth of gold bullion bound for the Far East was stolen from the Brink's-Mat warehouse, about one mile outside the airport perimeter, between 0630 and 0815 GMT.

Police have said a group of at least six men overcame the guards and successfully disabled a huge array of electronic security devices.

Insurers have offered a reward of £2m for information leading to the recovery of the 6,800 gold bars – which are all identifiable by refiners' stamps.

The members of the gang – who were all armed and wearing balaclavas – also stole £100,000 worth of cut and uncut diamonds.

They dressed in security uniforms to get into the warehouse and then terrorized the guards into giving them the alarm codes. All the guards were handcuffed, one was hit on the head with a pistol and two had petrol poured over them.

Once inside the safes, the robbers used the warehouse's own forklift trucks to transport the 76 boxes of gold into a waiting van.

The alarm was raised by one of the guards at 0830 GMT after the gang had left.

Scotland Yard Flying Squad chief Commander Frank Cater is leading the hunt for the thieves.

He said: 'There is no doubt they had inside information and were a highly professional team.'

The Brink's-Mat gang had expected rich pickings but they'd never imagined the extraordinary level of wealth they stumbled upon that day. Their audacious plot, ruthless in its conception and brilliant in its execution, had just landed them the biggest gold haul in British criminal history. The robbery would go on to make the names and fortunes of many of London's most notorious gangsters, but its bloody tentacles would spark a vicious, deadly, gang war in the London underworld that still rages to this day.

Police have always reckoned a six-man gang was involved in the Brink's-Mat robbery itself but only two of the actual robbers were ever convicted. Micky McAvoy and Brian Robinson were both jailed for twenty-five years. Inside man Tony Black – Robinson's brother-in-law – got six years for letting the robbers into the warehouse.

Black had been the predictable weak link when the police began reeling in the usual suspects. He summed it all up when he told police after being arrested: 'I'm feeling much better now. It's like a weight off my mind. It was just too big. I couldn't handle it. There's one thing though. I'm worried about these people, what they're going to do to me . . .'

As ex-robber Billy explained more than thirty years later: 'Those lads had pulled off a brilliant robbery. But then they went and got nicked very quickly and didn't have a decent system in place to smelt the gold down and turn it into hard cash.'

No wonder Reader and his Kent friend Kenneth Noye smelled an opportunity to make a lot of money . . .

CHAPTER SEVEN

PARTNERS IN CRIME

Brian Reader and Kenneth Noye attended a wedding in Kent in early 1984. Some of the guests knew the villains involved in the Brink's-Mat heist and there was a lot of talk and speculation about where all the Brink's-Mat gold bullion had ended up.

But when a photographer at the wedding took a photo of Noye among a group of guests, Noye exploded with rage, grabbed the camera from the photographer and ripped out the film.

Brian Reader watched the whole episode with mild amusement. He knew that Noye was a bit of a loose cannon, so he certainly wasn't going to reprimand him. Other guests at the wedding stepped away and tried to ignore the incident because many of them also knew how dangerous Noye could be.

Noye made it clear that he didn't like any photos of himself circulating because he didn't want them to fall into the hands of the police. He also implied that the wedding photographer might have been working for the police anyway.

Reader shared Noye's suspicious nature to a certain degree, though he did later admit to one associate that he found himself wondering why Noye overreacted so violently to such relatively harmless incidents. But then the London underworld was full of characters with hair-trigger temperaments like Noye, so Reader let it pass. Something he would later deeply regret.

The previous year – 1983 – both men had earned a small fortune from their VAT gold bullion scam. However, according to one associate from the Kent underworld, Reader and Noye managed to spend that money even faster than they earned it. The friend explained: 'Brian and Kenny were turning into right flash bastards. Everyone knew they was minted from gold dealing and a lot of villains started to get a bit envious.'

All this newfound wealth soon led to villas in Spain, speedboats, expensive cars. Noye owned half a dozen properties in the London suburbs and even bought his wife Brenda a £10,000 fur coat as well as a house for his mistress.

Brian Reader splashed out on the ultimate status symbol – a gold Rolls-Royce, which he insisted he only ever took out on special occasions. Reader was also said to be flashing a lot of cash around the pubs and clubs of South London. At one stage Reader and Noye were said to have owned seven cars between them.

Noye even knocked down his original detached house in the Kent countryside and built a completely new property in its place. He was also rumoured to keep wild animals such as tigers and wolves in the grounds.

And yet, despite all this influx of huge amounts of cash, neither man was renowned for his generosity. 'The pair of 'em were bloody tight fisted,' recalled one associate. 'Trying to get Brian and Ken to put their hands in their pockets for a pint in the pub was a bleedin' nightmare!'

It was clear to many in the South East London underworld that both men had developed an unhealthy addiction to money.

'They were always on the lookout for new earners, even when they were raking it in with the VAT fiddle on the gold. Basically they was greedy bastards,' added the associate.

But Brian Reader wasn't entirely comfortable with so much cash and eventually realized he needed to stop being so flashy because it was attracting all the worst sort of attention from criminals and police alike. So Reader moved from his classic detached Georgian mansion in Blackheath to a much cheaper house in more downmarket Grove Park, a suburb of South London sandwiched between Lewisham and Bromley. Reader liked its location because it was very convenient for driving to central London and Kent. Reader later told one friend he was also far happier in a more modest area, nearer to many of his more down-to-earth criminal acquaintances.

Having already let it be known they were prepared to help smelt down the Brink's-Mat gold, it was no big surprise when Reader and Noye were called to a meeting with a South London gangster rumoured to have been one of the gold bullion robbers. We'll call him The Fox here because even his real nickname would give away his identity. The Fox said he and jailed Brink's-Mat robbers Mickey McAvoy and Brian Robinson were looking for partners to help turn the Brink's-Mat gold into cash. Most of the bullion had lain untouched because both robbers had been arrested just weeks after the robbery and subsequently landed long prison sentences.

Reader and Noye were delighted to get involved. Not only could they turn the gold into cash and claim a large commission but they believed they could make an extra 15 per cent financial killing through the VAT scam, once the original gold had been smelted down.

As one old South London villain said years later: 'I could see the pound signs registering in their eyes every time they talked about the Brink's-Mat gold. It was a win-win deal for them and a lot of us were sure they'd make more money out of that gold than the poor bastards serving those long stretches for nicking it in the first place.'

Brian Reader immediately headed for his beloved Hatton Garden to look up some 'old friends', who would undoubtedly be able to help him smelt down the Brink's-Mat gold and eventually turn it into tens of millions of pounds.

The key to the success of the operation was to spread all the gold around to various locations in southern and western England, where it could then be smelted. It had been made clear to Reader and Noye that if any of the bullion went missing then they would be considered responsible and that could prove very costly for them.

Brian Reader was in his element. He was careful never to transport more than two bars of the Brink's-Mat gold at any one time. That way no one was ever likely to find it in his vehicle. A lot of the gold was stored in a secret underground cellar at Noye's isolated Kent farmhouse. From there, Reader took some of the bars to another notorious villain called John Palmer, who was based in the West Country. Palmer had a smelter on the premises of his £1 million Wiltshire farmhouse and was also prepared to transport small amounts of the gold abroad on a private jet he had access to at Bristol airport, near to where Palmer lived.

Many of the reconstituted gold bars were then smuggled out of the UK in the Tupperware lunchboxes of dozens of lorry drivers, who worked for a haulage company owned by one of Noye and Reader's oldest friends in the South East of England. The gold was then brought back into Britain from Holland and that's when the VAT was claimed on it by Reader and Noye.

Inside prison, the only two robbers to be convicted of the Brink's-Mat heist kept a close eye on developments through their own associates. No one completely trusted Reader and Noye. However, the two professional robbers had little choice but to use their 'services'.

Reader told one associate he drove between Kent, the West Country, South London and Hatton Garden on at least thirty occasions in the autumn of 1984. Some of the time he'd drive in his gold Rolls-Royce because it actually didn't look out of place among the wealthy gem and gold dealers of Hatton Garden. Other times he'd head down the M4 motorway to Palmer's home near Bristol in his more modest Vauxhall or one of the other cars he owned.

On one occasion, Reader broke his own rule and put too many gold bars in the boot of his Rolls-Royce because he was getting bored of driving back and forth to Hatton Garden and Wiltshire. But Noye stopped him on the long driveway of his Kent house and insisted Reader remove some of the bars. Noye laughed as he said Reader's Roller was so obviously overloaded it was virtually scrapping the tarmac. The paranoid Noye didn't want anyone to even try and guess what they were up to.

And in the middle of all this frenetic activity, Reader found himself going home at night to a sickly wife who needed constant attention. Lyn had developed diabetes and now the doctors were saying she needed an operation because of problems with her pancreas. So Brian Reader the cunning, calculating professional criminal turned into a caring husband every evening after he came home having ferried stolen gold bullion round half the country.

And back in the underworld, many heard rumours about Reader and Noye's Brink's-Mat gold bullion smelting operation.

And some of those villains got in touch with their 'friends' in the Flying Squad.

By early January 1985, Brian Reader had handled at least £4 million worth of the Brink's-Mat gold. Then he and Noye worked out they both seemed to be under round-the-clock Flying Squad surveillance. But neither of them was particularly bothered by it. They believed they'd set up such a brilliant filtering system for the gold that it would be impossible for the police to pin anything on them.

There was an added complication for Reader, though, because he was still technically on the run from those burglary charges he'd faced alongside his friend John Goodwin three years earlier. But the police who were now watching him and Noye weren't interested in such things. They wanted to recover the Brink's-Mat gold, so the charges against Reader were conveniently put to one side.

Meanwhile Reader and Noye amused themselves by leading their police shadows down a lot of 'dark alleys'. One time, Reader changed cars three times over a 20-mile journey just to confuse detectives. That provided a red herring which then enabled one of Noye's other associates to slip out of his farmhouse with another load of gold heading in the opposite direction.

During the first few weeks of January 1985, Reader and Noye led their police 'tails' a merry dance while attending meetings, some of which were held in Hatton Garden. Reader met with a gold dealer called Christopher Weyman, who ran a business called Lustretone Ltd, in Greville Street, just around the corner from 88–90 Hatton Garden. But none of these meetings provided Flying Squad detectives with any concrete evidence linking Reader and Noye to the Brink's-Mat gold (Weyman himself was later acquitted of involvement with the Brink's-Mat stolen bullion).

THE HISTORY

Reader became such a regular visitor to Hatton Garden at this time that he was on first-name terms with many traders. Reader and Weyman often joked about the best robbery targets in Hatton Garden itself, including the safety deposit vault at 88–90 Hatton Garden, which many crooks had had their eyes on for years. But for the moment Brian Reader had a much more lucrative criminal enterprise in mind.

Back in deepest Kent, specialist C11 undercover detectives from the Metropolitan Police's criminal intelligence branch had moved into position in a row of bushes by the public road by the entrance to the long driveway belonging to Kenneth Noye's home, Hollywood Cottage.

Just above the huge cast-iron gates that protected the entrance to Noye's driveway, a video camera disguised as a bird box was placed in an overhanging tree. Meanwhile over at the street outside Reader's large detached house in Grove Park, a variety of unmarked police vehicles kept watch after Reader got home from yet another trip to Hatton Garden.

And so the two men continued their cat and mouse games with the police. One detective later claimed Reader drove out of Noye's home one morning in his Rolls-Royce smirking at the police like the drug baron in *The French Connection* as he escaped the New York detective played by Gene Hackman on the city's subway system. The police were so infuriated they began pouring more and more officers into the gold bullion surveillance operation.

Many years later, Reader told acquaintances that he believed he and Noye made a lot of elementary mistakes while they were turning all that Brink's-Mat gold into cash. But the biggest of those mistakes was about to come crashing down around both men.

CHAPTER EIGHT

CASUALTIES OF WAR

At 6.12 p.m. on 26 January 1985, Brian Reader turned up at the front gate to Noye's isolated house in his Vauxhall Cavalier, pressed the intercom and was buzzed in. It was pitch dark. There was a sprinkling of snow on the ground and the temperature was so low, the spotlights at Noye's entrance illuminated the dense, misty air.

Once inside the house, Noye took Brian Reader into the kitchen to show him some photographs – taken earlier that month – of the cottage covered in snow. A cup of tea was made. Then Noye took Reader into his study to discuss gold bullion business.

Moments later, both men heard Noye's dogs making a commotion outside. Noye opened the study door and shouted to his wife: 'Brenda what's happening with those dogs?'

'They're down by the barn,' replied Brenda Noye. 'I'm not going down there. It's too dark.'

So Noye grabbed his leather jacket from behind a chair and left Reader and Brenda standing on the front porch of the house as he headed off down into the darkness towards the commotion.

As Noye passed his Ford Granada parked on the driveway, he

grabbed a torch from it and took a knife he'd been using earlier to clean the car's battery tops.

Holding both items in his left hand, Noye continued walking down the drive calling to the older of the dogs, Sam, and one of the puppies, Cleo. The other dog, Cassie, was still in the kitchen. Reaching the apple store area, Noye saw the dogs on a pile of sand barking into the shrubbery. He swung the torch in the same direction and moved further into the wooded area, letting the beam sweep across the ground in front of him.

Just then a noise to Noye's left attracted his attention and he swung the beam of light in that direction. It fell on a hooded figure just four or five feet away. Noye later claimed he immediately froze with horror as all he could see of the man were two eyeholes staring out from under a mask.

Noye insisted the intruder then struck him a blow across his face. Immediately after being hit, Noye dropped the torch, grabbed the knife from his pocket and put his left hand up to the other man's face and grabbed him.

Noye later claimed he used all his brute strength to smash his fists into the man's body over and over again. But still the man kept coming. Dressed in black, and with that mask on, the intruder seemed like a deadly giant as he lunged towards Noye.

On the porch of Hollywood Cottage, Brenda Noye heard the commotion and rushed upstairs to the couple's bedroom cupboard and took out a shotgun – one of at least half a dozen the couple kept hidden around the house. She also grabbed four cartridges from a nearby cabinet.

Outside in the garden, Noye was plunging his knife into the attacker, and in the tussle that followed both men crashed to the ground. The intruder fell on top of Noye, who stabbed him again and again. Noye broke free and started running away, looking back momentarily to see the figure staggering to his feet and moving towards the perimeter garden wall.

Loading the gun as she ran, Brenda Noye – in tracksuit and slippers – headed out of the house and down the drive. Brian Reader moved alongside her and she handed the weapon to him.

Halfway down the driveway, they met Noye.

'There's a masked man down there,' shouted a breathless Noye.

He grabbed the gun from Reader, dropping his torch in the process.

Noye quickly picked the torch up off the ground and began running back down the drive with Brenda and Reader close behind. Noye came across his dogs surrounding the masked figure, now lying slumped on the ground. Noye leaned down alongside the wounded man.

'Who are you?' shouted Noye. 'Who are you?' The intruder was still wearing his balaclava hood. Noye noticed a pair of night-sight binoculars around his neck.

Later Noye would claim that he thought he'd been dealing with a rapist or a peeping Tom.

'Who are you? Take that mask off!' shouted Noye. But there was no response from the man on the ground. 'Who are you? Take that mask off!' Noye repeated as he pointed the shotgun at the man. There was still no reaction.

'If you don't take that mask off and tell me who you are, I'll blow yer head off,' shouted Noye. Then, according to Noye's later testimony, the man groaned and began to take off his hood while mumbling the words: 'SAS.'

A beat of silence followed.

Then the man added: 'On manoeuvres.'

'Show us your ID, then,' ordered Noye.

Brian Reader and Brenda Noye looked on nervously.

There was no reply from the man this time. Under torchlight he looked deathly pale.

Brian Reader was worried. He sensed the intruder was probably a policeman.

Kenneth Noye, meanwhile, found himself bleeding from a cut near his eye and nose, injuries caused during his struggle with the man. Noye had also reached the same conclusion as Reader and he knew he needed photographic evidence of the struggle.

'Get a camera, Brenda, quick,' ordered Noye. And, as an afterthought: 'You'd better call an ambulance for him.'

Noye stood over the man for a few more moments, looking down at him. Then he knelt down and opened the man's jacket to get a closer look at the wounds he'd inflicted just a few moments earlier.

In a much quieter voice Noye then asked the intruder: 'What the fuck are you doing here?'

The man didn't answer. His head fell back awkwardly, so Noye put his arm under him to get him into a better position.

Brian Reader stood frozen to the spot. He could hear voices just beyond the garden wall and it was obvious they were policemen.

Moments later a police car smashed through the wrought iron gates to Hollywood Cottage, confirming Reader's worst fears.

Reader immediately turned and started running through the bushes alongside the perimeter wall of Noye's property. It's never been clear if Noye encouraged Reader to flee or whether Reader just took off. Moments later, Reader scrambled over the wall and found himself dashing across a snowy field. He'd run away once before and now he was about to try to do it again. If it meant a life on the lam then so be it.

In the deserted countryside beyond the perimeter of Noye's

house, Brian Reader ran through a small wooded area, almost falling into a stream. Then he jumped a gate and headed across snow-covered fields before eventually reaching the main A20 road, connecting London to the Kent coast.

The road was deserted. Then after a few moments, a vehicle appeared so far ahead of Reader that he couldn't make out whether it was a car or a van. Reader hesitated, then started waving his thumb in its direction.

Travelling towards him along the A20 from the London direction were Flying Squad detectives Alan Branch and John Redgrave in an unmarked car. Redgrave immediately recognized Reader from surveillance duties as they got nearer to the solitary figure who was thumbing a ride on the roadside. The detectives slowed their vehicle down gradually as they prepared to stop.

Reader recognized the make of car as being one often used by the police. He hesitated. Just then another car came round the corner from the opposite direction. Reader turned towards it and put out his thumb once again. The vehicle immediately came to a halt.

As the driver's window opened slowly, Reader leaned in.

'Any chance of a lift to London?' asked Reader.

'Yeah, get in,' replied the man at the wheel.

Reader had just slammed the back door shut and was taking a long sigh of relief when the driver revealed that he and his passenger next to him were Kent police officers. They asked Reader where he'd just come from.

'The pub,' replied Reader, indicating a tavern called The Gamecock, which they had just passed in the car.

The officers didn't believe Reader and he was then ordered to put his hands on top of the front passenger seat, despite his protestations of innocence.

Reader was then handcuffed and driven back to the car park at another nearby pub called The Portobello Inn, where other Kent CID officers were waiting. Reader later said he couldn't believe his bad luck to have had policemen coming in *both* directions when he stood there thumbing a lift.

Reader was then taken to Swanley police station where he was told he was being arrested on suspicion of assaulting a police officer earlier that night.

Reader responded: 'What?' The charges were then repeated. 'You must be joking!' he replied.

Kenneth Noye and his wife Brenda also ended up at Swanley that night. Noye – who'd earlier been transferred from Dartford police station – didn't even realize Reader was in an adjacent cell.

At 3.15 the following afternoon, Reader was seen by Detective Superintendent David Tully, of Kent Police.

When he was told that his wife Lyn had been arrested and was at nearby Gravesend police station, Reader immediately expressed concern because she was a diabetic and due to go into hospital the next day for treatment on her pancreas.

'I want you to know, Mr Tully, that she is a very sick woman and needs medical attention,' said Reader, whose concern was undoubtedly genuine, as his actions later in life would go on to prove.

Tully assured Reader he'd personally go to Gravesend to make certain she was all right.

Then Brian Reader tried to turn on the charm.

'This is a very serious matter,' he told the detective. 'I know a police officer has been murdered, and I was told I was responsible. I want you to know, Mr Tully, that I do not know anything about it and I did not have anything to do with it.'

Brian Reader then made a very uncharacteristic mistake. He

admitted that he and Kenneth Noye had been discussing the Brink's-Mat gold earlier that evening at Noye's house. Whether Reader did that deliberately in order to 'water down' his involvement with the death of the undercover policeman, we will never know.

Reader quickly realized his error because he then told the detective in a toneless voice he would not answer any more questions without his solicitor being present.

Police forensic examinations at Hollywood Cottage quickly connected Reader and Noye to the stolen bullion through globular fragments of gold discovered on the boot mat of Noye's Ford Granada and Reader's Vauxhall. Police also discovered eleven gold bars wrapped in red-and-white cloth hidden in a shallow gully beside the garage wall.

So Reader's confession at the police station wasn't a game changer but the police were able to use his admission to put pressure on Noye.

Reader later told one associate he believed he and Noye were being 'fitted up' for the murder of undercover officer Detective Constable John Fordham, whom they claimed they thought was a burglar. Reader was convinced the police wanted instant revenge for the death of one of their officers.

Detectives also said they'd found paperwork with telephone numbers that proved a further link between Reader and Noye. The safes in Noye's house were also inspected, and silver trophies and gold watches removed.

Brian Reader, Kenneth Noye and his wife Brenda were all charged with the murder of DC Fordham. Reader and Noye were also both charged with conspiracy to handle stolen bullion. Reader's wife Lyn was released without charge and later all charges against Noye's wife Brenda were also dropped.

One policeman who was present while Reader was at Swanley police station later recalled: 'Reader looked shaken to be in there. He clearly felt the killing of John Fordham was down to his mate Noye and it was irritating the hell out of him that they'd only been arrested because of something that wasn't even connected to the Brink's-Mat gold.'

Years later, Brian Reader told one associate that he believed if Noye hadn't discovered Fordham in his garden that night then he and Noye might never have been arrested on the gold bullion charges. 'The death of that copper was a disaster. It made the Old Bill go crazy and they were never going to let us out of their sights after that,' Reader told his associate.

The killing of an undercover policeman in the grounds of Kenneth Noye's home completely overshadowed Security Express robber Terry Perkins' trial at the Old Bailey during this same period. Perkins was very thankful because he wasn't seeking underworld fame. He liked to stay out of the press. It was bad for business.

CHAPTER NINE

BANG TO RIGHTS

Brian Reader and Kenneth Noye's trial for the murder of detective John Fordham took place at the Old Bailey in November 1985. At the request of the defence, other proceedings relating to the handling of the gold and VAT fraud were deferred to a later date.

The drama was played out in front of a jury of seven men and five women, packed press benches and a public gallery filled with well-known 'faces' from the criminal underworld. Security was so tight that each time Reader and Noye arrived or left in a prison van, streets around the court were closed off and armed police snipers posted at various vantage points overlooking the Old Bailey.

There were also genuine fears that someone might try and nobble the jury. This was partly fuelled when Brian Reader's old friend John Goodwin turned up in the public gallery at the Old Bailey on day one of the trial. Just a few years earlier Goodwin had been sentenced to seven years for jury nobbling in the burglary trial in which he and the then absent Reader had been co-defendants.

As a result, seventy-two police officers were assigned to jury protection duty during Reader and Noye's trial. It was a huge show of force, deliberately intended to tell the criminals that they should not even attempt to influence the jury.

Brian Reader's legal counsel insisted from the outset that his client had no case to answer. Reader exercised his right not to give evidence. It was a risky strategy but Reader was worried that the prosecution might trick him into saying something he would later regret.

Reader could only be found guilty *if* Noye was first proved to have murdered Fordham and *if* Reader was proved to have given assistance or participated in an assault with the intention of killing Fordham, or causing him serious injury. The court was told that Brian Reader had been seen to make a kicking motion by Fordham's undercover police colleague, Neil Murphy. But Murphy did not identify where the kick landed, and his claim had been made in a statement five months after Fordham's death.

The court also heard about Noye and Reader's criminal activities, when it was explained why the two defendants were under police surveillance. The prosecution claimed that the stakes were so high with the Brink's-Mat gold that Reader and Noye had no compunction about murdering anyone who might jeopardize their activities.

After twelve hours and thirty-seven minutes of jury deliberation, not guilty verdicts were returned against both Reader and Noye. The jury accepted that the killing had been in self-defence.

Brian Reader turned to the jury and said, 'Thank you for proving my innocence.'

Noye smiled, looked at his wife, then turned to the jury and said, 'Thank you very much. God bless you.'

The mood of gratitude was spoiled a few moments later when Reader and Noye stared menacingly towards the back of the court and then began sneering and mouthing obscenities at a group of Flying Squad detectives.

Brian Reader went home to wife Lyn after the end of the trial and withdrew completely from any criminal activities. He knew the police were watching him closely but more importantly he needed to give Lyn some loving care and attention. Her condition as a diabetic had worsened and those problems with her pancreas, which had first occurred during the gold bullion days, were ongoing.

To those who knew Reader well at this time, his actions were no surprise. One friend later said: 'Brian was a classic carer in many ways. He had this gentle side to him that very few people, apart from his family, ever knew about. After that trial he went out of his way to devote himself to Lyn and her health problems. Nothing else really mattered. You know, villains don't often make very good carers but Brian was different. He really did have that side to his character. I think it's why he so hated all the violence and the guns.'

Five months later – in May 1986 – a supremely confident Brian Reader and Kenneth Noye strolled back into the dock at the Old Bailey's Number 12 court to face charges relating to their Brink's-Mat gold bullion-smelting activities and the VAT fraud. Both men had the aura of invincibility about them following their earlier acquittal. Alongside them in the dock were five other fellow Brink's-Mat-connected conspirators.

The loss adjusters handling the Brink's-Mat insurance claims were so concerned that the accused men might be acquitted they'd already launched a civil action against them. In a High Court action, a judge agreed that the assets of all seven – including Noye and Reader – should be frozen pending an outcome of any civil hearings.

But such moves were of no great consequence to professional criminals like Reader and Noye because all their property and vehicles were registered in other's people's names. And they didn't use regular banks to keep their cash safe, either.

Noye, Reader and one other man were eventually found guilty of conspiracy to handle stolen bullion and avoiding VAT. Reader was also convicted of dishonestly handling £66,000.

Pointing to the jury, Reader exploded, as the verdicts against both men sank in.

'You have made one terrible mistake. You have got to live with that for the rest of your life,' said Reader, angrily.

He was then described by the judge as Noye's 'vigorous right-hand man', before being jailed for a total of nine years, including an extra year for handling that cash.

Noye – who was later sentenced to fourteen years in prison – screamed at the jury: 'I hope you all die of cancer.'

Reader's twenty-year-old son – also called Brian, but known as Paul – scuffled with police officers as the sentences were announced.

'You've been fuckin' fixed up!' he screamed.

Paul Reader was arrested for contempt of court and later bound over in the sum of £100 to keep the peace for twelve months. Reader's son and his loyal wife Lyn had attended every day of the hearing, which seemed to prove that despite everything, Reader still retained very close links to his family.

Lyn was besieged by the press following the trial and even turned down an offer of £1,000 from one tabloid who'd specifically demanded a photo of Reader supping champagne. Paul Reader was encouraged not to follow his father into crime and got himself a job as a stagehand at the Barbican theatre in London shortly after this.

Once incarcerated, Brian Reader calmed down and took the pragmatic route by sensibly deciding to keep his head down and serve his sentence in the hope that if he avoided trouble he could be released within four or five years with remission.

In Brian Reader's world this wasn't really such a bad result. Sure he'd be away from his family but he'd make sure they were well looked after while he was inside. Reader was very careful not to boast to anyone about how much money he'd made out of his Brink's-Mat bullion activities. But it was presumed in the London underworld that he would be 'minted' once he was released.

In prison, Reader initially enjoyed the fame of being 'one of the Brink's-Mat boys', as everyone connected to that robbery was known inside jail. But he switched back to being more low profile as news of the fate of other criminals handling the Brink's-Mat gold began filtering into prison.

Feuds had been fuelled when a significant quantity of the gold bullion 'went missing' during the period Reader was involved with smelting it down. The Brink's-Mat robbery had turned from the job everyone wished they'd been on to the one no one wanted to touch with a barge-pole.

Reader was understandably worried that he might end up a victim of what people in the London underworld now called 'The Curse of Brink's-Mat'. Noye was typically more defiant and warned that if anyone came after him there would be hell to pay.

Inside prison, Reader linked up again with Security Express robber Terry Perkins. The pair had a lot in common, thanks to their connections to the UK's two most lucrative robberies of recent years, which also guaranteed them a measure of respect from most other inmates.

Perkins is today remembered fondly by former prisoners who knew him at that time. They describe him as 'a very old-school

London criminal gent'. Other inmates were well aware that Perkins was already a wealthy property developer but say that he always retained a 'warm personality' and never looked down on other inmates.

Perkins' cell became renowned for meetings during grub and slop-out sessions. However, some recall Perkins often looking a bit sickly due to his 'dodgy ticker'. He had a genuine heart complaint, which inhibited his ability to do any over-exertion.

Meanwhile in the outside world, crime – like everything else – was booming. London in the late 1980s was virtually wall-to-wall with lucrative robbery targets.

In the summer of 1987, an Italian-born 31-year-old career criminal based in London called Valerio Viccei decided to stash his stolen money from recent crimes plus a gun in the Knightsbridge Safe Deposit Centre, just opposite London's most upmarket store Harrods. There he discovered that owner Parvez Latif had a weakness for cocaine and that his business was losing money. So handsome Viccei homed in on Latif – and even began a secret affair with Latif's girlfriend.

Latif told Viccei all about the riches hidden in the boxes inside the safe deposit vault. It was, in the words of one detective who investigated the case, 'a no-brainer' for a career criminal like Viccei on the lookout for his next big payday.

On 12 July 1987, Viccei and an accomplice entered the Knightsbridge Safe Deposit Centre and requested to rent a box for their valuables. After being shown into the vault, the two men produced handguns and subdued the duty manager and security guards. The pair then hung a sign on the street-level entrance explaining that the Safe Deposit Centre was temporarily closed, while letting in further accomplices.

Security guard uniforms, metal-cutting equipment, walkie-talkies and the owner's complicity ultimately enabled Viccei and his gang to clear 114 boxes over a weekend inside the vault. The victims included royalty, celebrities, millionaires and criminals. No shots were fired and no one was injured. To many it seemed like the perfect crime.

The haul was so vast that Viccei filled his bath with bank-notes and covered the floor of his flat in Hampstead, North London, with glittering jewels. One diamond alone was worth over £4 million.

The true value of Viccei's haul will never be known as more than thirty keyholders failed to come forward following the robbery. In some ways that made it an even more perfect crime, because the police would never know exactly what had been stolen. Viccei's haul was eventually valued at £40 million (equiv-alent to at least £140 million today).

Prison inmates Brian Reader and Terry Perkins avidly read every word of the newspaper reports of Viccei's exploits. His crime hit a nerve with them as safety deposit box vaults were perfect targets because they often contained valuable items that would never be reclaimed by their owners, even in the event of a robbery. That meant no one – not even the police – could ever accurately establish the true value of what had been stolen.

Three days after the Knightsbridge robbery, police forensic officers found a bloody fingerprint on one of the safety deposit boxes. It turned out to be a match to a set the Italian authori-ties had sent over a few weeks earlier belonging to wanted bank robber Valerio Viccei. By mid-August 1987, several of Viccei's London accomplices were under Flying Squad surveillance, but detectives believed that Viccei himself had already fled to Latin America.

However, Viccei was then spotted by Flying Squad detectives driving around London in his red Ferrari. When officers swooped on Viccei in Park Lane, in the centre of the capital, they found £2 million of valuables stolen from the Knightsbridge vault in the boot of Viccei's car. Only £10 million of the £40 million stolen from the Safe Deposit Centre was ever recovered. Viccei was eventually sentenced to twenty-two years for his part in the heist.

The key to the Knightsbridge job had been the way Viccei turned over the inside man Parvez Latif (he ended up getting sixteen years for his part in the robbery). It was something that Brian Reader and Terry Perkins discussed at great length. As ex-robber Billy later explained: 'An inside man was essential for this sort of job but they were also a bleedin' liability because they usually ended up crumbling under pressure from the police.'

Viccei's only mistake in the eyes of old-school villains Reader and Perkins was that he was a 'flash git'. Ex-robber Billy explained: 'Viccei should have kept a lower profile. He'd have got away with it all if he hadn't started driving around London in a red Ferrari. But you gotta admire the fella's bottle and after all, he did pull off one hell of a job.'

In Viccei's case, no amount of cash could have prevented him from dying in a hail of bullets in a shootout with Italian police in 2000.

What comes around . . .

CHAPTER TEN

BANDITS HIGH

Back inside prison, Reader and Perkins were noticing a seismic change in the criminal underworld. Drugs were overtaking robberies as the most lucrative source of income for London's professional criminals. Even Charlie Wilson – one of the legendary Great Train Robbers – had become a drug baron in the late 1980s. But he paid the ultimate price for crossing another gang of cocaine smugglers in 1990 when he was killed by a hitman in the garden of his home near Marbella, on the notorious Cost del Crime.

Reader and Perkins concluded that the 'drugs game' was full of nasty, trigger-happy South Americans and to be avoided at all costs. Many inside the London underworld naturally presumed that Reader was able to avoid the drugs business because he still had access to a lot of money earned through handling the Brink's-Mat gold. But no one knew for sure.

In the middle of all this, Reader received news in his prison cell about the murders of at least three of his old criminal associates involved with the handling of the Brink's-Mat bullion. None of this sat easily with Brian Reader. He was genuinely worried that his name might be on some kind of 'hit list'.

On top of this, the worldwide publicity Kenneth Noye had

sparked by stabbing undercover cop John Fordham in his garden had also infuriated the gang behind the actual robbery. They blamed Noye for the police's continued obsession with finding the gold, believing that the killing of a copper had galvanized the police at a time when they were struggling to crack the case.

But in one sense at least Brian Reader was lucky compared to Terry Perkins and Kenneth Noye because he was serving a shorter prison sentence. Of course, that was only good news if Reader could ensure his own safety once he was back in the outside world.

By the time Reader got out of prison in 1991, drugs had indeed taken over much of the London underworld. He was still appalled by them and steadfastly avoided linking up with anyone involved in that 'game'.

But even more worrying for Brian Reader was his discovery that in the outside world there were a lot of people claiming he and Kenneth Noye were police informants. No doubt both men had 'done a bit of back scratching' with a few policemen down the years. But neither of them looked on that as being anything more than 'part of their job' in order to keep in the loop with what the police were up to, or so they later claimed.

Brian Reader considered he'd already paid a huge price for getting involved with Kenneth Noye and he feared that it was only a matter of time before the police came knocking on his door once again. There were rumours flying around Kent and South East London that a unit of Flying Squad detectives had been specifically assigned the task of getting Reader back into prison because of his alleged connection to the death of John Fordham.

Sure enough, the police soon began turning up at Reader's home at all times of the day and night demanding answers to questions about crimes he knew nothing about. Though Reader kept his cool, his patience was wearing thin. He'd even moved with Lyn to an even cheaper area to try and convince the underworld and the police that he did not have access to any of the Brink's-Mat cash. His new house was a detached property in the far from glamorous Kent town of Dartford. Reader had made sure the house was in his son's name, just in case anyone suggested it had been bought with the proceeds of crime.

In some ways, Brian Reader believed he'd been a lot safer inside prison. Now he was out, he felt increasingly vulnerable and he began seriously contemplating leaving the country altogether. It had got so bad that Reader avoided many of his favourite pubs in Kent and South East London for fear of other criminals with some twisted score to settle as a result of that missing Brink's-Mat gold.

It was a tough time for Reader. His income was apparently non-existent. He wanted to avoid all the traditional criminal activities in case the police came down on him. And in every direction he turned, Reader kept coming across old associates, now dealing in drugs.

Cocaine had been quickening the spirits and brains of South Americans for at least four thousand years when the drug barons emerged in the second half of the last century. The coca plants themselves grew virtually everywhere in the moist tropical climate of the Andes – Peru, Ecuador, Chile, Bolivia and Colombia – but the really good quality produce tended to come from areas not too high above sea level. Growing the coca leaf was never a problem. But at that early stage the drug was extremely bulky, so interim laboratories, usually portable, were built close to the growing fields where the leaves were compacted into cocaine paste, which could be smuggled far more easily. And the biggest challenge for cocaine production was the transportation. Pack animals and planes were (and still are) the best way to move that cocaine paste.

Creating street cocaine required one more operation, which involved dissolving the base in ether then combining it with acetone and hydrochloric acid. Then it was allowed to sit out and dry into a white, crystalline substance.

The combined costs of the coca leaves, the chemicals and the cheap labour in South America added up to less that £1,000 for a kilo of 100 per cent pure cocaine, which would then be sold out of the country for £4,000. Once transported to the US or Europe, it would then go on the wholesale market for £35–50,000 a kilo.

The cocaine would then be 'cut' a number of times by interim 'handlers' to boost the weight and maintain the profit margin. The end product often contained no more than 15–20 per cent actual cocaine. It was, in the words of ex-robber Billy, 'a licence to print money'.

No wonder a bunch of washed-up London villains – many of whom were known to Brian Reader – did their sums and worked out that selling 'marching powder' for £60 a gram would generate street profits in the UK of £200–300,000 per £20,000 worth of cocaine.

Finding the right supplier, though, was the key. Without that source, none of it meant anything. 'Don't worry, my friend,' the cartel men told Brian Reader's old gangster mates on the Costa del Crime. 'We can get you all the cocaine you want, if you have the money.'

Up until this time in the 1990s, the UK cocaine market had been supplied by a host of different criminal gangs. The South

Americans avoided supplying the UK directly because they knew that, as foreigners, they would stand out and be asking for trouble. The Latinos needed British 'partners' they could trust, facilitators who could get the drugs into the country safely and in much larger amounts than had been done previously. The old-school villains assured the cocaine cartel reps in Spain that they knew who to bribe and who to avoid in Britain.

Once the UK end of the operation was properly up and running, the money would start pouring in. As one former drug smuggler later explained: 'You need to be patient with the drugs trade. Have a plan and stick to it like glue. Then, if you play your cards right you'll get fucking rich beyond your wildest dreams.'

As any self-respecting professional London villain will tell you, when robberies began being replaced by drugs as the London underworld's most lucrative source of income, the stakes got much higher and the criminal-on-criminal murder rate skyrocketed.

Brian Reader hated the way that drugs had changed all the rules. 'Bleedin' drugs,' he told one Kent associate. 'In the old days it was simple. You did the job, nicked the stuff and then got on with the rest of yer life. But drugs are different; there's always someone lurking just behind you wanting to rip you off or grass you up or kill you.'

As ex-robber Billy also later said: 'The Colombians were ruthless and they struck more fear into the London villains than any copper. But there wasn't much else most of them could do to earn any decent money back then. A lot of the old-timers even started dipping into their own produce and getting off their heads. Then they'd get paranoid and trigger-happy on all that gear.'

No wonder the drug trade in southern Spain was considered

by many professional criminals – including Brian Reader – to be a lethal business.

So, at an age when most people were contemplating a life of quiet retirement, a small group of greying British villains in London and Spain joined the European-wide multimillion-pound cocaine industry. One bunch of Spanish-based British drug barons even tried to set up a private school for all their children based in the heart of the Costa del Sol.

One Kent criminal now in his mid-eighties ran a team of smugglers called 'The Organisation' who were renowned for transporting all types of drugs and other contraband across continents without any problems. Reader had known the owner of The Organisation since the 1950s, when they grew up together in the suburbs of South London.

Reader became a frequent traveller between Spain and the UK in the early 1990s. He tended to stay in one particular villa near Marbella, which he either owned or rented. One of his oldest associates told me: 'Brian was unusual in that he had never taken drugs in his life and looked on them as a mug's game. He understood that drugs were a product to make money out of but he couldn't really understand why anyone would want to take the risk.'

Then one incident in Spain convinced Brian Reader that it was time to get as far away from the drug-riddled Brits on the Costa del Crime as possible.

Reader's associate explained: 'An old South London villain who we all knew had bought into a shipment of nose gear which then went missing while it was in his custody, so to speak. Well, there was hell to pay after that. The Colombians still wanted their money and this man was expected to "punish" his smugglers for losing it. Then it was suggested that maybe the smugglers had nicked it and sold it on for themselves. This old fella was caught right in the middle of it all. It was doing his head in. In the end he paid off everyone including the Colombians and realized that despite all the promised riches from drugs he'd ended up as broke as the day he'd started in the business.'

So Brian Reader headed back to his old manor in Kent and South East London. But there was little for him back in the UK, except the deadly threat of some bitter and twisted villains still convinced he'd ripped off the Brink's-Mat gold. Within days of getting home, Reader was finding himself watching his back even more than when he left.

It soon got so bad that Reader started casting around for somewhere else to head for. Eventually he settled on Northern Cyprus, a place he'd been told about by a family of South London Turkish criminals he'd known for many years. It was, they said, a sunshine paradise with a dark core, which enabled most people to do what they liked without any interference from the state. To Brian Reader it sounded like the perfect location.

CHAPTER ELEVEN

TIMESHARE OR BUST

The island of Cyprus has been divided since 1974 when Turkey invaded the north in response to a military coup on the island, backed by the Greece's military junta. The island was then effectively partitioned with the northern third inhabited by Turkish Cypriots and the southern two-thirds by Greek Cypriots. In 1983, the Turkish-held section of the island declared itself the Turkish Republic of Northern Cyprus. The status of Northern Cyprus as a separate nation was recognised only by Turkey, which kept around 30,000 troops there.

Northern Cyprus was filled with unspoiled beaches and the tinpot Turkish-backed so-called government who ran it were keen to encourage any wealthy foreigners to set up home and businesses there because they were trying to develop it as a tourist destination. Reader had been enticed to the island in the mid-1990s by promises of enormous tax breaks. Whatever money he had left needed to be invested in something long term. So he decided to open a timeshare resort. It was going to be Reader's 'get out of jail card' in order to escape the threats and cold weather back home in 'Blighty'.

Reader had for some time been nurturing an obsession with creating a business that could rival the runaway success of his old criminal associate John 'Goldfinger' Palmer, whose nickname came from his alleged involvement with the Brink's-Mat gold bullion. But it was Palmer's extraordinarily lucrative timeshare business in Tenerife that had earned him a combination of respect and envy in the London underworld. At the height of his notoriety in the 1980s and 1990s, Palmer was said to be worth at least £300 million. He owned a Learjet, two helicopters and a yacht. Palmer even occupied 105th place on the 1996 *Sunday Times* Rich List — a position he shared with the Queen.

Reader planned to construct seventy apartments and villas and then convince tourists that they'd make dream homes in the sun. Timeshare meant they'd only be buying the rights to spend one week a year in those holiday homes. Reader believed he could then sell the same holiday home fifty times over, giving him more profit than any criminal enterprise.

Reader also saw his timeshare project as the perfect refuge; a place where he could make a fortune, enjoy the sunshine and leave all those dodgy deals and psycho villains in London behind. Reader even persuaded some friends and relatives to come over from South London to help run the resort. Reader convinced himself that within five years he'd be as rich as his old associate Palmer and he'd finally be able to put his feet up after nearly half a century of ducking and diving.

However, problems with builders and the mandatory bribing of local planning officials meant the resort took a lot longer than expected to complete. But Brian Reader wasn't too worried. Northern Cyprus was an extremely cheap place to live. He felt a lot safer there than in the badlands of South East London, so he was happy to bide his time

*

Back in the UK, Reader's friend Terry Perkins had found the last couple of years of his prison sentence for the Security Express robbery very hard to deal with. His old resentments about the length of his jail term were making him extremely restless. Nothing could make up for the wasted years he'd spent inside and things weren't helped when an application for early parole was rejected by the prison authorities.

As he told a friend many years later: 'I went a bit loop the loop. I got it in me head that I'd never get out.'

So in mid-1995, Terry Perkins absconded from Springhill Open Prison in Buckinghamshire, heartily fed up of hearing how his mates like Brian Reader were lapping up the Mediterranean sunshine. Perkins had already been given temporary release from prison but had failed to return after this expired.

Even the police and the prison staff were taken aback by Perkins' escape. He'd been a model inmate and his decision to abscond had come completely out of the blue.

'Average height, well built, with greying hair, blue eyes and sporting several distinctive tattoos,' read the description issued by the authorities in the wake of Perkins' disappearance.

Terry Perkins' break-out didn't even get much publicity. Britain had moved on from the heady heist days of the 1980s, so his notoriety as one of the Security Express robbers didn't really mean much any more.

In any case he was a small timer – publicity wise – compared to fellow gang members Ronnie Knight – husband of famous actress Barbara Windsor – and Krays associate Freddie Foreman. An in-depth book about the Security Express robbery had been published before Perkins' escape. But there weren't even any photos of him in the book and he barely got a mention.

And Terry Perkins didn't act or feel like a man on the run.

No one came looking for him and he decided that rather than do the expected thing and head for the sunshine on the Costa del Crime, he'd travel to Portugal where there were a lot less villains and police lurking round every corner.

Perkins ended up buying a villa in the Algarve region in the south of the country where he spent at least three months every year. He travelled in and out of Portugal without ever being stopped at passport control. And he even earned himself a few thousand pounds every year by renting out the property to other Brits whenever he was back in London.

Perkins' decision to go on the lam had been vindicated to a certain degree. The police had never tried to pull him in and he'd turned over a bit of a new leaf, thanks to his property empire in London and Portugal. True, he missed the excitement and glamour of being a professional villain but he certainly didn't miss the days, months and years he'd spent under lock and key.

On 19 May 1996, the murder of a motorist, Stephen Cameron, during a road rage incident on a Kent motorway junction close to where Brian Reader still owned his house in Dartford, sparked a massive police manhunt. It was to dominate UK newspaper headlines and TV news bulletins for many weeks.

A middle-aged motorist had become involved in an altercation with another younger driver on a slip road off the M25 motorway, near Swanley. During the fight, the older man had stabbed and killed the other motorist with a knife.

When Kenneth Noye turned up unexpectedly in Northern Cyprus, Brian Reader had no idea that his old friend was the police's main suspect for that road rage killing. Noye had only been out of prison for less than a year.

Noye was named in the media as the number one suspect a

couple of days after he arrived in Cyprus. Reader was stunned. He'd been with Noye when he'd killed undercover policeman John Fordham just ten years earlier and now Noye had been accused of another very similar attack with a knife that ended in the death of another man.

Noye insisted to Reader he'd been set up by the police in revenge for the Fordham killing. But it soon became clear to Reader that in all probability Noye was the killer. Noye was labelled in the British press as 'Public Enemy Number One' so he wasn't too welcome in Northern Cyprus because his presence was attracting all the wrong sort of attention on the island.

Back in South East London, Kenneth Noye was not surprisingly considered a 'fuckin' liability'. Reader loyally tried to help his old friend but he was mightily relieved when Noye flew off in another criminal's private jet. Noye had concluded the island wasn't a safe enough place for him to hide out from the British police.

Not long after this, Brian Reader discovered that making millions out of a timeshare resort wasn't going to be as easy as he had thought. Reader was ripped off by local cowboy builders as the cost of his development spiralled. Then his old associate John 'Goldfinger' Palmer gleefully rubbed salt in his wounds by informing Reader that North Cyprus didn't even attract enough tourists to make his timeshare resort viable.

A run-in with another group of local builders followed and there were supposedly trumped-up claims that Reader had threatened some residents on the island. Over on Tenerife, John Palmer heard about Reader's demise. 'He should have stuck to VAT fiddles on gold. He was in way over his head [in timeshare],' Palmer told one West Country criminal associate many years later.

Brian Reader's business collapsed before the resort even opened. The abandoned carcasses of his buildings were left scattered half built across a deserted piece of 'prime wasteland' sold to Reader at what later turned out to be an inflated price. Reader had discovered the hard way that his reputation meant nothing in this lawless territory, so he reluctantly accepted a knockdown price for the land from a local developer and quit the island.

Battered and bruised from his experiences in Northern Cyprus, Reader decided it was time to go home to the shallower waters of Dartford. His wife Lyn was much happier back in England and Reader's number one priority had always been to look after her. Lyn's health was not good but Reader was happy to be her carer. He did so, safe in the knowledge that his wife was the only person in the entire world he really trusted.

CHAPTER TWELVE

MISSED OPPORTUNITIES

Back in London, Brian Reader's favourite area of Hatton Garden hit the headlines for all the wrong reasons in 1998 when a well-known diamond dealer was murdered. In a classic gangland shooting, a hitman pumped four bullets into the man outside his North London home before escaping on a waiting motorbike. It emerged that as well as trading in precious stones, the victim was financial adviser to a group of notorious London criminals with close connections to Hatton Garden.

After the murder, it was also revealed that the victim was also suspected of fraud and money laundering 'on an international scale'. The man was said to have met with his crime bosses three or four times a week and arranged for more than £25 million of black money to be hidden in property deals and offshore accounts.

Mind you, those sorts of big money deals must have seemed like a pipedream to Brian Reader at this time. He was back in Kent, struggling to make a living for the first time since he was a teenager. Having been off the manor for some years in Northern Cyprus, Reader now found himself totally out of the loop when it came to the South East London underworld.

Reader hadn't even managed to hold on to his membership

of the Freemasons, thanks to his links to the Brink's-Mat gold and a certain Kenneth Noye. And of course Reader had lost a fortune on that disastrous timeshare resort. He wished he could kick back and relax after a stressful forty-year career but now retirement wasn't even an option.

In 2000, Reader's friend Noye was jailed for life at the Old Bailey for the murder of that innocent motorist on the M25 slip road. Back in grim old Dartford, Reader struggled to pay the bills and maintain his rambling, rundown house despite having bought it for cash many years earlier.

Reader eventually opened a second-hand car dealership in Dartford. He made a point of telling his closest associates he hoped he could make a few bob and keep his head above water. He didn't want anyone in South East London or Kent thinking he still had any money left over from handling the Brink's-Mat gold.

But flogging used cars wasn't as easy as it had been back in the old days. By the late 1990s, many new regulations had been put in place to prevent the sale of 'dodgy motors'. Reader found all the paperwork a nightmare. Back in the 1970s and 1980s, he'd flog a car with false registration documents and then move on to other things without any repercussions.

And just around the corner from Dartford, in the criminal badlands of Kent and South East London, yet more villains linked to the Brink's-Mat gold were paying the ultimate price for their connection to the raid. Reader knew most of them and he was terrified. One man was shot dead outside his minicab business just a few miles from Reader's home. Another was gunned down on his yacht in the Mediterranean. Reader wondered if he was going to be next.

He was also kicking himself for not putting more of his money into the UK property market before he did his flit to Northern Cyprus. Many of his associates had invested their 'black' money in property and hung onto it as prices skyrocketed in London and the South East of England. Reader was, in the words of one associate, 'completely stuffed'.

By this time Brian Reader was in his early sixties. He felt drained and cut off from the London underworld he'd once played such a prominent role in. A new breed of younger, more clinical villain was appearing on the scene. Like so many older citizens, Reader's 'services' were, quite simply, no longer required. In the eyes of many, his 'skills' belonged to a bygone era.

It wasn't just the South East London and Kent underworld that was changing. Brian Reader's favourite stomping ground of Hatton Garden had undergone something of an image makeover. The old-fashioned 'dodgier' traders were still around but the 'front of shop' staff were much more visible. Flashy criminals, Russian oligarchs and overpaid City bankers began to form the hard core of Hatton Garden browsers by the end of the 1990s. With new jewellery shops opening virtually every month, Hatton Garden and its surrounding area had become the perfect place to buy a 'sparkler'.

It was well known by this time that a lot of the Brink's-Mat gold bullion had 'journeyed' through Hatton Garden. But that wasn't the only reason for Brian Reader's connection to the area. The vast majority of jewellers and gold traders operating in Hatton Garden were (and still are) undoubtedly honest, hardworking types. Many saw the 'modernization' of Hatton Garden as a healthy development, which brought in a larger range of customers. Others were not so sure.

The gem trade still greatly appealed to criminals because, as banking regulations got tighter, it was one of the few remaining businesses where large cash transactions could be carried out with complete anonymity.

Cash was still king in Hatton Garden.

'It was all based on trust so there was no paper trail,' one money-laundering expert explained. 'These sorts of transactions are carried out in an environment of almost complete secrecy and Hatton Garden had become a very cash-intensive market-place in the late 1990s.'

Ex-robber Billy set the scene perfectly: 'There was one family of villains who based themselves actually in Hatton Garden. They'd gone from small time duckers and divers to running some very flashy clubs and bars stretching from Tottenham in North London all the way across town to west London in the 1990s. They thought they was on a roll, invincible. That's when gangsters are at their most dangerous.'

Everyone in Hatton Garden knew who this family of villains was. But no one ever mentioned their names and most tried to go about their everyday business as if they didn't even exist. But in reality they were extremely active in the underworld and few ever had the courage to cross them.

Brian Reader was acquainted with a couple of members of this crime family directly through his Brink's-Mat gold bullion dealings. And he knew they were a nasty bunch capable of anything if people got in their way. Typically, Reader had always managed to placate them but now he was aware that they had effectively 'taken over' the Hatton Garden area.

Yet despite all this, Reader still felt Hatton Garden suited him down to the ground. After all, it had been a very profitable place for him until Kenneth Noye stabbed that policeman to death.

During the late 1990s, Reader met up once again with his old prison pal from North London, Terry Perkins, still officially on the run after earlier absconding from open prison. Both men were struggling to make a living and looking around for some 'new opportunities'. One of their favourite topics of conversation was the Hatton Garden Safe Deposit company's underground vault on the corner of Hatton Garden, which they'd first talked about in prison ten years earlier.

Reader's association with Perkins was certainly unusual as far as other professional criminals were concerned. Most London villains would never team up with a criminal from another part of the capital. But Reader had long since ignored such 'rules'. East. West. North. South. Reader didn't care where they came from so long as they helped him earn some much-needed cash.

So it was that Brian Reader found himself wandering up Hatton Garden one afternoon day-dreaming about that underground vault just thirty feet beneath the very pavement he was walking on. Reader had casually spoken to a few of the Hatton Garden regulars he'd met down the years and they'd openly confirmed that the vault was used by many diamond dealers to store their valuables. Reader also knew that criminals – including members of that family who ran their empire from Hatton Garden – also used the vault for 'safe keeping'. Reader and Perkins knew only too well that meant a lot of stolen property was stored in the metal boxes inside the vault.

A few days later, Brian Reader and Terry Perkins put a proposition to an underworld financier who we'll call The Man. They needed some upfront cash as 'development money' to finance preparations for a raid on the Hatton Garden Safe Deposit vault.

But The Man didn't want to know. Reader and Perkins were yesterday's villains in his opinion. He even suggested they should accept a 10 per cent commission from a younger team of robbers and walk away from the job. Reader and Perkins were outraged that they were considered over the hill. They were about to storm out of the meeting when The Man suggested they should reconsider their plans for another, much more potentially dangerous reason. He pointed out that the crime family who ran their business in Hatton Garden didn't like anyone committing crimes on their 'patch'. The Man said that if Reader and Perkins valued their lives they should try and find somewhere else to steal from.

But Reader and Perkins would have none of it. They still saw themselves as master craftsmen and they didn't think anyone else had the right to stop them using their skills to their best ability, wherever the opportunity arose. As a result, raiding that vault beneath Hatton Garden became even more of an obsession.

Both men went back to The Man and warned him in no uncertain terms that if he tipped anyone else off about their plans for the Hatton Garden vault there would be trouble. The last thing they wanted was to help a bunch of younger villains pull off a job that was *their* idea and, more importantly, they didn't want anything to do with that crime family. The Man told them he had many other targets for his boys. He didn't need to 'nick' work off Reader and Perkins, he said.

So Reader and Perkins went back to the drawing board, spurred on in part because out on the streets of London, the art of armed robbery was making a bit of a comeback.

In February 1999, a gang of old-style blaggers stopped a security van carrying £10 million in Nine Elms, South London by blocking off both ends of a busy main road alongside the River Thames. The plan was to use a stolen lorry carrying trees –

which camouflaged a huge metal spike welded into the chassis – to split open the security van's rear doors. However, an irate motorist running late for work removed the ignition keys from the unattended tree lorry as it stood blocking the road. At a stroke, the robbers' plan fell apart and they fled empty-handed, making their escape in dramatic fashion on an inflatable speed-boat moored on the nearby River Thames.

But the same gang behind that failed Nine Elms ram-raid soon had another much more lucrative target in their sights; they planned to rob the Millennium Dome – on the southern bank of the river in North Greenwich – which had been spe-cially built as part of London's celebrations for the new century.

Two members of the gang visited the De Beers Millennium Diamond Exhibition at the Dome and filmed the vault with a camcorder. On display were jewels as well as the Millennium Star, a flawless 203.04-carat diamond with an estimated value of £200 million and considered one of the most perfect gems in the world. It was protected by a specially built £50,000 cab-inet featuring reinforced glass three-quarters of an inch thick, as well as a sophisticated security system. Its makers claimed it could foil any 'known tool' for at least thirty minutes.

But the gang's ringleader believed he could weaken the glass with three shots from a powerful Hilti nailgun. Then they'd use a sledgehammer to break the 'warmed-up' glass. The technical aspects of the job later greatly interested Brian Reader, who himself would one day use other Hilti tools during the Hatton Garden Job.

However, Scotland Yard's Flying Squad had been told all about the Millennium Dome gang's plans by an informant and just before dawn on 7 November 2001 more than two hundred officers gathered at the site. The police operation was codenamed 'Operation Magician' and included forty specialist firearms officers. Some were hidden behind a secret wall within the Dome building. Others were dressed as cleaners concealing their guns in black plastic bags and rubbish bins. A further sixty armed officers were stationed around the Thames and twenty on the river itself.

Two minutes into the raid, dozens of armed police threw distraction devices into the vault before entering it and overpowering the robbers, ordering them to drop their weapons and come out immediately. None of them put up any resistance. The Flying Squad had no doubt the Millennium Dome raid would have been the biggest robbery since the Brink's-Mat job in 1983 if it had been successful. The main robbers were later jailed for fifteen years each at the Old Bailey

The failure of the Millennium Dome raid had a far-reaching effect on the London underworld frequented by Brian Reader and Terry Perkins. Younger gangs of London robbers turned their attention to other more risky but softer targets, such as businesses selling high-end luxury goods; top of the range cars; jewellery; gold and, of course, cash. But it wasn't that different from the 'good old days' when Brian Reader's associates would blow open the back of security vans or charge across a pavement brandishing sawn-offs for a bag of swag.

In 2001, a 25-year-old estate agent was stabbed to death in South London in front of his fiancée as he parked his car outside his home. His two teenage assailants were only after his £30,000 Audi. They stole it on behalf of a gang of professional car 'handlers' who shipped the car abroad to Brian Reader's one-time Mediterranean bolthole of North Cyprus, en route for the Middle East. Carjacking was soon being committed left, right and centre.

The police eventually came down heavily on the carjacking gangs, thanks to CCTV footage, sophisticated in-car tracking devices and DNA. Old-school professional criminals like Brian Reader were outraged by the nature of carjacking: 'We thought it was a bloody liberty,' said ex-robber Billy. 'The coppers had to get these characters off the streets because they'd stepped across the line. Nicking from a bank or a security van or a jewellery shop was fair game but threatening ordinary citizens in their cars was completely out of order.'

Meanwhile Brian Reader and many of his older associates continued to struggle financially as the face of the London underworld changed almost beyond recognition. One bunch of old-timers whom Reader knew even resorted to dealing in counterfeit cash to make a living.

In May 2002, two elderly villains were arrested by Scotland Yard's newly formed National Crime Squad at a counterfeiting factory in Canning Town, in the heart of the East End. Police found £921,000 in forged £20 notes but there were also enough blank notes to print at least another £8 million in fake currency.

One of the old lags even escaped from prison while awaiting trial. Brian Reader and many of his now elderly contemporaries loved this story because they still got a vicarious thrill every time one of their mates got one over on the 'cozzers'.

In the middle of all this, Reader and Perkins were still trying to raise the funds to put together a proper plan to raid the Hatton Garden Safe Deposit vault. They'd thought a lot about The Man's advice not to commit crimes on the manor 'belonging' to that crime family. But there was no point in telling the family what they were up to, unless their raid was actually going to happen.

Then in 2003, Hatton Garden was 'infiltrated' by another middle-aged man with exactly the same ideas as Reader and

Perkins. This character initially went by the name of Philip Goldberg and he began appearing in the area in the early spring of that year. Goldberg was a dapper looking gentleman in his fifties, dressed in a dark suit, a tie and a homburg hat. He also used the names Luis Ruben, and Ruben Luis. He didn't stand out among the traditionally dressed men of Hatton Garden, many of whom were Orthodox Jews, and he often sealed deals with a handshake and the Yiddish words '*Mazel und broche*' (luck and blessing).

Goldberg bought diamonds for jewellers to examine and, much like any dealer, he would frequently enter the grand stone doorway to 88–90 Hatton Garden and disappear down the dark green linoleum staircase to the basement of the Hatton Garden Safety Deposit Company Ltd, where he would visit his four strongboxes in the vault.

Goldberg's final visit to the vault occurred at 9 a.m. on the last Saturday of June 2003. It was of course the Jewish Sabbath – and too early for the shopping crowds – so Hatton Garden was largely deserted. It wasn't until the following Monday morning, when a customer entered the vault and found his box glued shut, that a robbery was uncovered.

At least £1.5 million in jewellery and cash had vanished from several boxes. The well-dressed Mister Goldberg had vanished too, in what was one of the best-planned and most audacious one-man jewel thefts in the history of Hatton Garden.

Reader and Perkins were sick to their stomachs. They'd missed a golden opportunity, which might never come their way again. And worse still, the robbery resulted in many Hatton Garden stores introducing much tighter security to get onto their premises. This included CCTV cameras, plus a series of steel doors which each had to lock shut before the next could be accessed.

However, some useful details did emerge from the publicity that surrounded the Goldberg case. Press reports revealed that the safe deposit vault worked on a two-key system: customers had one individual key, and the deposit staff had another key, which was the same for all the boxes. Without both being used at the same time, the box could not be opened. Even if someone got hold of a copy of the safe deposit's master key, he would still have to obtain copies of the individual keys for a box to be opened.

Following the robbery, Hatton Garden was buzzing with theories. Most presumed Mister Goldberg had a copy of both the relevant keys. Some even suspected he'd knocked a key out of someone's hand and then gave it back after taking an impression on wax in his palm.

It was also revealed that there were no CCTV cameras in the vault for privacy reasons. That meant no video footage of the robber in action. Reader and Perkins also noticed that reports said Goldberg hadn't had to use force to open the boxes, which meant he must have had both sets of relevant keys.

Reader and Perkins tried to put a brave face on it by promising each other the vault would eventually be worth another crack once the dust had settled. However, Reader believed it would take at least two years for the boxes in the vault to become full enough again for a raid to be worthwhile committing.

Many in Hatton Garden were convinced that Mister Goldberg got away with a lot more than the police estimated because many of those boxes contained illicit goods the owners of which wouldn't want to admit anything to the police.

Goldberg disappeared into thin air and was never brought to justice. Reader and Perkins made their own enquiries about the master thief because they wanted to ask him a few 'questions'.

But Goldberg was never located and he remains a wanted man to this day.

But that robbery had another disturbing knock-on effect. The crime family running their empire from Hatton Garden picked up a rumour about Reader and Perkins' interest in robbing the Hatton Garden vault. The gang hauled the two men into their offices and made it abundantly clear that no one else should even attempt to rob the vault because they kept a lot of their 'property' in boxes there and it was their territory. *They* would decide if or when such a raid would take place.

Reader and Perkins nodded politely and afterwards decided to put the Hatton Garden Job on ice for the time being. But they both agreed that one day they would go back and have another crack at it.

CHAPTER THIRTEEN

ITCHY FEET

Back on the streets of central London, drug prices were tumbling and the so-called art of robbery continued to make a comeback, albeit in many different guises. After all, the same old targets still existed. And they didn't come much more obvious and lucrative than Heathrow airport, the location for the Brink's-Mat robbery more than twenty years earlier. It remained a transport hub for tens of millions of pounds worth of goods each day.

In 2002 and 2004, two robberies at Heathrow – or 'Thiefrow' as it had become known in the wake of the Brink's-Mat heist – flagged up a new breed of robbers, who were making fortunes right under the noses of more 'seasoned' gangsters like Brian Reader and Terry Perkins.

One of the two Heathrow robbery gangs even came from within West London's Asian community. For elderly professionals like Reader and Perkins this was totally bemusing. Only *certain* types of people were supposed to be blaggers, yet a bunch of inexperienced Asians had shown everyone how it should be done.

In 2005, Reader and Perkins heard rumours about a massive job in the pipeline that involved a raid on a Securitas cash deposit warehouse deep in the Kent countryside. When a couple of experienced professional robbers known to Reader and Perkins made an approach to one of the relatively younger South London 'faces' in the gang, they were told nothing was happening and that it was all gossip. The old-school criminals pressed hard and even tried to muscle their way onto the job but they ended up making themselves look desperate, which didn't do them any good.

It later emerged that the younger villains didn't trust the old-timers. They'd heard from their own criminal families how many so-called professional villains back in the seventies and eighties would happily grass their mates up to the police if it suited them.

But there was an even more significant reason why the old 'faces' were not required for the Kent job. The younger robbers involved had, albeit reluctantly, joined forces with a crew of Eastern European gangsters because the 'job' had come through an Albanian inside man, who worked at the Securitas depot, located near the town of Tonbridge, in Kent.

On 21 February 2006, the gang kidnapped the depot manager and his family and forced him to hand over the codes for the building's alarm system. Later it was claimed the Eastern Europeans in the gang had insisted on a full-scale 'tiger' kidnap which involved one team holding the family captive while the other team escorted the manager to the depot so he could punch in those vital codes needed to gain access to the vault.

The masked-up gang arrived at the depot at 1.28 a.m. and left at 2.43 a.m. In just 75 minutes they took £52,996,760 in cash but left behind another £153,833,020.73 purely because they'd all agreed in advance not to stay on the premises for any longer than a set amount of time.

Police eventually located some of the vehicles linked to the heist and then stumbled on £1.4 million in cash from the robbery in a white Transit van in the car park of a hotel in Ashford, Kent. The van also contained a machine gun and a black balaclava with one of the robbers' DNA on it. The main suspects were soon rounded up. In June 2007, three of the robbers were given indeterminate sentences with a minimum of fifteen years. The Albanian-born inside man who had previously worked at the depot was jailed for twenty years.

Brian Reader and Terry Perkins couldn't help admiring the gall of the Tonbridge 'team', although they reckoned the local villains had been asking for trouble by hooking up with Eastern Europeans and that was why they all ended up being arrested.

Then there was also the small matter of the 'inside man'; Reader and Perkins believed the only way to pull off the perfect robbery was to *not* use an inside man. Such characters remained the biggest thorn in the side of any modern blagger. After all, it was nearly always the 'inside man' who ended up spilling the beans to the police.

London's economy continued to boom, thanks to the large number of foreign billionaires invading the UK's capital city. This influx of new, brazen wealth encouraged the expansion of high-end jewellery stores by companies such as Graff's, who by this time had premises in many of London's wealthiest districts. These contained millions of pounds' worth of gems, which could – in theory – be accessed through one flimsy door into the street.

Graff had already been subjected to a series of robberies at its stores across the world, during which jewellery worth tens of millions of pounds had been stolen. Those raids had included a $38m (£24.5m) raid at a Graff's store in Tokyo and a $13.5m (£8m) heist in its Dubai store. But it was the raid in which gems worth £20 million were stolen from the company's Sloane Street branch in London's Knightsbridge in 2007 that made the London underworld sit up and take notice.

The blaggers had been allowed into the store by a security guard, who believed they were genuine customers because they pulled up outside in a chauffeur-driven dark-blue Bentley Continental Flying Spur, worth £118,000. One of the two robbers was a middle-aged man wearing a distinctive Panama hat, which also helped fool the security guards.

After brandishing silver handguns and forcing staff to lie face-down on the floor, the robbers stole rings, bracelets, necklaces and earrings. This included a necklace decorated with 270 diamonds with a collective weight of more than 155 carats, which alone was worth many millions of pounds. The crime remains unsolved to this day; the man in the Panama hat was allegedly linked many years later to the Hatton Garden Job because CCTV footage seemed to show similarities between him and one of the raiders.

As ex-robber Billy later explained: 'Those jewellery store robberies took a lot of bottle and were a big risk in many ways. London had turned into a bleedin' billionaire's paradise and every villain out there wanted to get a piece of the action.'

Numerous similar robberies occurred in London over the following couple of years but the most notorious of all was on 6 August 2009, when two sharply dressed men in virtually identical grey business suits arrived in a taxi outside another branch of Graff's in New Bond Street, Mayfair.

It was 4.40 p.m., just before the main rush hour out of the city began. The two men were so cocky and confident, they even paid their £9.20 taxi fare with a £20 note and told the cabbie to keep the change – the best tip he'd ever received. The driver later said they were Londoners.

Once inside the Graff's store, both men pulled out handguns and forced staff to the floor. Shop assistant Petra Ehnar was 'petrified' when one of the robbers thrust a gun in her back and ordered her to empty rings, necklaces, watches and earrings from display cases. In all, forty-three pieces of jewellery worth a total of £40 million were put in their bag. One diamond necklace alone was valued at £3.5 million and the haul included a total of 1,500 individual diamonds.

Within hours, police located one of the gang's getaway cars and discovered a pay-as-you go mobile phone, wedged between the driver's seat and the handbrake. Anonymous numbers stored on the mobile phone quickly enabled the police to discover the identity of the robbers and they were rounded up. The gang's ringleader was eventually sentenced to twenty-three years in prison. His two accomplices were each jailed for sixteen years after being convicted of conspiracy to rob. Another robber got twenty-one years.

Brian Reader and Terry Perkins were astounded that the May-fair robbers could pull off such a brazen job in broad daylight. Not surprisingly, the names of the 2009 Graff robbers were unfamiliar to them because they were all under 30 years of age. And the robbery blatantly hammered home to Reader and Perkins that maybe it was time to throw in the towel.

But, as ex-robber Billy pointed out: 'These guys didn't have pension schemes. They had to live by their wits until the day they died. That meant always being on the lookout for an earner. The funny thing is that as you get older you start getting more reckless, instead of less. The risks don't matter if you're cruising into the last ten good years of yer life. Why not have a go at something big? What's the harm in it?'

Brian Reader's life at this time certainly must have seemed mundane and meaningless compared to the way it had once been. He'd spent much of 2009 nursing his beloved wife Lyn, who had cancer. Reader had truly adored Lyn and was devastated when she died at the end of that year. An avid crossword puzzler, he'd sit alone at the kitchen table in their home most days writing her pet name again and again instead of the answers to the clues.

Reader's used car business in Dartford had been put on the backburner while he nursed Lyn and now it was struggling to stay afloat. His reputation in the South London underworld seemed almost dead and buried. Reader and Perkins dearly missed that magic word the 'buzz'. They longed for some excitement and a challenge in their lives.

Then in July 2011, Terry Perkins got a nasty blast from the past. He was still technically a wanted man after walking out of that open prison back in 1995 just before the end of his heavy sentence for the Security Express job. And one day the police came calling at his home in Enfield. Why they'd left it so long was anyone's guess. Perkins just presumed it was some vindictive copper's idea of a joke.

Perkins was rearrested and ended up getting a four-week prison term for that earlier escape. Perkins wasn't even made to serve it immediately and ended up going into custody voluntarily just after Christmas 2011, where he was duly locked up for a month and released on 7 February 2012.

But this incident reawakened Terry Perkins' burning resentment about his original Security Express sentence. He'd never forgotten watching all the killers and paedophiles in prison get out quicker than him back in the 1990s. Being put back in prison almost twenty years after his so-called escape seemed pathetic to Perkins. Now he longed to stick two fingers up at the establishment one last time.

*

Brian Reader and Terry Perkins got a timely reminder that they weren't the only old-school professionals looking for 'work' when a gang of aged 'Essex Boys' pulled off a bullion heist in Belgium, in October 2011.

The men – with the help of a lorry driver inside man – grabbed millions of pounds' worth of silver in a carefully stage-managed hold-up. But shortly afterwards they started being shadowed by police, who'd got a tip from an informant after the raid. Days later, detectives swooped on an apartment and a hotel room in Antwerp and most of the bullion was recovered.

Six members of the gang – who included the stepfather of two stars of TV's *The Only Way Is Essex* – were later sentenced to a total of more than twenty-three years for their roles in the heist.

Reader and Perkins sneered at the Essex 'team' for trying to pull off a job abroad and had little sympathy for them. But others pointed out that at least they had the bottle to try it. Reader and Perkins did a lot of talking about the old days but they seemed reluctant to get stuck in again, even though they were both in desperate need of money.

Then on 9 May 2012, seven men – including a 71-year-old Hatton Garden-based fence – were jailed for a total of sixty-four years for their involvement in ten smash and grab raids on luxury goods stores in central London. The Hatton Garden connection confirmed that the area remained a hotbed of criminality, which meant a lot of valuable gems were probably once again being stored in those metal boxes inside the Hatton Garden Safe Deposit company's underground vault.

Terry Perkins was pumped up after spending that month in jail as punishment for walking out of an open prison nearly two decades earlier. He was angry and resentful. He was in danger of turning into the ultimate grumpy old man. But after reading about that jailed Hatton Garden fence he decided it was time to do something to break the cycle of boredom which had enveloped his life.

PART
TWO

THE
JOB

'What d'you think this is? The wheel of fortune? You think you can make your dough and fuck off? Leave the table? Thanks Don, see you Don, off to sunny Spain now Don, fuck off Don. Lying in your pool like a fat blob laughing at me, you think I'm gonna have that? You really think I'm gonna have that, ya ponce. All right, I'll make it easy for you. God knows you're fucking trying. Are you gonna do the job? It's not a difficult question, are you gonna do the job, yes or no?'

Don Logan in *Sexy Beast*

CHAPTER FOURTEEN

ALL WOUND UP

In late 2012, Brian Reader fell out of a tree that he was cutting in the back garden of his house in Dartford, fracturing his neck. He was at the end of his tether. He'd lost his beloved wife. He'd just been diagnosed with prostate cancer and neutropenia, a blood condition that makes the sufferer susceptible to infections. Life didn't really feel as if it was worth living any more. Reader's mind flashed back to the good old days when he was living fast and enjoying a highly profitable life of crime. He told his friend Terry Perkins he longed for one last 'hit' of happiness before he died. The doctors had said he might last another five years, but Brian Reader already felt half dead.

It was a gang of German robbers who finally convinced Reader and Perkins that it really was a matter of now or never. It irritated both of them immensely when, in January 2013, raiders drilled through 80cm of reinforced concrete to enter the vault of the Volksbank, in Steglitz, South West Berlin. They opened 294 security deposit boxes, stealing diamonds, gold and silver valued at more than €10 million (£8.3 million).

Noted ex-robber Billy: 'The key to that job was the equipment they was using. The lads looked closely at the technical details mentioned in the press, including the drill they used to get through that thick concrete wall.'

A few weeks after the German robbery, someone – never identified – began taking a much closer look at the Sudanese family who now owned and ran the vault in Hatton Garden. It turned out that the son of the owner was the manager in charge of the day-to-day running of the business. His name was Manish Bavishi and he lived in a large detached house in North London.

It's not known who was directly involved but a break-in occurred at the house in the spring of 2013. The police were called to the incident and recorded it at the time as an 'aggravated burglary'. That meant whoever carried out the raid was known to have been armed when they entered Mr Bavishi's home.

It seems highly likely that the 'robbers' who entered Manish Bavishi's property took imprints of some keys, which would have then enabled those people to gain access into the main building where the Hatton Garden Safe Deposit vault was located thirty feet below ground level.

Back in the suburbs of North and South London, Brian Reader and Terry Perkins were now utterly convinced that if they didn't get a move on and hit that Hatton Garden vault then someone else would beat them to it yet again.

Terry Perkins was also still wound up like a coiled spring. He even told Reader one day that he wanted to hit the vault because he'd just discovered that his daughter's engagement ring – bought from Hatton Garden – had a fake among the six mounted stones. 'They deserve all they get, Dad,' was his daughter's response when he jokingly mentioned that 'someone should rob the place'. It was no laughing matter to Perkins. He was so outraged that he'd been conned in such a blatant manner that he felt he had 'permission' to steal the contents of the Hatton Garden vault.

However, Reader and Perkins first needed to get some financial backing if they were finally going to pull off their audacious crime. So they took a very long, deep breath because it was time to enter the lion's den.

Brian Reader and Terry Perkins had agreed they should first make a courtesy call to the crime family who'd run their empire from Hatton Garden for so many years. It made sense to 'sign off' the vault job with them first, despite their reluctance to do so in the past. In any case, they'd run out of potential sources to finance the job so maybe they could get an investment direct from the family.

Reader and Perkins were advised by a middleman that they should fly out to Southern Spain to meet one of the family's most trusted employees, who we'll call Lenny. They could run the job past him and maybe he'd green light an investment as well.

Reader and Perkins arrived on different flights from London at Malaga's newly rebuilt airport in mid-2014. They even deliberately stayed at separate hotels to avoid any of the British police units often working in Southern Spain. They located near the seedy Puerto Banus area, a man-made port close to Marbella, which had seen more London robbers come and go than Parkhurst Prison, on the Isle of Wight.

Reader and Perkins were stunned by what they saw on the recession-hit Costa del Crime. Many of the older criminals had disappeared or died, often abandoning their mansions in the hills behind Marbella because of the property slump, which had left million-pound homes worth virtually nothing on the open market.

As a result, Southern Spain was playing host to younger, flashier criminals who'd gradually eroded the power of the traditional old-school Brits. These new 'faces' were the sort of characters who'd walk into a bar or club and shoot someone to send out a message to rivals: "Don't fuck with me". Only a handful of the London veterans remained but they kept mainly in the background as fixers and organisers, hiding behind legitimate businesses or working as middlemen for mainly Eastern European and Russian drug barons.

At his home in the mountains high above Marbella, Lenny immediately disarmed Reader and Perkins by announcing he had cancer, but assured them that the family were very much prepared to invest in the Hatton Garden Job. Reader tried to empathise with Lenny by talking about his own brush with cancer but Lenny clearly had other things on his mind. Lenny's criminal pedigree was impressive. He'd originally been a master robber from North London. Then he'd gone into the drug trade big-time. He'd been caught by police many times but always managed to wriggle out of criminal charges, thanks mainly to the family's close 'connections'.

Lenny told Reader and Perkins he'd thought he would never have to work again after the last big shipment of coke. But his fortune had been hoovered up by ex-wives, children, grandchildren, mistresses, his own love of cocaine and the Blair government's Proceeds of Crime Act, 2002, which had left him stranded in Spain.

Lenny told Reader and Perkins he was sick and tired of getting his fingers burnt in drug-smuggling deals run by twitchy, coked-up young Albanians, who couldn't be trusted to look after their own grannies.

THE LOCAL: the Old Wheatsheaf pub, in Enfield, where the old codgers spent time planning the raid.

2015/05/18 12:45:36

PREPARING FOR THE DROP-OFF: Kenny Collins and Hughie Doyle behind the Old Wheatsheaf pub, where chirpy Irishman Doyle had his workshop.

GETAWAY VEHICLE: The white van driven by Kenny Collins in Hatton Garden.

TARGET: entrance to rear of Hatton Garden Safe Deposit Ltd. The small door in the metal archway leads to the yard and the wooden doorway, the black door to the right of that leads directly to the fire escape where the safe was found.

AWESOME KIT: the Hilti DD350 drill used to rip open the vault wall.

PLAYING THE GAME: CCTV footage of raider Danny Jones inside the vault building and then keeping an eye on the time.

FORT KNOX: the formidable vault door which was next to the tunnel in the wall.

WE'RE IN: this is what it looked like to the raiders when they finally broke through the concrete wall and inner steel lining of the vault.

BENDING THE RULES: this security door couldn't stop the old codgers from carrying out their mission.

AFTERMATH: the raiders left behind this scene of chaos and destruction in their wake.

JONES AND HIS STASH: Edmonton Cemetery, where Danny Jones hid his share of the loot and tried to pull a fast one on the police.

EJB/031115/4

EJB/031115/2

JONES' STASH: some of that jewellery, recovered from Danny Jones' stash.

FLOPHOUSE: the property in Sterling Road, Enfield, where three of the mob were nabbed by police who found some of the loot at the same time.

THE SLAUGHTER: bags found in the living room of the house in Sterling Road, Enfield, where the gang planned to distribute the loot.

GUV'NOR'S MANSION: police raid gang leader Brian Reader's large detached home in Kent.

2007.09.17 13:36:15

CAUGHT ON CAMERA: secret police video surveillance footage of (left to right) Terry Perkins, Kenny Collins and Brian Reader in the Castle Public House, Pentonville Road.

OUT AND ABOUT: more secret photos of (below left) Brian Reader at Scotti's Cafe in Clerkenwell Green, 17 April 2015, and (right) Kenny Collins, also at Scotti's.

THE JOB

Perkins and Reader ran through all the details of the job. They explained that they also needed some extra cash to keep them going for at least three months after the job was carried out, because they didn't want to touch any of the loot until the dust had settled.

Lenny then invited Perkins and Reader to a slap-up dinner in one of Puerto Banus's most expensive restaurants, where they swopped 'war stories' without once uttering another word about the Big One. That would come later.

Ex-robber Billy later explained: 'I heard it was a funny old trip. They had to keep skating around the main subject because there were a lot of grasses in Puerto Banus. You certainly didn't go shootin' yer mouth off in a restaurant filled with people. One old copper I knew thirty years back once told me that the Sweeney paid people at that very same restaurant to report back anything they heard.'

Perkins, Reader and Lenny ended up that night at a club owned and run by a onetime drug baron from Perkins' old manor in East London.

'I know that place myself,' explained ex-robber Billy. 'It's tucked away down a dusty track on the road to Estepona. Full of women dressed to the nines and no doubt on the hunt for a rich punter. The owner had used it to launder a lot of the cash from his drug deals.'

The three men eventually retired to a back room to hammer out an agreement, and that was when Lenny asked Perkins and Reader if they had an inside man to guide them into the vault.

'Bollocks to that,' replied Perkins. 'We'll work out our own access. Inside men are a fucking liability.'

Lenny mulled over their reaction and then came up with what he described as 'a proposition'. In exchange for financing the Hatton Garden Job, Lenny wanted Perkins and Reader to guarantee they would nick a specific box in the vault, which was 'of interest' to the family.

While Perkins and Reader stopped for a few moments to mull over what they'd just heard, Lenny punched out a number on his throwaway mobile phone and told a voice at the other end of the line: 'I want you to meet two of my good mates. I think you might be able to help them.'

Seconds later a tall, slim, upright man walked into the backroom of the club and introduced himself to Reader and Perkins as 'Basil'. They screwed their eyes up suspiciously. The man had strange-coloured hair poking out from under a baseball cap and his facial features were almost indistinguishable, thanks to a large pair of sunglasses. Reader later told one friend: 'He looked like some kind of evil clown. Tall, awkward sorta bloke. But he smiled a lot.'

Lenny said: 'Basil here has got something that might be of great interest to you two gentlemen.'

Perkins and Reader looked across at each other quizzically.

The man who called himself 'Basil' opened the palm of his hand to reveal two keys, like a magician revealing his latest trick.

Then he said proudly: 'With these I can get you in the building, whip round to the fire exit and, hey presto, let you all in. Simple as that.'

Lenny then cut in. 'Basil here is gonna be on the job with you. He'll get you in. He also knows all about how to handle the alarm system. That's guaranteed. But I also need him there to collect that very special box I mentioned earlier.'

Lenny looked across at Reader first and then Perkins – straight in their eyes.

'Are you happy, lads? We finance it all and you just help Basil here get something we need. Is that all right?'

The two men hesitated.

'Basil knows the inside of that building like the back of his hand,' said Lenny. 'He'll knock out all the alarms and sort the lift out for you and all we want in return is for him to take that one box away with him. Whatever you take is yours.'

Perkins looked across at Reader. It all sounded too good to be true.

But then on the other hand they were two old age pensioners with nothing to lose.

Reader and Perkins nodded slowly at each other. Then they leaned forward to shake hands with the two other men.

Lenny laughed and said quietly: 'You won't regret this, boys.'

And with that, Terry Perkins and Brian Reader returned to their hotels, packed their bags and headed to Malaga airport where they flew back to London on the first available early morning flights to Gatwick and Stansted.

They weren't exactly 100 per cent happy about Basil. But they realized that his access to the building would short-cut a lot of problems. In any case, Reader and Perkins knew that without the crime family's approval for the job it would never happen, so they really had little choice in the matter.

Back at their homes in the suburbs of Kent and North London, Reader and Perkins each began to work out the finer details of the Hatton Garden Job. Their families knew they were up to something, but hoped the two old-timers would work out for themselves that at their age it was all a pipedream.

Reader and Perkins put a lot of time and effort into examining every aspect of the Hatton Garden Safe Deposit company. The vault itself was housed in a seven-storey building, which accommodated sixty other businesses, including watch traders and diamond wholesalers. Small studios, large enough for two craftsmen, could be rented for £10,000 a year. One building expert they knew told the two men that the concrete wall next to the safe would be heavily reinforced with springs (coils of metal inside the concrete) and they would not only need a specialised drill but also the correct diamond tipped heads to pierce the wall.

So with Lenny's cash advance burning a hole in their pockets, Perkins and Reader then decided it was time to start recruiting the rest of the Hatton Garden team. Naturally, they were both worried about sharing their plans with anyone but they needed some decent 'soldiers' otherwise the raid would never get done.

'It's a Catch 22, isn't it?' explained ex-robber Billy. 'You gotta recruit some "workers" but that's always a big risk in case they don't sign up and then start blabbering to other people about what's happening.'

So the two old age pensioners headed for Terry Perkins' favourite pub . . .

CHAPTER FIFTEEN

FINDING THE TROOPS

The Castle, just off Pentonville Road, in Islington, in the heart of what had once been the criminal badlands of North London, isn't exactly the most low-key place to recruit villains for a major crime. The pub itself had turned into a trendy 'gastropub' thanks to soaring local property prices which had sparked an invasion of the area by middle class professionals.

First recruit for the gang was 60-year-old Danny Jones, an experienced North London professional criminal. Perkins had shared many boozy evenings with Jones in The Castle down the years. And the Hatton Garden Job would not be the first time Jones had been involved in a plot to drill into a subterranean vault. Several years earlier he'd been arrested in connection with a similar scheme. On that occasion the plot was foiled before it got off the ground.

Danny Jones had served a few prison terms in his time and knew all about Brian Reader from a disaffected acquaintance of his in the next door cell during one of Jones's periods 'inside' at HMP Maidstone. Jones's lengthy criminal record dated back to 1975, with convictions for robbery, handling stolen goods and burglary. He'd been jailed for five years on 21 July 1982 at

Snaresbrook Crown Court for stealing jewellery worth £92,000 from a Ratners jewellery store.

Jones told Reader and Perkins he was definitely up for the job and immediately said he'd start researching the internet for the right kind of equipment. He even mentioned a book he had called *Forensics for Dummies* about police forensics, which would help ensure they didn't leave any evidence behind after the job. Jones liked to 'big himself up' so he pointed out the world was now filled with electronic gadgetry, which hadn't existed when Reader and Perkins were at their prime. Both men admitted they had little idea about such stuff and were happy to pass on that responsibility to Jones.

Jones, a father of two, lived in a large detached £2 million mansion near Perkins' semi-detached home in Enfield, North London. In some ways, he was more like an overgrown schoolboy than a professional criminal. Jones refused to speak to people after 5 p.m. every day. He'd use the prison phrase 'bang-up' to describe the evenings when he would rarely answer the door or phone. He spent most of the time watching crime documentaries, reading true crime books and viewing films noirs on the internet.

Jones also had a disarming habit of talking to his white-haired terrier Rocket as if it was human, which didn't go down too well with some of the regulars at the The Castle. Jones also happened to be as tight-fisted with money as Brian Reader. One of Jones's friends later claimed that Jones would not 'borrow or lend him anything', saying he 'buys his clothes out of Oxfam'. The friend added: 'Danny Jones is renowned that he wouldn't sleep if it cost him a penny . . . he certainly wouldn't give me anything.'

The eccentric Jones also had a penchant for sleeping in his dead mother's dressing gown and often walked around his house wearing a Turkish fez hat, similar to the trademark headgear of comedian Tommy Cooper. One of Jones's friends later said that he was so obsessed with the army that he'd often sleep in a sleeping bag on his bedroom floor, presumably wearing his dead mother's dressing gown. Oh, and on those occasions he used to go to the toilet in a bottle.

No wonder Jones's wife was considered long suffering. It was later said in court that the poor lady was so agoraphobic she rarely ventured outside the couple's house. It was claimed she was always on at Jones about the state of his clothes and the mess he'd left in the kitchen. One of Jones's oldest friends later described him as 'a very sensitive guy, a very funny man. Everyone who knew Danny would say he was mad. He's eccentric.'

Shortly after he 'signed up' for the team, Danny Jones insisted on reading Reader and Perkins's palms one inebriated evening in The Castle. No one knows what secrets Jones uncovered about his associates but presumably they ignored all the warning signs with a hearty laugh and a slap on the back.

In any case none of this eccentricity seemed to put off Perkins and Reader. Far from it. They believed you had to be a bit of a nutter to be a villain in the first place.

So over pints of lager and glasses of vodka and tonic, the men outlined their plans at The Castle each Friday in the early autumn of 2014. Brian Reader avoided alcohol because of medication for his various ailments and drank tap water instead, which saved him a fortune because he was never obliged to buy a round of drinks.

It wasn't long before they'd recruited another old 'face'. Kenny Collins was well known to all the men but Brian Reader had pushed for him to join the gang because they went back a long way. Aged 74, Collins had a long history of crime, including a £300,000 jewellery raid in West London in 1988, for which he'd been sentenced to nine years in prison. He'd also been done for handling stolen goods and fraud dating back to 1961. Collins was well known in criminal circles as a break-in expert; he'd also made money from touting football tickets and was, according to one friend, 'the man with the hardest head and the biggest heart in London'.

But what Collins didn't make clear to the three other members of the gang was that his morbid obesity had left him suffering from severe hip problems. He often used a walking stick, which he kept in his car so no one would know he was virtually a cripple.

The gang's next recruit was the relatively young and spritely Hugh 'Hughie' Doyle, aged 48. He'd originally known all the gang members through monthly drinking sessions at The Harlequin pub near Sadler's Wells a few years earlier. Doyle ran his own plumbing firm but was a 'bright spark' who could provide the perfect venue for the gang to plan the job and then possibly even store the loot. Collins reminded the others that Doyle was a 'straight shooter' with no criminal record, so the police would be unlikely to suspect he was up to no good.

Doyle's colourful background made him a bit of a fish out of water compared to the others. After first arriving in London from Ireland as a teenager, he'd squatted with friends in Belsize Park, North London, in one of the Iranian government's abandoned houses, following the overthrow of the Shah. Then they moved into a Chinese Embassy building on the edge of Regent's Park from where they were eventually evicted. Doyle initially found work in the printing business in the City but, worn out by the commuting, he'd retrained as a plumber, which gave him more time at home with his family and their cocker spaniel.

THE JOB

Dyslexic Hughie's business was called 'Associated Response' and he was known as a 'perfect gentlemen' to the customers whose drains he unclogged. Online reviews of Doyle's company described him as 'a knight in shining armour' and a 'very hard-working and trustworthy individual'.

Hughie Doyle's lock-up building for his plumbing business was located just behind a pub called The Old Wheatsheaf, near his home in Enfield. Jones and Perkins lived nearby. The gang wanted to use the building for meetings whenever they needed to avoid being overheard in The Castle and as a place to test out all the equipment they'd need for the Hatton Garden Job.

The final recruit to the Hatton Garden gang was Danny Jones's old friend Carl Wood, 58, considered 'a bit of a dark horse' right from the onset. He'd been Jones's drinking partner for more than thirty years and his role was to do the donkey-work as the gang set about the physically draining task of breaking into the vault.

Carl Wood certainly had the right criminal pedigree. In 1993 he'd stood trial with two police officers who'd teamed up with another crook in a bid to recover £600,000 owed to the same man by an underworld financier.

They'd been caught by police corruption busters, who secretly filmed the entire transaction. Wood was heard bragging how he'd beat the debtor with an iron bar after claiming he owed him £80,000. Wood was jailed for four years for his role in the plot.

Carl Wood also hid his health problems from the rest of the gang, apart from Jones. He suffered from Crohn's disease, which reduced his capacity for hard work. Danny Jones had helped Wood after his original diagnosis by taking him out for walks and encouraging him to keep fit and healthy. Wood received a disability pension of around £320 a fortnight for this ailment and later said he found the disease 'very painful and debilitating', adding: 'It feels like a mouthful of ulcers with a bottle of vinegar in your mouth.'

Wood had pushed for a place in the gang after Jones had let slip to his old friend that he was taking part in something that involved a lot of money. Jones even mentioned to Wood that if he got him a couple of rings from the heist then 'all your problems are gone'.

Wood was then given the 'thumbs up' by his old friend Billy Hickson, a legendary underworld 'face' who was convicted of handling some of the proceeds from Terry Perkins' £6 million Security Express heist back in 1983. Ironically, Hickson was later alleged in court to have also been a member of a gang of robbers known as the 'armed wrinklies', because they disguised themselves by whitening their hair with talcum powder and exaggerating their wrinkles with make-up in order to look older than their real ages. The case against Hickson for membership of the 'armed wrinklies' gang was eventually thrown out because of question marks over some of the evidence in Hickson's original trial.

Carl Wood believed the Hatton Garden raid would be the answer to all his money problems, and he got into the obsessive habit of trying to work out how he would spend all the money he presumed he was going to make from breaking into the Hatton Garden vault. Wood's ever mounting debts and the costs of keeping his mother with Alzheimer's in a care home near his Hertfordshire home were driving him to distraction. He owed almost £9,000 to Barclays, more than £3,000 to NatWest, up to £2,000 for a Christmas loan and almost £9,000 to a friend.

*

Three of those now in the Hatton Garden Mob – Perkins, Doyle and Jones – came from the North London suburb of Enfield, which had a strange but highly relevant connection to the London underworld's preoccupation with money. Enfield had the distinction of being the first place in the world to have an ATM or cash machine. It was officially opened in June 1967 by Reg Varney, an actor and personality most famous for his lead role in slapstick TV comedy series *On the Buses*. This historical event is still marked by a silver plaque on the wall of the Barclays Bank to this day.

So with their main 'team' now in place, Terry Perkins and Brian Reader began trying to work out when and how to actually pull off the Hatton Garden Job.

It didn't take long for the strange and distant Carl Wood to upset the apple cart, though. Ex-robber Billy explained: 'Wood was stony broke and owed money everywhere and he started pushing for them to do the job immediately. He was eventually told to shut the fuck up or get off the team. Brian and Terry were the ones who'd make that decision, all in good time.'

Brian Reader's health seemed to be further deteriorating. He'd never completely recovered from the energy-sapping treatment he'd earlier undergone for prostate cancer. Terry Perkins wasn't exactly fit and well, either. He'd had heart problems since before the Security Express raid but now he was also on a daily shot of insulin for diabetes. As a result, Perkins felt exhausted most of the time. Another reason why Reader and Perkins refused to rush into doing the raid was that they'd decided not to do it in the winter. They had visions of heavyweight Kenny Collins slipping head over heels on icy pavements in Hatton Garden.

Brian Reader was paranoid about other villains trying to muscle in on the job. He and Perkins had accepted Lenny's man

Basil because he had the keys to the entrance to the building and apparently knew a lot about the alarm system. But they didn't trust Lenny or his crime family bosses not to screw them over.

However Reader's biggest fear was that a bunch of foreign criminals might hear about the job on the grapevine and try to take it over. Exactly that had just happened to one of his oldest mates, whose criminal enterprise had resulted in a deadly shootout in a car park in Essex.

It certainly wasn't safe out on the streets when the 'foreign boys' were in town.

CHAPTER SIXTEEN

THE CROSSING

The fear of a foreign 'invasion' had driven both Reader and Perkins to recruit old-school local 'English' criminals right from the start. Reader had a huge bee in his bonnet about the foreign villains in the South East of England. He considered them to be 'psycho bunnies', intent on murder and mayhem. Reader and Perkins and many other professional criminals believed that the Dartford Crossing – right on Reader's doorstep – had single-handedly helped all these foreign gangs to invade the old country.

The Dartford Crossing connected the counties of Kent and Essex and had been opened in 1990 by Her Majesty the Queen to great fanfare. With 160,000 vehicles using it every day, it was Europe's busiest river crossing. But Reader was convinced it provided a transport hub for killers, kidnappers, drug smugglers and people traffickers going backwards and forwards across the English Channel via the nearby ports of Dover and Folkestone. As a result, Eastern European gangs were now trying to take over the previously partitioned criminal badlands of Kent, Essex and London.

Reader cited the record-breaking £53 million Securitas robbery back in 2006 as a classic example of the 'foreign invasion' he was always banging on about. The robbery had been committed by a gang of Eastern European and local criminals. But the chilling fallout from that job had sent a shiver down the spine of many older London villains. One British member of the robbery gang disappeared soon after the raid and was presumed dead. Another criminal connected to the robbery was murdered by a hitman on the Costa del Sol. A London gangster also linked to the heist was almost killed in a hit-and-run murder attempt outside a Kent pub that was notorious as an underworld haunt. And then a fourth man connected to the Securitas heist killed himself after threats to his family by Albanian gangsters.

Brian Reader and his pals had been appalled by the way the Eastern Europeans had handled the fallout from the Securitas raid. Ex-robber Billy explained: 'The Albanian mafia financed the Securitas robbery and then accused the Brit robbers of grassing their men up to the police. That's why this all kicked off in the first place. The Albanians told the Brits they'd be "running" Kent and Essex and most of London by the end of this decade. It was fuckin' outrageous.'

Many of Brian Reader's now elderly contemporaries had stepped back and watched as these cold-blooded foreign criminals swaggered through their home territories over the previous ten years. One gang of Albanian burglars even raided the known homes of a number of Essex and Kent criminals and stole hundreds of thousands of pounds worth of goods.

'They just kept taking the piss,' explained ex-robber Billy. 'Those bastards were using the Dartford Crossing to let us know they knew where some of us lived.'

Another Albanian gang – dubbed by the tabloids as 'modern-day highwaymen' – posed as police officers and cruised the M20 and A20 in Kent looking for cars with foreign visitors before forcing them to stop and robbing them of all their valuables.

Then in the early summer of 2014, a seven-man gang of Eastern European robbers mounted a daring heist inside the Lakeside Shopping Centre, in Essex, long considered a safe haven for local criminals and their families.

Ex-robber Billy later explained: 'They'd come swaggering onto our territory where we went with our families in broad daylight. They were sending out a message to us that they could do what the fuck they wanted.'

Billy added: 'One of my oldest mates sat down with one Eastern European gangster to try and work out a peace deal around this time. This bloke pulled out a shooter and told my pal that his wife and kids would be killed if he didn't step away from his territory. His territory? We're talkin' about part of South East London here. It was outrageous. A bloody liberty.'

Official UK government figures estimate there are now more than 2,000 foreign organized gangs operating in the UK and the majority of those criminals come from Eastern Europe. That means more than 40,000 hardened foreign criminals have 'targeted Britain', according to those Home Office figures. Of those, more than 8,000 individuals are classified as 'high harm' gangsters.

One Kent police officer, now retired, said: 'It must have been hard for old villains like Brian Reader and Terry Perkins. Once they'd been the kings of the castle, virtually untouchable and getting on with committing their crimes in a professional and efficient manner. Then along came the foreign boys waving guns around and telling the old British boys to get the hell away from their territory.'

But not even this so-called 'foreign invasion' was going to stop Reader and Perkins carrying out the Hatton Garden Job.

Back in London, Reader and Perkins stepped up the pace as they surged through the planning stage of the raid. Now there really was no turning back. In any case, Lenny's 'investment' on behalf of that crime family had locked them all in. The family were expecting delivery of that box, which Basil was going to take with him from the vault.

Talking of Basil, he was nowhere to be seen after that initial meeting in Spain. When Perkins and Reader contacted Lenny to ask why Basil had not been in touch, they were told not to worry because he would pop up when the time was right.

Over the following few months, Reader, Perkins, Jones and Collins carried out numerous reconnaissance trips to Hatton Garden. They examined the vault building from all angles, worked out the weak points and logged the movements of each member of staff at the Hatton Garden Safe Deposit company and all the other firms working out of the same building.

But gang member Carl Wood was not among them during these trips. He rarely met up with anyone in the gang apart from his good friend Danny Jones. Instead, Jones would brief Wood at garden centres in North London. On other occasions Jones kept Wood in the loop by phone on a 'need-to-know basis'.

It seemed to some of the others that Wood wasn't as 'committed' as the rest of them. Friends and associates have since said he dreamed all day and most of the night about the money he was going to earn from the raid. And within weeks of joining the Hatton Garden gang, Carl Wood attended the Adventure Travel Show, at the Kensington Olympia, featuring 'once-in-a-lifetime travel experiences' in apparent anticipation of his future wealth.

Meanwhile ringleader Terry Perkins was proving particularly fastidious when it came to the final stages of the planning. Ex-robber Billy later explained: 'He'd spent a lot of time in prison thinking through all the mistakes he'd made on the Security Express job and he wanted to make sure that this time there were no errors.'

Brian Reader's reputation as the 'master cutter' meant he was responsible for operating the high-tech equipment that would be needed to breach the vault. Jones had come up with the name of the best drill – a Hilti DD350 – for the job by scanning the internet for days and nights. Reader then said he'd find one for the gang to steal.

Reader initially visited a number of large building sites in London, Birmingham and Manchester looking for the particular drill, which was renowned for piercing even the thickest concrete walls. Only a few hundred of the Hilti DD350 drills existed throughout the world. Reader knew it was only ever used on major construction developments, such as office and apartment blocks. With the correct set of diamond-embedded tips, the Hilti could slice open a hole through the two-metre-thick reinforced concrete wall that surrounded the underground vault.

Having failed to find a Hilti drill in those faraway locations, Reader began spending his afternoons shuffling around the City of London casually 'inspecting' construction sites in his old-fashioned tweed jacket, corduroy trousers and traditional brown leather lace-up shoes.

In December 2014, Reader stumbled upon a Hilti DD350 drill in a new office block development in New Fetter Lane, less than a half a mile from Hatton Garden. The gang later turned up in a van to steal the drill and another £63,000 worth of equipment, including the diamond-tipped drill bits which were most often used by construction crews converting former banks into hotels or permanent housing. The thieves who raided the site drove a van similar to the one later used during the Hatton Garden Job. CCTV clearly showed the van parked nearby for just two minutes while two hooded men entered the premises.

City of London police later called to the site didn't even think about the equipment being used to break into a vault. The Flying Squad were not informed about the theft until days after the actual Hatton Garden raid had been carried out.

It must have all seemed so exciting compared to Brian Reader's mundane existence back in Dartford: every morning he'd stroll down to his local newsagent to buy himself a newspaper – usually the *Daily Mail* because that had been his late wife Lyn's favourite – and a pint of milk and then wander back home for a slice of toast and a cup of piping hot tea. Reader's only other regular domestic activity at this time involved visiting his local 'Monday Club' in Dartford where he met other recently bereaved old folk to talk about how much they missed their loved ones.

When Brian Reader was asked about his career before he retired he told the other old folk that he owned a second-hand car business. A few of them had no doubt heard the rumours in Dartford about Reader's real 'career'. But no one there would have dared asked him about it.

CHAPTER SEVENTEEN

TRUE PROFESSIONALS

Just after Christmas 2014, Reader, Perkins, Jones and Collins all met at the lock-up belonging to plumber Hughie Doyle to do a 'test run' with the Hilti drill, which they believed could penetrate the vault's two-foot-thick concrete wall. The drill weighed 5½ stone (35kg) and generated such heat when it was operated that it needed a constant supply of water to keep it cool. The gang unpacked the drill and set it up round the back of the building, which stood about thirty yards from The Old Wheatsheaf pub.

Reader insisted he knew how to operate the drill and stepped forward to start it. But he then struggled for more than half an hour to fire the machine up. Reader was about to abandon the test run when Jones stepped forward, opened up his laptop and studied a YouTube clip of the drill he'd found earlier that day.

The drill started almost immediately but Jones was respectful enough to then let Reader step forward to operate it alongside him. It almost flew out of their hands as it spun at 600rpm. Jones assured them it would not overheat because of that water cooling system but he reminded them all to make sure it was topped up at all times, otherwise the drill would likely catch fire.

The drill head was then pointed into a concrete wall behind

the building. The gang was stunned by the speed with which the drill began penetrating the wall, but eventually stopped the machine in case the noise of it alerted the attention of anyone nearby. In fact, loud drilling was later reported by neighbours of the ordinary-looking pub outbuilding in that suburban North London street.

Ex-robber Billy later explained: 'It was a monster of a thing and the lads were almost scared of it at first. But once they got it going they knew it would be the key to their success.'

Now that most of the equipment for the job was in place and stored at Hughie Doyle's lockup, Terry Perkins wanted to nail down the perfect date to carry out the raid. He earmarked the Easter Bank Holiday of April 2015. Perkins told the other gang members that on a Bank Holiday weekend, local traders would put much more cash, gems and precious metals into boxes than on a 'normal' weekend. Perkins also mentioned that Pesach (the Jewish holiday of Passover) was celebrated from 3 to 11 April that year, which would mean even more gems would be left in the vault because that holiday was a whole week when certain shops would not be open.

When another gang member pointed out that perhaps the Flying Squad might put two and two together because the Security Express heist had been the only other time when a robbery gang struck on an Easter Bank Holiday, Perkins laughed it off.

Ex-robber Billy explained: 'Terry was obsessed with doing it on that weekend. He said it had to be on the first big Bank Holiday of 2015 and he refused to listen to anyone who doubted his plan.'

Not surprisingly, Perkins and Reader still had concerns about Lenny's man Basil, who was still nowhere to be seen. Lenny had also not been answering their calls. Then one afternoon in

THE JOB

January 2015, Lenny called Perkins and announced that Basil would meet them later that very day.

At that meeting, Basil briefed Perkins, Reader, Jones and Collins clearly and precisely about the layout of the seven-storey building that housed the vault. It was clear to the others that he'd been inside it many times before.

Basil said he'd disable the alarm system and he also outlined the route that the gang would be expected to follow once he'd let them inside the building via the fire exit. Basil also informed them that he and one other gang member would use a ladder to clamber down the lift shaft once it had been disabled and then the others could break down a metal gate that would enable them to come into the vault area via the building's courtyard.

Brian Reader pointed out that the Hilti drill would take many hours to bore a large enough hole in the concrete wall to enable anyone to get into the actual vault. Basil said that since he and Danny Jones were notably thinner than the others they should be the ones to go into the vault through the hole, to save time.

Basil also repeated that he was only there to get one box and then he'd be off. He helpfully suggested to the others that everything else should be transported by wheelie bins back up to the ground floor fire exit.

Then Basil took a long deep breath and the tone of his voice changed. Ex-robber Billy takes up the story. 'He said that they could only nick the boxes on the right side of the vault and that they must only take seventy specific ones. He said he'd give them the numbers on the night of the job.'

The other gang members looked surprised. Not even Reader and Perkins were aware of these new 'rules'. They asked Basil why they were being told to target such specific boxes.

'But he completely ignored the question and just repeated

that that was the deal. There was no room for negotiation,' added ex-robber Billy.

Moments later, Basil left the meeting. Reader and Perkins then found themselves having to explain to Jones and Collins that without Basil, they couldn't get access to the main building so doing what he'd said was a small price to pay for that access.

Jones and Collins were clearly just as disturbed by Basil's briefing, and Collins later intimated he wanted to get out of the job there and then. But Terry Perkins then stepped in and assured them it would all go like clockwork, as long as each of them did their jobs properly. He also warned them there was no turning back now. The job was set in stone.

On Friday, 16 January 2015, Terry Perkins, Danny Jones and Kenny Collins all met at The Castle pub. Perkins had earlier rung Collins to suggest they needed to 'have a chat'. The three men sat in a corner of the main bar and talked quietly among themselves.

At ten o'clock the next morning, Carl Wood and Danny Jones spoke on the phone to discuss the raid.

A week later, on Friday, 23 January, Terry Perkins phoned Brian Reader on his son Paul's mobile phone to discuss how their plans were progressing. Reader was the only member of the gang who didn't have his own mobile phone. He'd decided many years earlier that the police could track him through a mobile phone, so he could live without one.

That evening Collins, Perkins and one other member of the gang met again at The Castle. Other locals in the pub began to wonder what they were up to.

At 6.10 p.m., Terry Perkins again called Reader Paul's mobile and the two men spoke about the job as Perkins stood outside the pub. At 7.27 p.m., Collins left The Castle and headed home. The others left shortly afterwards in their own vehicles.

The following afternoon, Saturday, 24 January, Carl Wood and Danny Jones spoke on the phone once again, this time for nearly four minutes. Their conversations were gradually taking on a fresh urgency because the date for the Hatton Garden Job was approaching.

During the last week of January 2015, Hatton Garden jeweller Lionel Wiffen began to notice that a number of suspicious looking people seemed to be showing a lot of interest in 88–90 Hatton Garden, where he'd had his workshop for the previous thirty years. At first Mr Wiffen didn't pay much attention, but he kept seeing cars slowing down as they passed the building and occasionally men would stop on the pavement outside the building and seemed to be examining the side entrance.

On Thursday, 12 February, Carl Wood made a brief visit to Hatton Garden to check the location out. He then spoke to Danny Jones on the phone for three minutes and 36 seconds about various aspects of what he'd found during that reconnaissance trip.

The following morning, Wood and Jones spoke yet again on the phone and later that day a meeting was held at The Castle between Jones and Perkins. Following this meeting, Perkins' blue Citroen Saxo headed over to the Hatton Garden area before he returned home to Enfield.

The following day, Sunday, 15 February, Terry Perkins travelled in his Citroen to visit a man at a metal company some miles from his home. It was, the prosecution later claimed, a venue the gang would use to start disposing of the contents of the safety deposit vault.

Later that same day Danny Jones phoned Perkins to tell him his thoughts about a range of issues relating to the job. The intensity of the build-up to the raid was clear to all those involved. It had in itself turned into virtually a fulltime job, even though they were still more than a month away from putting all their plans to the test.

Then the gang got a big break; Kenny Collins managed to get hold of a key to the building opposite 88–90 Hatton Garden that would be the perfect lookout post. It's not known how Collins obtained those keys, but the building did have a past connection with the crime family who were helping finance the raid through their man Lenny.

Armed with the keys, Collins was dispatched to check out the building late at night and on at least half a dozen occasions over the next couple of weeks he watched all the comings and goings at the seven-storey building opposite his lookout post.

Sometimes Perkins joined Collins as they spent hours monitoring the vault's staff and movements, a tactic that Perkins had successfully employed during the Security Express robbery in 1983.

At midday on Tuesday, 17 February, Collins and Jones drove down to Hatton Garden once again and carried out a detailed reconnaissance close to the seven-storey building that housed the vault, as well as the surrounding area. They checked for any weak spots that might prove a problem on the day of the actual raid. They were, in the words of one former robber, 'covering all exits'. It was later stated in court that 'in all likelihood' Terry Perkins was also with them during this trip.

Later that same day, Jones called Carl Wood and updated him about the trip to Hatton Garden. During this period, Jones always contacted Wood after visiting Hatton Garden.

Perkins and Reader consistently encouraged the other gang members to get a proper feel for the place. As ex-robber Billy later explained: 'You can't just swoop into somewhere, commit a big crime and then swan off without a care in the world. You need to know the area like the back of your hand. That's why it was so important to visit Hatton Garden over and over again.'

On Tuesday, 24 February, Kenny Collins travelled back to Hatton Garden for yet another look at the area before then driving north in his white Mercedes to The Castle pub, where Jones and Perkins joined him. Once again they went over all the details, examining everything in minute detail. Collins even told them all about jeweller Lionel Wiffen, who had an office off the main courtyard at 88–90 Hatton Garden. He warned the others that Wiffen often worked very late but he never left any later than 9–9.30 p.m.

Throughout March, the gang members kept to a similar routine as they worked hard to cover all the angles for the job. Collins ended up 'scouting' the Hatton Garden area at least half a dozen more times, always parking his distinctive white Mercedes round the corner and then hobbling awkwardly along the pavement, checking out the area. Meanwhile Wood, Jones and Perkins kept in regular touch with each other by phone, as well as holding face-to-face meetings.

In mid-March, residents in the Hatton Garden area reported a 'peculiar' power cut, which gave the impression someone or something had caused a major power surge, blowing out all the electricity in the area. No one to this day knows if this incident was linked to the Hatton Garden gang.

CHAPTER EIGHTEEN

TIME GENTLEMEN, PLEASE

On the evening of Friday, 20 March 2015, Woods, Jones and Perkins all visited Kenny Collins' home in Bletsoe Walk, Islington, which was close to The Castle pub. Later that same evening, all four men left the house and drove in Collins' white Mercedes to Hatton Garden, arriving at approximately 9.15 p.m. Collins' car left the area at around 9.40 and was back in the vicinity of Bletsoe Walk just ten minutes later.

That evening, Kenny Collins invited his friend Billy Lincoln round to his house and mentioned very casually to Terry Perkins that Lincoln was going to be the gang's driver. Perkins was far from happy to find that a complete stranger had now joined the gang. Perkins later recalled: 'I said, "'Ere, how does this fucking Bill [Lincoln] know about anything?" I went upstairs to have a shower, right, and when I came down there was a bloke here who I never knew, which was Bill, and Kenny [Collins] had told him everything.'

Round-faced, overweight Billy Lincoln had close family links to Collins. Lincoln's aunt Milly Garrett lived with Collins as his common law wife at Collins' home in Islington. Lincoln had a string of convictions for attempted burglary, burglary and attempted theft between 1975 and 1985, but his most recent conviction was for battery in 2013. The proud Eastender had attacked a gang of youths with a chair because they were causing trouble on his street in Bethnal Green. Married father-of-two Lincoln was even known as 'Billy the Fish' at the famous Billingsgate fish market where he would buy haddock, kippers, eels and salmon to sell on to friends and family members.

Lincoln liked to relax at the Georgian Porchester Spa, Queensway, a Turkish baths specialising in 'Schmeissing' (a Yiddish term for the treatment where men are beaten with a large soapy brush). Lincoln's reputation as 'Billy the Fish' was enhanced at the baths because he used to arrive with salmon to sell to his fellow bathers.

But Billy Lincoln kept quiet to the others about some serious health issues; he suffered from sleep apnoea, bladder problems and severe osteoarthritis, which had necessitated a double hip replacement. As a result of Lincoln's ailments, he was unable to work and received both disability living and employment support allowances. Lincoln had also recently been involved in an incident with his grandson – the 'light of his life' – which saw the child end up in an induced coma in hospital. Lincoln had been asked by his daughter to look after the youngster but he was unable to, and while under the care of someone else the then two-year-old suffered a head injury.

Kenny Collins had planned for his share of the Hatton Garden loot to be transported by Billy Lincoln via Lincoln's nephew Jon Harbinson. Cabbie Harbinson had held a Hackney Carriage licence for the previous twelve years and usually worked in the afternoons and evenings around the eastern side of London, including the City and Liverpool Street station. (Harbinson was later cleared of any involvement with the gang.)

The following day, Tuesday, 31 March, a woman depositing

some jewellery at the Hatton Garden Safety Deposit premises noticed that the lift inside the building was taking an unusually long time to arrive on her floor. When it finally turned up after some six or seven minutes, the doors opened to reveal a man in his mid-sixties with white hair and wearing blue overalls standing inside the lift. He was surrounded by tools and building equipment.

It later occurred to the woman that it must have been hard for an elderly man to get into the lift without someone loading the tools around him. The workman smiled apologetically, because there was no room for her to get in, and the doors closed.

Terry Perkins fitted the description of that man perfectly. At 4 p.m. the same day, Perkins' car was recorded driving north of the North Circular Road, on the A10 once again en route back to his home in Enfield. Gang member Carl Woods' car was also recorded driving just south of the North Circular near the A10, a few minutes earlier.

At 12 a.m. on Wednesday 1 April – April Fool's Day 2015 – electrical cables under the pavement in Kingsway, near Holborn underground station, burst into flames, which shot out of a manhole cover after an apparent gas main burst. It was just a short distance from Hatton Garden. A Metropolitan Police helicopter helped guide the fire services to the source of the blaze. Several thousand people had to be evacuated from nearby offices, and local theatres cancelled performances. There was also substantial disruption to the telecoms infrastructure and emergency services were tied up for days. One ex-Flying Squad officer later claimed critical wiring might have been destroyed on purpose, leaving the vaults at the Hatton Garden Safety Deposit Ltd easier to access.

Back in that small outhouse building behind The Old Wheatsheaf pub in Enfield, north London, the Hatton Garden gang were going through their final preparations. They discussed how the vault was accessible through three doors: the first barred like a prison cell, the last made of metal, 18 inches thick. They'd been over it many times before, but Perkins and Reader wanted to make sure everyone knew what their jobs were off by heart.

Ex-robber Billy explained: 'The fellas said afterwards it was the best organized job they'd ever been on. Each member of the gang had a specific task and they were expected to perform it to the best of their abilities. In a way it was like being back in the armed forces. A couple of the lads – including Brian – were old enough to have been called up in the 1950s, so they knew all about discipline.'

On the morning of Thursday, 2 April, all the gang members told their wives and girlfriends they were off 'to do some work' and wouldn't be back for a couple of days. Some of the wives already suspected what was happening, but kept their thoughts to themselves because they knew only too well what would happen if they confronted their husbands. Reader later claimed to one friend that he 'talked' to his late wife Lyn that day. He often 'spoke' in his head to Lyn from beyond the grave. But Reader never actually told anyone if Lyn approved of his plan to carry out the biggest burglary in British criminal history.

That morning Brian Reader and Terry Perkins met with the others for a final run-through at Hughie Doyle's lock-up behind The Old Wheatsheaf. Perkins told them they could well end up with cash and jewels worth as much as £50 million. Danny Jones shouted 'Yes!' and leapt to his feet. He was as excited as a teenager going out on his first date and the others had to tell him to shut up and sit down.

Perkins also mentioned in more detail what they'd do with the most valuable gems immediately after the raid. He wanted to get them woven into rudimentary costume jewellery and then given to women to wear on budget flights to Europe. There the jewels would be recut and sold on – sometimes back through Britain.

No one has confirmed if Basil was present at this last gathering but it seems unlikely. The other gang members still looked on Basil with great suspicion and wondered if he was even going to show up for the actual break-in planned for later that very day. When one of the gang suggested to Perkins and Reader that Basil might be an undercover cop, they laughed off the idea and it was never mentioned again.

Brian Reader then warned the others that if any of them were tempted to pocket anything out of the sight of the rest of the gang they would be 'hung, drawn and quartered'. They were also warned that if they opened any of the boxes on the right hand side of the vault – which they'd been specifically told to ignore – they would also be taking their lives into their own hands.

But most important of all, Brian Reader made it crystal clear he wanted to avoid any violence. He'd seen enough death and destruction with his own eyes thanks to the likes of Kenneth Noye and others. He assured the gang they wouldn't encounter anybody and that the job had been specifically designed for that reason. Reader also knew only too well that sentences would be much longer if weapons were carried and that could mean never living to see the spoils of their work.

One of the gang members later told ex-robber Billy that Reader then said to them: 'We're all too fuckin' old for a fight, anyway!'

As the gang got up to prepare to leave Doyle's outhouse, each of them turned to the other and nodded silently. They'd all agreed to leave separately and then meet up in St John Street near Hatton Garden at 7 p.m. that evening.

Billy said: 'It was calm and cool in there apparently. No hugging before the game like those poncey Premiership footballers. Nah! These were old men steeped in crime, who had a job to do and a lot of risks to take. They didn't have time to be emotional about it.'

As they were all about to depart, Brian Reader turned to the other gang members and casually mentioned that he was travelling to Hatton Garden by train and bus later because he didn't like driving in the London traffic. The others nodded very slowly but said nothing.

Reader then proudly informed them he'd got himself a stolen Freedom Pass at his local pub a few nights earlier, so there would be no trace of his movements. It seemed almost comical to the others that the so-called 'Guv'nor' of the entire job was using a pensioner's travel pass to reach the scene of what they all hoped would turn out to be the world's biggest burglary.

Then, as the six men turned to head towards the exit, Terry Perkins said there was one last important thing they all needed to do. The gang looked at each other with quizzical expressions on their faces.

'Phones gentlemen, please,' said Perkins, who'd not mentioned to any of the others that this was the eve of his 68th birthday.

Each man produced his own mobile phone and placed it in a brown cardboard box that was handed around between them – except Brian Reader. He proudly reminded them all he didn't use a mobile phone.

The men left the lock-up in north London and went off in their own separate directions.

A couple of hours later, gang member Carl Wood found himself pacing up and down at his home in Cheshunt, desperate to get going on the job. Eventually, he picked up the landline phone in the hallway and made a call to Barclaycard to find out the exact status of his latest debts owed to the bank. Wood ended that conversation happy that within a few days he would have it all sorted out. He felt bouncy and light-headed after the putting the phone down, excited that all his money problems would soon be over. Or so he thought.

At just after 5 p.m. that same day, Brian Reader struggled a bit for breath as he boarded a number 96 bus outside his home in Dartford Road, swiping the travel card he'd bought at his local pub. A few minutes later he took a train to London's Waterloo East station. Reader exited Waterloo East at 6.31 p.m. Less than half an hour later – at 7.02 p.m. – he boarded the 55 bus. To the other passengers he was just an elderly man and it's even possible someone gave up their seat because of his age. That bus took Reader to St John Street, which was a five-minute walk from Hatton Garden.

Over at 88–90 Hatton Garden, building supervisor Carlos Cruse was checking the courtyard and the basement before closing up. He could clearly see the Hatton Garden Safe Deposit company's full-time security guard Kelvin Stockwell carefully locking the vault ahead of the Bank Holiday weekend. Stockwell set the alarm as he'd done every night for twenty years and the electric door to the vault slid closed.

Carlos Cruse waited for the guard to leave the building and then activated the magnetic glass internal door and departed the building through the main doors, which closed and locked automatically behind him.

Less than two hours later – at approximately 8.25 p.m. – a

white van driven by Kenny Collins pulled up in Leather Lane just around the corner from 88–90 Hatton Garden. Two minutes later, Danny Jones and Carl Wood got out of the vehicle.

Walking along another street near Hatton Garden at that moment was Brian Reader. He'd dumped the long overcoat he'd been wearing earlier to reveal a hi-visibility jacket with the word 'GAS' written on the back. He was also wearing a yellow hard hat. The outfit seemed incongruous combined with his jazzy looking stripy socks and expensive brown leather shoes, as well as a distinctive coloured designer scarf.

CHAPTER NINETEEN

NO TURNING BACK

On that same evening of Thursday, 2 April 2015, jeweller Lionel Wiffen was working late as he often did at his workshop, overlooking the courtyard at 88–90 Hatton Garden. He was still wondering about all those strange occurrences over the previous couple of months.

Earlier that very week, Mr Wiffen had noticed yet more random vans and sometimes taxis driving slowly past. In some cases, they'd stopped for a few moments before moving on. He'd also seen people sitting in cars parked on the other side of the road. He later recalled: 'They seemed to be looking over every time I opened my door.'

Less than fifty yards away from Mr Wiffen's workshop, at just after 9 p.m., the white Ford Transit van parked on Greville Street just near the corner with Hatton Garden. Danny Jones and his old friend Carl Wood got out and walked down the street towards 88–90 Hatton Garden. Brian Reader and Terry Perkins remained inside the van.

Wood was dressed in dark clothing, with a hi-visibility waistcoat, navy baseball cap and spectacles, and carried a black backpack. Later he'd put on a white surgeon's style mask and dark gloves. Jones was wearing a hooded jumper with white writing, striped trousers (although the stripes were not always visible in subsequent CCTV footage), a hi-visibility waistcoat, red trainers and a navy baseball cap. He was carrying a blue Nike bag and red toolbox.

They strolled around observing the area close to the seven-storey building that housed the vault before walking around the block and back down Leather Lane, where they returned to Greville Street once again and got back into the parked van.

Nearby, the man known only as Basil strolled casually along Greville Street, with a bulky black plastic sack strategically placed on his shoulder so that any overhanging CCTV cameras would not be able to capture an image of his face. Basil was wearing a blue jacket and dark trousers but it was his salmon-coloured hair visible beneath a black cap that seemed most incongruous. Many later said it must have been a wig. Basil was also wearing see-through latex gloves.

When Basil reached the corner of the street, he moved across the pavement towards the front entrance to 88–90 Hatton Garden. Footage from overhanging CCTV cameras record the moment Basil unlocked the main entrance to the building. Once inside the front door, Basil was confronted with a magnetic glass door that needed a four-digit pincode. It's not clear if he had the code or used a tool to get in. But from there he crossed the lobby and unlocked another door that led downstairs to the courtyard and the basement entrance to the Hatton Garden Safe Deposit company's offices.

Then he heard a noise and stopped and waited.

A few yards from where Basil stood, jeweller Lionel Wiffen locked up his workshop and departed the building at 9.21 p.m. via a fire exit. Moments after Mr Wiffen had shut the exit door behind him, Basil was spotted by CCTV cameras in the court-yard heading for the same fire escape.

In the street outside, Wood and Jones got out of the white Ford Transit van, which was parked close to a public telephone box. Jones then whispered something into a walkie-talkie as he surveyed the area.

Moments later – as if by magic – the doors to the fire exit swung open just as Terry Perkins and Brian Reader also got out of the van. Diabetic Terry Perkins patted the pocket of his jacket just to make sure he was carrying the insulin he needed. All four men then began unloading equipment and tools from the double doors which they'd opened at the back of the vehicle.

Brian Reader's stripy socks and smart brown leather shoes seemed even more out of place compared to the trainers being worn by other members of the gang. Tufts of white hair were visible beneath Reader's hard hat as he stooped and struggled for breath, while trying to unload a bag of tools from the back of the van. Perkins later said that Reader didn't really do much to help. Next to him, Perkins looked more like the consummate professional dressed in dark clothing, with hi-visibility waist-coat, a yellow hard hat and white surgeon-style mask.

The men lugged bags of tools out of the van as well as two large black plastic wheelie bins and some long metal joists. As the gang ferried everything from the back of the van in through the fire escape entrance, they tried not to hurry so as to avoid attracting any attention. Finally they took out a long canvas bag containing the Hilti DD350 drill. It took three of the men to get it out of the van and in through the narrow fire exit.

Just inside the fire exit, the long metal joists were then speed-ily ferried down the stairs to the building's courtyard. They were to be used by the gang to jam open the lift doors in order to gain access to the basement.

In the corridor by the fire exit, Danny Jones stopped in his tracks and looked around in an agitated state. Then he spoke to Perkins. Standing nearby were Reader, Wood and mystery man Basil.

Outside the building, Kenny Collins drove slowly off in the white Transit van and headed towards nearby St Cross Street.

Back in the corridor, Jones and Perkins continued their 'discussion'. Suddenly, Jones turned and moved off back up towards the fire exit. The others looked to Perkins for a reaction.

In St Cross Street, Kenny Collins pulled up in the van and parked it carefully. Then he switched off the engine and got out. He was just about to lock the vehicle when Danny Jones suddenly appeared in the street. Collins looked up, alarmed. Jones moved alongside him and grabbed the van keys out of Collins' hands, informing Collins the gang had forgotten something.

Jones ripped open the double doors at the back of the van, snatched a green crate and slammed the doors shut.

Moments later, he was back at the fire escape door of 88–90 Hatton Garden, which had been left jammed open. Once back in the corridor on the other side of the fire door, Jones beckoned Wood over towards him. He then placed the crate in one of the wheelie bins and the two men carried it down the stairs to the courtyard.

Outside, driver Kenny Collins had locked the van and was waddling awkwardly along Hatton Garden towards the crossing with Greville Street. He was wearing a green quilted jacket, a flat cap and carrying a brown briefcase that contained a cheese sandwich and a flask of hot tea. Not long after this, Collins huffed and puffed as he walked up to the front door of the 'lookout' building opposite 88–90 Hatton Garden.

Collins spent some time at the door trying to open it before finally getting in. The studio and offices on the first floor of the building provided Collins with a clear view of the front and rear entrances to 88–90 Hatton Garden, where Perkins, Reader, Jones, Wood and Basil were already hard at work.

Collins settled into his perfect vantage point by a first-floor window, put his feet up on a window ledge and waited. He knew that he'd be there for quite some time, so he'd save his sandwich and tea until later. Collins had a walkie-talkie, which was only to be used if there was a problem. Two other members of the gang in the basement opposite had walkie-talkies for that same purpose.

While some of the men continued lugging the bags, tools and other equipment downstairs to the courtyard, Basil peeled off towards the lift with Danny Jones. He then expertly disabled the lift to make sure the car remained stuck on the second floor. The door sensors were left hanging off, so that the doors would stay open. The empty lift shaft would provide the gang with a short drop down from the ground floor to the basement from where they could let the others in from the courtyard. Ironically, the lift hadn't been down to the basement since an armed robbery back in the 1970s.

There were no CCTV cameras actually inside the Hatton Garden Safe Deposit company's offices because customers preferred it that way due to the 'sensitive' items they stored in the vault's boxes.

Having disabled the lift, Basil and Jones used a portable ladder to climb down the empty lift shaft to the basement to save time. At the bottom, the shutters to the lift door were jammed open so roughly from the inside by the two men that they buckled. Above them, on the ground floor, one of the men left a handwritten note stuck next to the lift entrance. It read: 'Out of order'.

Basil then located the electrical equipment cupboard beneath the stairs in the basement. He expertly cut the grey telephone line cable coming out of the alarm box and the GPS aerial was broken off, significantly reducing its signal range.

Basil calmly removed the cover of an electrical box underneath a desk, which powered the outer sliding iron gate at the entrance to the vault area from the courtyard. Further wires were cut. This would cut the power to the electronically operated metal gate, which would enable it to be pulled open manually.

With the alarm apparently switched off, the others wrenched open the metal door that separated Basil and Jones from the rest of the gang and they all poured into the office area. But Basil hadn't completely disabled the alarm system. The breaching of that metal door allowed the weakened alarm system to send a radio signal to the security company monitoring the vault. A text was then automatically sent to the local police station informing them that there had been an 'incident' inside the vault area.

The gang, completely unaware the alarm had been tripped, continued with their mission.

CHAPTER TWENTY

TOO CLOSE FOR COMFORT

The gang next broke off the lock on the wooden access door to the vault area. This left a big open doorway, through which they could move larger items, as well as providing easier passage to and from the vault area.

Two of the raiders then cut through a second sliding iron gate on the perimeter of the vault with an angle grinder. Once that was snapped off its hinges, they used heavy-duty industrial metal cutters to get through the main door to the vault company offices.

Now – for the first time – they faced the biggest obstacle of all: the two-foot-thick concrete outer wall of the vault.

No one at the nearest police station, nor at the headquarters of the security company who managed the vault, had noticed that text message about a possible break-in at the vault building.

Meanwhile, thirty feet below Hatton Garden, two members of the gang carefully removed the cumbersome Hilti hi-tech drill from its canvas cover. Brian Reader licked his lips and stared down at the machine. He could feel his heart pounding. After all these years of talking about this job, it was finally actually happening in front of his eyes.

Opposite Reader, an equally breathless Terry Perkins took an insulin bottle out from his trouser pocket and told the others to look away while he jabbed a needle into his arm. Without this medication, he'd told them all earlier, he'd be 'a goner'.

The gang knew they needed to drill three adjoining circular holes in the wall itself. Those holes needed to be at least 50cm deep, 25cm high and 45cm wide so that they provided a big enough space for the slimline Basil and Danny Jones to climb through. Special diamond-tipped drill bits of that width had also been specially stolen earlier. The three holes would be drilled separately, which would then be knocked into one large opening. It was going to be a long night.

Reader had earlier warned the others that drilling through concrete would be extremely noisy and was probably the most risky aspect of the job. But that night the gang had an extraordinary stroke of good fortune because at nearby Farringdon station the noise of construction work on the underground Crossrail project was being blamed, by most Hatton Garden residents, for all the loud noises in the area.

Reader, Perkins and Jones were all confident the drill would easily penetrate the wall but no one was absolutely sure how long it would take.

Initially, the gang was stunned by the loud noise of the machine and of course they had no idea that the noisy Crossrail work was going on nearby. When they'd tested the drill a few weeks earlier on that wall behind Hugh Doyle's workshop, the noise had been dissipated into the outside air. But now they were in a very enclosed space and the decibels were literally bouncing off all four walls. Every fifteen minutes Reader and Perkins stopped to allow the drill to cool down, even though Jones assured the two elderly villains it would not overheat because of its water cooler. The others suspected Reader and

Perkins just needed an excuse to have regular breaks because they were finding it so exhausting.

Basil stood back in a corner of the room, watching the others intensely with his fingers in his ears to drown out the din.

At first, the drill seemed to make little impression on the concrete wall. The men wondered if perhaps they'd misjudged its performance or picked the wrong diamond drill head. Each time they stopped to see if a hole had started to appear, there was nothing other than a slight dent. Then, after more than an hour, a small split appeared in the wall and tiny splinters of grey concrete began bouncing off the drill piece.

After another hour and a half, the drill had almost completed the first of the three holes right through to the other side. Reader and Perkins told the others not to get too excited yet as they still had to drill two more identical holes. They all stopped for a break at just before 12.20 a.m., still unaware that their initial break-in had sent an SMS text alarm call to the local police.

Across the street, Kenny Collins was struggling to stay awake after he'd stuffed back that cheese sandwich and a cup of tea. Hatton Garden was deserted and his head was starting to droop with tiredness. Every now and again he fell slightly forward and woke up with a start. At one stage, he tried to slap some water on his face to wake himself up, but that didn't make much difference.

Thirty feet beneath the pavement, the gang were back drilling. In the far corner, Basil watched them all through narrowing eyes. Every now and again the others looked across at him with irritation. They still didn't feel comfortable having him there – not to mention the fact that he did very little to help.

At the local police station, the text from the alarm company had finally been noticed three hours after it had sensed movement in the vault area. The officers on duty had checked their desktop computer for references to this particular alarm and decided from the file that this was not a 'priority alarm system', so they ignored it. The call was recorded and transferred to the police's Computer Aided Dispatch system. The grade applied to the call meant no police response was deemed to be required, although a call did finally go out to the alarm company advising them to send a vault security guard to have a look at the outside of the building, just to be on the safe side.

Down below street level, the gang were taking another break, this time for some refreshments. The drill was heavy and extremely tiring to operate. Perkins and Reader glanced up at Basil when they stopped but he didn't even look back at them. Reader was feeling particularly breathless again, so he was glad of a break.

Across the street, Kenny Collins was now sound asleep and snoring loudly. He didn't even notice vault security guard Kevin Stockwell pull up outside 88–90 Hatton Garden in his car. It was 1.15 a.m.

Downstairs in the basement, the raiders thought they heard the sound of a car pulling up and then the movement of someone above them. When two of the gang pulled out spanners from their tool bag, Reader told them to put them away. He's said he wasn't too concerned because they hadn't heard anything from Collins on the walkie-talkie. Whoever was up there was only walking around the outside area at the front of the building.

The last thing Brian Reader wanted was any violence. Just then Basil chipped in with a comment that stopped all the others in their tracks. He said that even if it was the security guard, he'd only look at the outside of the building and then leave. Ex-robber Billy later said that it was clear to the others that Basil knew everything about the building.

Upstairs, Stockwell checked the front area of the building as he walked outside and then around to the fire exit, which appeared to be locked. Stockwell later recalled: 'I got out of the car, went to the front of the building. I pushed through the doors, they was secure. I went round to Greville Street (fire exit) and I looked through the letterbox. All I could see in there, the light was on, was a metal box on the floor and a bicycle.'

Stockwell's main priority had been the front doors to the building and since there had been no sign of a break-in, he presumed the alarm had tripped itself and then turned itself off. The fact that there had never been any other 'false alarms' since the new system was installed in 2007 did not enter his head.

In fact it later emerged that the vault company's insurers had insisted the police would be the only ones to enter and investigate any call-outs, not the private security guard. The guard's instructions were probably something along these lines: 'Do a security sweep of the outside of the building, and if no signs of break-in, continue normal patrol. If signs of break-in, call the police and observe the building from a safe distance.'

After completing all the standard checks, Stockwell phoned the vault manager and son of the owner, Manish Bavishi – who was on his way to the building in his car – to say that everything appeared secure and it must have been a false alarm. Stockwell later recalled: 'He said he was about five minutes away. I told him the place was secure and he said you might as well go home.'

So both men returned home in the early hours of that morning, completely unaware that a gang of thieves were drilling holes in the concrete wall of the supposedly impregnable vault.

Incredibly, a few minutes after the security guard left, raider

THE JOB

Carl Wood was caught by CCTV cameras having a cigarette in the corridor next to the fire exit.

As soon as they felt there was nothing to worry about on the street above them, the gang restarted drilling the second of the three adjoining holes they would need to get access to the vault itself. There were no more interruptions that night.

However, unknown to the raiders, their drilling was having a major impact on the sleeping habits of a couple living just opposite the fire exit to the main building, in Greville Street. John Han, a 26-year-old data scientist, later recalled: 'I did think at the time: "Who the hell does drilling at this hour?" Mr Han and his girlfriend assumed the noise was connected to repair work in the area following a power blackout a few days earlier.

Thirty feet beneath a deserted Hatton Garden, the gang were soon making speedy progress, thanks to their 'monster' drill. By approximately 5 a.m., they'd completed the third of the required holes. Using sledgehammers, they further smashed the remaining concrete separating the three holes to make the opening big enough for Basil and Jones to worm their way through.

But they weren't through to the vault quite yet.

CHAPTER TWENTY-ONE

SLEEPING DOGS LIE

The gang had created a 25cm by 45cm hole in the wall but the steel inner lining of the vault still separated them from tens of millions of pounds worth of loot. The gang had been expecting this because they knew that the grey steel cabinets holding the safety deposit boxes were anchored up against all four walls of the inside of the vault. The steel 'skin' weighed several tonnes and was bolted to the floor and the ceiling. Shifting it would be no easy task, but the gang had come prepared by bringing a Clarke pump and hose attached to a hydraulic ram. Reader had admitted to Perkins a few days before the raid: 'If that doesn't do the trick then we're fucked.'

Before continuing, Perkins then heard his walkie-talkie crackling. He waited to see if there was anyone on the line. There wasn't, so he called Kenny Collins to check if anything was happening outside. Collins didn't answer his walkie-talkie at first because he was fast asleep. When Perkins tried it again, Collins came on the line trying to sound alert and awake.

'You been akip, Kenny?' asked Perkins suspiciously.

Collins denied it and swore on his kids' life he hadn't been asleep.

Reader then enlisted Jones and Wood to help him set up

the pump with its heavy hydraulic ram by using some of those same metal joists they'd lugged from the van earlier to anchor it into position. Reader looked exhausted but as ex-robber Billy later explained: 'The rest of them were running on adrenalin by this time. It's better than any drugs.'

Basil sat in a corner of the room throughout, without offering to help. The others looked back in his direction every now and again. They later recalled he gave out a vibe that he was the man in charge, even though it was very much Reader and Perkins' job.

With all the equipment now in place, there was an expectant hush in the room. Reader pressed the starter on the machine but nothing happened. He tried over and over again but the device refused to fire up. Two of the gang swore out loud with frustration. For the first time since the unannounced visit by that security guard more than four hours earlier, there was tension in the air.

Reader tried the starter button again and this time it fired up. Jones and Wood cheered. For the next hour, the hydraulic ram smashed backwards and forwards through the triple hole in the concrete wall. But the steel 'skin' refused to bend, let alone snap.

When Perkins demanded the machine be speeded up, it made a terrible clunking noise and completely died. Reader and Perkins tried for at least fifteen minutes to restart it but it had totally expired. Basil sat in the corner of the room throughout this period, with a grim look on his usually cheery face.

Infuriated, Reader turned to Perkins, shrugged his shoulders and told the others to smash their way through the steel 'skin' of the vault with the same sledgehammers they'd just used on the last bit of the concrete wall.

So for at least the following half an hour, Reader stood back exhausted as the rest of the gang frantically hammered awkwardly through the hole onto the steel inner skin like miners trying to get through a collapsed tunnel. It was hot work and every now and again Reader – still struggling for breath – leaned down at an awkward angle trying to examine the open hole to the metal 'skin' on the other side.

The temperature in the room rose steadily while the air was being sucked out of the atmosphere by the five sweating men as they tried in vain to smash their way through the steel skin.

As ex-robber Billy later commented: 'It musta been doin' their heads in. They was so close and yet so far.'

Suddenly, Carl Wood threw down his sledgehammer and began walking round in tight circles 'screaming like a pig', according to later conversations between the raiders. Jones pulled him to one side and told him to sort himself out.

Basil looked the most pissed off of all of them. Sensing tension among the 'troops', Reader and Perkins told Jones and Wood to stop completely. It was pointless. Reader, catching his breath, told them they'd all have to pull out.

Basil shook his head but said nothing. He then narrowed his eyes and squinted at each of the others in turn.

The other men all looked across at Reader with grim expressions. All this effort and they were about to abandon 'The Big One' – the job they believed was going to eclipse all others.

Basil then spoke for the first time in hours. His voice was cool and unflustered. He insisted all was not lost and told the other men they should get some replacement equipment and then return the following evening. He pointed out that the Bank Holiday meant there was no big risk attached to them returning to the scene of their crime. But the others looked far from convinced.

THE JOB

When Basil noticed Reader and Perkins rolling their eyes at the ceiling as he spoke, his tone changed.

Ex-robber Billy later explained: 'He told them that Lenny and the family wouldn't have it if they abandoned the job. And they all knew what that meant.'

The gang had always presumed the Hatton Garden raid would be a 'one-hit job'. That meant getting in there and getting the job done in one go. Returning the next day seemed like complete madness to them but it didn't look as if they have any choice in the matter.

Brian Reader then sat back exhausted and let Terry Perkins explain the situation. He deferred to Basil every now and then as he explained the situation to the others. As ex-robber Billy later added: 'They knew they'd be topped if they refused.'

Reader and Perkins realized that whatever was in the one security box that Basil was supposed to pick up had to be extremely valuable. But it felt to them as if they'd surrendered all their power to Basil and the crime family. As Billy explained: 'They felt like they'd been stitched up like a kipper. The golden rule in this game is "never return to the scene of a crime" and these lads had just been told they had to do precisely that.'

At just after 7.30 a.m., Kenny Collins was contacted by walkie-talkie and told to stand down, unaware that the gang had not managed to steal anything. He waddled out of the building opposite and went to collect the gang's white Ford Transit van.

At 7.51 a.m., the gang began pulling out from the premises, hopeful that with any luck their activities would remain undiscovered and they could return again with new equipment. But they all knew the risks would have gone up tenfold by the time they came back.

'I s'pose at least they knew they could get straight back in

SEXY BEASTS

and a lot of the hard work had already been done,' Billy later reasoned. 'Someone I know asked them afterwards if they'd have gone back if Basil hadn't been around, and on balance they reckoned they probably still would have. But the trouble was that the decision had been taken out of their hands and that was hard to swallow.'

Reader, Perkins, Wood and Jones all bundled into the white van and told Kenny Collins to drive them to his home in nearby Islington. He asked them where the loot was. None of them answered but just told him to drive. As the van moved off, they watched the mysterious Basil drifting off by foot in the direction of Holborn Circus.

It was only then the gang told Collins what had happened. He was stunned but said little in response. At Collins' home, they were subdued and exhausted. But they knew they needed to work out their next move. They were all having difficulty concentrating on the matter at hand. And every time they thought about what had just happened, they concluded that going back to the vault might well turn out to be a suicide mission.

Terry Perkins did, however, manage to make light of the fact that, to counter any potential health problems, he'd have to take twenty pills between then and when they returned to the vault. He said: 'If I don't take 'em, you'll have to carry me out in a wheelie bin.'

Shortly after the gang had left 88–90 Hatton Garden that morning, jeweller Lionel Wiffen returned to his workshop, completely unaware that anyone had broken into the premises. He was surprised and 'a little worried' to find the fire escape door had been left ajar.

He had never found it open before so he crept in through the open fire exit for a look around, even peeping through a hole in one of the doors to the basement area where the vault was located. But he later said he didn't spot 'anything untoward'. Mr Wiffen locked the fire exit door in Greville Street when he left that evening after preparing his premises for an electrician booked to visit his workshop the following day.

Back at Kenny Collins' ex-council house in Islington, Brian Reader looked especially shattered. He'd seemed a bit unsteady on his feet when they got out of the van earlier. The others said nothing out of respect because they knew how important this job was to him.

Reader then confided to the others he didn't know if he could handle the physical side of another night trying to break into the vault. The raid had taken a huge toll on him, he said. None of the other gang members argued with Reader because he looked so knackered. Reader also pointed out that he could prove a dangerous liability to them, if he collapsed with a heart attack in the middle of the job.

The rest of the gang were worried in case Basil and his crime family bosses got nasty if they returned the following night a man short. Reader tried to reassure them he would handle Lenny and the family once the job was over. But it was a massive call for Reader, especially since his decision might also endanger his chances of getting a share of the loot. That hadn't been discussed yet but it was no doubt on all their minds.

Brian Reader was old-school through and through, and he no doubt hated having to pull out because he felt enormous loyalty towards the others, especially Terry Perkins. Perkins respected Reader too much to try and make him change his mind and totally accepted his reasons for quitting. So getaway driver Bill

Lincoln – who'd been waiting at Collins' house after the raid – was ordered by Terry Perkins to give Reader a lift to London Bridge station, where the 76-year-old made his way home to Kent using his trusty stolen travel card.

Back at Collins' place, Perkins and Danny Jones started discussing the new plan for the return trip to the vault. Wood and Collins looked on slightly dazed by it all. Wood had remained very quiet throughout the stay at Collins' house but his outburst in the vault room had been noted by the others. Then, following Reader's departure, he started saying he wasn't happy about everything.

When Wood asked Perkins for his mobile phone back, Perkins laughed and pointed out that wouldn't be happening until they'd completed the job. Perhaps surprisingly, it never occurred to anyone – not even so-called techno wizard Danny Jones – that they'd have been better off ditching the phones altogether and then buying new ones.

The following morning, Easter Saturday, 4 April – Danny Jones and Kenny Collins drove to West London to buy a brand new version of the faulty Clarke pump that had let them down on the first night. There was no time to cast around for one to steal from a building site. Their 'window' of opportunity for the biggest payday of any of their lives was about to close.

The first tool shop they tried didn't even stock the Clarke pump. They were then directed to a store called Machine Mart, in the suburb of Twickenham where it was available. Danny Jones signed for the equipment using the name *V. Jones* – a cheeky reference to British gangster film actor and former footballer Vinnie Jones.

But then he gave his own address and provided his own credit card for payment. Why he did this we will never know but it was one of the most elementary mistakes any of the gang made. How could a team of supposedly professional criminals make such an error?

Early that Saturday evening, a series of phone calls were exchanged between various members of the gang before Collins drove Perkins, Jones and Wood back to the Hatton Garden area in his white Mercedes E200.

At least this time they didn't have to wait for old-timer Brian Reader to get the train and catch a bus.

CHAPTER TWENTY-TWO

DÉJÀ VU

Back in the vicinity of Hatton Garden once more, the four gang members checked out the area very carefully, just in case anyone had been alerted in the thirty-six hours since they'd pulled out.

After circling the area a number of times, Collins' white Mercedes drove back to Islington. As ex-robber Billy later put it: 'They must have felt right weird. Here they were all over again, not even knowing if anyone had stumbled on anything. But they hadn't got this far just to turn back and call it a day. No way. They wanted what they'd come for the previous day and nothing was going to stop them. But of course they still had the problem of Basil and his bosses.'

No one had seen or heard from Basil since the end of the raid the previous day, when he'd wandered off alone down Hatton Garden. Then just as the four walked back into Collins' home, the landline phone on the hall table started ringing. It was Basil. He told Perkins he'd meet them all outside the building the same way he had the first night of the raid. Wood said he smelt a rat and started suggesting that maybe it was all a trap. Perkins and Jones told him to shut up.

Forty minutes later, the gang were back in the Hatton Garden area in the white Ford Transit van. They pulled up in

Greville Street, near to that now very familiar fire exit. Carl Wood immediately got out and tried the fire escape door – which jeweller Lionel Wiffen had earlier locked. Wood started pushing it with his shoulder but it wouldn't open. Perkins and Jones then joined Wood in the street and there was an intense conversation between them. Wood pointed out the exit had been deliberately left unlocked the previous day just in case 'keyman' Basil didn't show up. Now it was locked. Someone must have seen what they were up to?

Perkins reminded Wood through gritted teeth they were waiting for Basil and they were running a little early. But Wood shook his head from side to side and got even more agitated. Later the rest of the gang questioned Wood's bottle, one observing that 'his arsehole went'.

Wood was convinced someone else had been in the building since their departure the previous day and he warned the others that whoever was there would have been sure to notice the break-in. Wood believed they were probably all being set up to be arrested. He told the others he wanted out. 'We've been stitched up,' Wood said.

Terry Perkins and Danny Jones later discussed the fallout from Wood's decision. Perkins said to Jones: 'He thought we would never get in ... I said give it another half hour. We've done everything we can do, if we can't get in, we won't be able to get in will we?'

But Wood was having none of it. He thrust his finger in the direction of Terry Perkins and mouthed the words 'fuck off' before turning his back and walking away from the gang members.

CCTV footage later showed Wood stomping away from the area to the left of Leather Lane, beyond Hatton Garden. He was never seen again on CCTV and by all accounts had nothing more to do with the job. The others were stunned by Wood's decision but continued waiting for Basil, no doubt fearful that his crime family bosses might 'punish them' if they weren't there when he arrived.

Billy explained: 'Some people says Wood bottled it. But that's a dangerous assumption to make about an old pro like him. Maybe he wasn't well? Maybe he'd forgotten something? But the trouble was that the others were shit scared that Basil's crime family bosses might seek retribution if the job didn't go ahead. They had to wait for Basil.'

At 9.17 p.m. – not long after Carl Wood had stormed off into the night – the others noticed Basil wandering along the street towards them, apparently without a care in the world. He was carrying the same black sack from the previous night, once again cleverly angled on his shoulder to make sure his features could not be seen on CCTV. Basil's 'drifty' walk was significant because it suggested that perhaps he was a lot older than anyone else realized. But he was also no doubt extremely fit as the others never saw him struggle for breath, unlike old boys Reader, Perkins and lookout Collins.

Basil calmly nodded at the other gang members standing by the van and headed straight around towards the front entrance to 88–90 Hatton Garden. He then let himself in and took the same route through the building as on the Thursday evening. A couple of minutes later, Basil opened the fire escape door to let in the others, who immediately made their way through the building, with Kenny Collins once again resuming his role as lookout in the building across the road.

CCTV footage from that second night showed gang member Danny Jones carrying in a different black holdall from the first night. It contained the brand new Clarke pump and hose bought that morning in Twickenham.

Once back in the basement, the gang again set up the metal joists they'd brought in before to anchor the pump and hose on the wall opposite the vault in order to get maximum traction from the hydraulic equipment. Other gang members looked on tensely as Perkins finalized the preparations.

Ex-robber Billy later explained: 'Apparently the atmosphere was much more tense than the first night. They was worried they might have been set up or that the crime family would show up and blow them all to smithereens.'

Self-confessed eccentric Danny Jones took on a more pivotal role on the second night; however. He seemed even more determined than the others that this time there would be no turning back. According to Billy: 'He wanted to pull the job off more than anyone else. Fuckin' mad bastard.'

Jones and Perkins later discussed how the group began trying to breach the vault on that second night. Jones reflected to Perkins: 'So they put the work down to me and you, they was sitting, going "put a bit here, try a bit there".'

At first the men tried to force the ram to push the metal skin of the cabinet over. The others looked on impatiently, including Basil, who kept glancing at his wristwatch, which was making them all feel even more nervous.

But when that didn't work, Jones got impatient and finally said: 'Let's smash that up.'

Gradually the machine began ramming further and further into the steel outer skin of the cabinet, which lined the vault wall.

Jones shouted: 'Smash that up now, put that down, it's fuckin' workin'. It's workin', it's workin', you got to take it off, it ain't ping back.'

The machine rammed deeper and deeper into the steel skin of the cabinet until it all came crashing down in one piece, leaving a big opening straight into the vault itself.

Jones later recalled that moment in conversation with Perkins: 'Remember me saying that "it ain't fuckin' come back, we're in, we're in", and then you started pumping again, "get some more, get some more". Ain't it?'

The three couldn't quite believe they'd finally done it and for a few moments they all stared in complete disbelief at the scene that had unfolded in front of them. For the first time, they could see right inside the vault beyond the three holes they'd punctured in the thick concrete wall on the first night. Next to the hole was the huge impregnable vault door still tightly closed.

Basil then reminded them they were working against the clock and they needed to get a move on. He was sounding more and more as if he was the man in charge. So, as had previously been agreed, the two slimmest men in the gang moved towards the hole.

Basil was the first one in. Then came Danny Jones who struggled more because he was bigger than Basil. Once in the vault itself, Basil immediately started looking for one specific box on the left side of the vault. Meanwhile Jones – with a scrap of paper in his hand containing all the relevant numbers – headed to the right-hand side as per their agreement. (No one knows to this day why they targeted those specific boxes but it was later noted that virtually all the boxes stolen or ripped open were in the 900 numbers range.)

Neon light from the overhanging lights bounced off the shiny steel front doors of all almost 1,000 safety deposit boxes that lined all four walls of the vault. Many of the boxes were locked with two keys. Other safes had dials.

In the first box ripped open by Jones, he discovered a cassette tape, which looked from the label as if it was 'someone confessing to something'. Jones looked at it for a moment and then decided to leave it somewhere it would be easily found. It was of no value to them.

Jones was soon smashing the locks on the doors and ripping out the actual boxes. He then opened them with an angle grinder and a crowbar. He later said it was like 'popping open boxes at Christmas time'.

Meanwhile, Basil had leant down and was pulling out a specific box in front of him. His movements were a lot more subtle than Jones's. It looked to the others as though he was being careful because he didn't want to damage anything fragile in the box.

Across the vault floor, Jones was yelling 'Yes!' every time he opened a box while filling a bag with jewellery and cash.

A couple of feet away, Basil pulled his target box carefully out from among the boxes lining the left side of the vault. Then he gently placed it in the sack he'd brought with him. He hadn't bothered opening it. Then he moved towards the hole in the wall where Jones was already passing the first bag of loot through to Perkins.

Jones turned and passed Basil as he returned to the right side of the vault, still armed with that scrap of paper containing the numbers of the security boxes they'd been allowed to steal. Basil leaned in to the hole, pushed his sack through the opening and then scrambled through.

On the other side of the vault, Perkins was examining the contents of the first bag Jones had pushed through. He began discarding the cheaper looking jewels in a heap of rubble in the corner of the room. Only seven of the seventy-three boxes grabbed that night turned out to be empty. Those who attended the scene afterwards said it was clear the raiders had known which boxes to target.

Basil sat himself down in the corner of the office and watched Jones through the hole as he continued ripping open the boxes. He seemed curious about what Jones was taking out of them.

Some boxes were taken unopened by Jones and dropped in bags. This also further suggested another ulterior motive for the burglary. One ex-Flying Squad officer wondered after the raid: 'I can see why one specific box was targeted but why didn't they bother opening a lot of the other ones? After all, the boxes were relatively bulky, so they wouldn't have been able to get as much loot into those wheelie bins.'

Undoubtedly, the contents of those boxes would have been enormously varied. Clients were paying £300 a year for a medium-sized box, and while many belonged to Hatton Garden traders, others had been leased to private individuals, whose items could be anything from guns to gems, a lot of those items most probably stolen.

One gang member later told one of ex-robber Billy's closest friends what happened next: 'After we'd emptied seventy-odd of the boxes it shoulda felt great but the presence of Basil had reminded us that this job was far from complete. Here we were, the fuckin' geniuses who'd pulled off the crime of the bleedin' century but all we could think about was, "will we live to see any of this?"'

There had been at least 900 safe deposit boxes in all in that vault and no one knows why the gang stopped at just seventy-two. As another retired Flying Squad officer commented afterwards: 'It just doesn't make sense. Why go to all that trouble of going back a second time and all the risks involved and *not* grab as many boxes as you can?'

*

Basil remained in the corner of the room beaming over his sack of swag. Then he stood up and calmly announced he was off. No one bothered saying goodbye to him and he disappeared in the direction of the courtyard. Perkins and Jones presumed they would never see him again.

As Basil passed the vault's security office a few moments later, he walked in and calmly grabbed the hard-drive for the CCTV cameras and dropped it casually into his sack. This might come in handy one day, he thought.

About fifty feet above on the other side of the road, Kenny Collins was given his orders to pull out via a crackling walkie-talkie message from Perkins. He left his lookout post in the building opposite and headed back towards the white van parked around the corner.

Back in the vault, Danny Jones hesitated as he was about to clamber back through the hole in the wall. He wished he had a camera with him because, as he later said, it would have made the most sensational selfie ever taken.

Jones and Perkins packed all the bags containing the stolen items into their two large wheelie bins and other assorted bags. Terry Perkins finally mentioned it was his 68th birthday to Jones. It was the second time in his criminal career he'd celebrated his birthday while committing one of the biggest crimes in UK history.

Jones and Perkins dragged their wheelie bins and bags up to the corridor just inside the fire exit door on the ground floor.

Outside, a CCTV camera captured Collins pulling up in the white van outside the fire escape just as Perkins and Jones appeared at the doorway. They gave Collins the thumbs up and speedily loaded the wheelie bins and bags into the back of the van. Then all three jumped in the vehicle and drove off.

It was 5.45 a.m.

CHAPTER TWENTY-THREE

ANTICLIMAX

One of the raiders later described the Hatton Garden Job like this to ex-robber Billy: 'Once we'd got in the van everything seemed a lot better. I can't put it into words really. First my eyes went watery and supersensitive to light. Then I got that little "PING" and that's when I really felt on top of the world. We'd done it. Basil had gone and good riddance to him. Now we could get on with the rest of our lives.'

But the gang had left behind a lot of equipment including drills, as well as crowbars and the angle-grinders, which had been used to force the boxes open. They've never explained why they did this. Many believe they were so desperate just to get out of the building after Basil had left that they simply didn't have time to pick up their stuff.

Billy later explained: 'The lads were bricking themselves in case Basil and that family decided to call the police the moment Basil was off the premises. That's the way those bastards are. You can't trust them an inch and the lads left the building double quick as a result. In any case there were only two of them left and they must have been fuckin' knackered.'

Less than half an hour later – at 6.12 that Easter Sunday morning – a moped ridden by a man who never took off his helmet was seen pulling up near 88–90 Hatton Garden. The driver walked down the alley at the side near the fire exit, hung around for twenty minutes and then rode off. It is not known if 'Moped Man' was connected to the gang or the crime family who introduced them to Basil and helped finance the job.

Jeweller Lionel Wiffen – who himself kept a box inside the vault – arrived at his workshop in the same building at 7.30 a.m. that morning. It was less than two hours after the raiders had departed. He once again found the fire escape door open. Wiffen later said: 'I was more nervous than I was the day before. I thought I would go to the caretaker and find out who he had given the key to.'

Mr Wiffen once again peeked into the basement area, but did not notice anything unusual, so he simply bolted the fire exit again and went back to his workshop.

A couple of miles away, the gang arrived at Collins' Islington home where they could rest up, eat and watch a bit of telly, safe in the knowledge that no one back in Hatton Garden had a clue what they'd been up to. Perkins had looked forward to this moment for so long, but now it felt like a huge anticlimax. They'd undoubtedly pulled off a brilliant job but had they 'sacrificed' themselves to a cold-blooded family of criminals?

With his favourite song – Sinatra's 'Mack The Knife' – playing in the background, Perkins handed Jones and Collins back their mobile phones and began reiterating to them the weaknesses in the Security Express job and how he wasn't going to make the same mistakes this time around. That meant ensuring everyone got their own share of the loot immediately, even though it would all be brought back together at a later stage and turned into cash.

In many ways this decision was down to trust – or rather a

lack of it. All three appreciated that it would be premature and clumsy to immediately go out into the underworld and start fencing all their loot. But everyone knew that there would have been problems if one member of the gang was allowed to keep everything in one place. It was also better to spread it around in case the police came calling.

Some of the items they looked at initially that morning included precious stones, such as £15,000 sapphires and diamonds, watches by Breitling, Omega, Tag Heuer and Rolex, gold rings, earrings, necklaces, bangles and brooches. There were bundles of brand new £50 notes, US dollars and Euros, as well as platinum and small bars of gold bullion.

Perkins was just beginning to relax and savour the moment when he got the phone call he'd been dreading. The crime family – who'd introduced them to Basil and his keys and expertise in exchange for him taking that one security box away in a sack – informed Perkins that there had been a 'change of plan' and they would like all the most valuable gems to be given to Basil, so he could get them shipped abroad immediately.

Perkins was outraged and told the deadpan-voiced caller to 'fuck off' before slamming the phone down. But the same man called back and pointed out that the family had in their possession a hard-drive from the CCTV cameras inside the building and the footage clearly showed them all 'in action' and would no doubt provide the police with a lot of useful clues as to their identity.

The crime family 'spokesman' then tried to soften the blow by assuring Perkins that everyone in the gang would still get their fair share of the money raised from the sale of the most valuable gems. But Perkins knew that would never happen. The initial elation he'd felt when he got to Collins' house had turned into a feeling of complete and utter doom. They'd been hijacked by a 'family of psychopaths' rumoured to have murdered dozens of their underworld rivals over the previous thirty years.

Some of the gang later admitted that at that moment they began to wonder if being banged up in prison wasn't such a bad option. It had to be safer than out on the streets of London, where someone could walk up to you and shoot you in the head and then disappear off into the traffic on the back of a scooter.

Moments after the call, mystery man Basil turned up with a couple of armed weightlifter-types and expertly separated all the most valuable gems from the rest of the loot. Basil told them he was taking it all abroad that very night. He said the family would ensure the gang got their fair share of the money once those gems had been turned into cash. Not for the first time did Terry Perkins not believe a word of it.

As ex-robber Billy later explained: 'There was no point in grabbing Basil and threatening to top him because they all knew the family wouldn't have cared but would have come after them with a vengeance. No, they were left with no choice but to agree to let him have those gems. They musta felt sick to the stomach.'

Perkins looked at the expression on the faces of Jones and Collins and knew they shared his dismay. It would take a miracle and a shootout at the OK Corral to get back their fair share of the proceeds from the Hatton Garden Job. Collins began shaking as it all started to dawn on him. Jones on the other hand was furious but Perkins told him to calm down. He didn't want any problems while Basil was still there.

They all knew that the appearance of the stones he was about take with him would have to be drastically altered. That meant it would be even harder to know what pieces had been sold on for what prices. The most likely long-term marketplaces were China, Hong Kong, India, Russia or the Middle East, where there was strong demand and plenty of money. In those places the people who bought them probably wouldn't go to the trouble of trying to properly identify them.

But for a powerful crime family, getting the stolen goods out of the country would be 'a doddle'. As Billy explained: 'The same people who import drugs and weapons into Britain would take it all out in the other direction. It wouldn't be in a box in the back of a van — it'd be mixed up with something like a furniture consignment.'

After Basil had left Kenny Collins' house, Terry Perkins tried to put a brave face on it all by encouraging Collins and Jones to take their share of what was left with them, along the lines they'd already discussed. The subject of Basil and the family was dropped as the gang tried to rapidly sort through all the items.

Jones even tried to raise a laugh about the jewellers and businessmen foolish enough to think their valuables were in safe hands in the Hatton Garden vault. Jones said of one box holder: 'I'll tell you what he lost, shall I? £1.6m worth of gold he lost plus £70,000 in notes, he's lost a chunk that cunt there.'

The atmosphere in Collins' house remained as flat as a pancake. Perkins ordered the other two to make sure their share of the loot was put somewhere very safe. He also told them to go back to their normal lives for the time being.

Perkins warned them not to talk to anyone and pointed out that for the moment they should not communicate with each other; they were to be very careful of Basil and the crime family and to only break their self-imposed phone silence if they were approached by them. Perkins then humbly apologised for what had happened.

THE JOB

Jones and Collins urged Perkins not to beat himself up about it because hopefully they'd all end up with a decent payday, thanks to what they each had in those bags.

But as ex-robber Billy later pointed out: 'They was gutted. All that effort and planning and those other bastards had taken it over. Trouble was that no one dared take them on because it was as good as signing yer own death sentence.'

So Perkins, Jones and Collins went their separate ways, each armed with a huge bag of swag and an even bigger dose of paranoia.

Collins' share would be picked up within hours from the corridor of 'driver' Billy Lincoln's terraced house in Bethnal Green and then taken 'elsewhere'.

Danny Jones split up his share of the loot immediately he got home and took some of it to his brother's loft and hid three bags at a local cemetery. The other two carefully hid their shares of the loot in an assortment of places ranging from behind skirting boards to under dog kennels. Terry Perkins even kept back a bag for Brian Reader: after all he'd come up with the idea for the raid in the first place, so Perkins felt strongly he should get the same as the others.

Perkins, Jones and Collins all later admitted they were mightily relieved to get back to their families, and for the moment they tried their hardest not to think about the raid. Or at least not until the newspapers and TV heard what had happened. Perkins even managed to get a message to Brian Reader to say they'd pulled off the job, but they agreed to give each other a wide berth for the moment. Perkins assured Reader he would look after his share of the loot. Reader had no choice but to believe his friend.

CHAPTER TWENTY-FOUR

KEEPING UP APPEARANCES

At just after 8 a.m. on Tuesday, 7 April 2015, security guard Kelvin Stockwell arrived at the Hatton Garden Safe Deposit building after the long Easter weekend. He'd already noticed office manager Keefer Kamara, who'd let himself in through the front entrance.

It was only when Stockwell went downstairs and entered the main office area that he noticed the wooden door that led into the company's main room had been smashed open. Inside the room, there was a huge hole in the concrete wall, big enough for people to squeeze through.

Stockwell later explained: 'On the floor were tools, cutting material so I went straight into the yard to get a signal and phoned the police.'

Within minutes police cars had arrived at the scene and officers quickly established what had happened. Inside the building, the communal lift had been disabled and was jammed on the second floor. The police and security guards concluded that the suspects had used the lift shaft to climb down into the basement. There, they had forced open the lift's shutter doors. The enquiry was immediately handed over by local police to the Flying Squad and more than a dozen detectives were quickly on the scene.

*

THE JOB

In the suburbs of North and South East London, members of the gang had had forty-eight hours to get their lives back on track before the raid was finally discovered. Ex-robber Billy explained: 'That gap between the Sunday and the Tuesday was crucial. It enabled them all to set up watertight alibis and most important of all, make sure all the loot had been put somewhere very safe until the inevitable "heat" died down.'

Back in his house in the Hertfordshire commuter belt, Carl Wood was, in the words of one criminal associate, 'fuckin' brickin' it'. He knew he'd made a serious error by quitting before they got into the vault that second night, and now he was very worried that he might be looked upon as a potential informant by the other gang members. He still had no idea if they'd got in and snatched any loot.

That same day – 7 April – Wood rang Barclaycard again about his debts. This time he was doom-laden because he presumed he wasn't going to get a penny from the raid. He knew he'd blown the Hatton Garden Job by not going back and now he was a facing a complete financial meltdown. Wood eventually convinced his bank to agree to let him pay back his loan at the rate of £1 a month. But he was very scared that the Hatton Garden gang or Basil and his crime family bosses would come after him sooner rather than later.

Meanwhile, at his semi-detached house on a quiet suburban street in Enfield, Terry Perkins was feeling very wobbly for a whole load of different reasons. Not only was he worried about Basil's bosses breathing down his neck but he was still unhappy with the way Kenny Collins had brought Billy Lincoln in as the gang's driver just before the job went ahead. Perkins was worried that Lincoln might be a weak link if he started blabbing to anyone about his involvement.

Then Perkins noticed a Sky News bulletin announcement on his TV screen. A Scotland Yard spokeswoman was telling a battery of journalists and cameramen: 'At approximately 8.10 today police were called to a report of a burglary at a safety deposit business at Hatton Garden. The Flying Squad is investigating and detectives are currently at the scene. It appears that heavy cutting equipment has been used to get into a vault at the address, and a number of safety deposit boxes have been broken into. Enquiries are ongoing.'

Terry Perkins knew it was coming but it still knocked him sideways to see it all over the TV. Now the big guns would start firing and he just hoped that he and the rest of the gang could handle the approaching storm.

The first Flying Squad officer on the scene was Detective Constable James Day. He later told how he immediately concluded that because there had been no damage to the door to the main entrance of the building, the raiders must have had inside help. DC Day was also intrigued by the way the gang had ripped out the CCTV system's hard-drive in the belief that it controlled all of the cameras in the building. What police didn't realize was that the footage from two of those cameras was being used as a bargaining tool by Basil's crime family bosses.

The police were left only with recordings from just one camera inside the courtyard plus a camera owned by a nearby jewellery shop called Braganza, and footage from another camera belonging to an independent company called Premises 21, based on the second floor of the building that housed the vault.

Newspaper and television reporters swamped Hatton Garden within minutes of Scotland Yard's live announcement.

Local gem dealers quickly began speculating about who might

have carried out such a daring raid. Many spoke about the last big robbery at the same vault back in 2003 when a conman posing as a customer called 'Mister Goldberg' stole jewellery, cash and valuables worth an estimated £1.5 million after emptying a number of safety deposit boxes.

Back inside the vault itself more than two dozen police officers and forensic staff were methodically recovering, recording and packaging more than four hundred pieces of potential evidence, to be profiled for DNA, fingerprints and other forensic tests. Specialist police photographers mapped out the crime scene with tape using hi-tech digital cameras to film every inch of the inside of the premises. It took the police more than a day just to work their way through the site as boxes and junk had been left everywhere by the raiders

The police refused for the next three days to allow anyone into the vault while they examined it. As a result, it was some time before they were able to reveal which boxes had been stolen, and how many. This left many Hatton Garden traders unsure if their boxes had been taken or not. Initially most presumed the raiders had opened every one of the boxes but, of course, that was not the case.

On the afternoon of 7 April, specialist officers in white forensic suits could be seen coming and going from 88–90 Hatton Garden with evidence bags and safety deposit boxes. There was no visible damage to the outside of the property, other than a loose wire hanging out of the side of the front entrance door.

It wasn't until the following morning that the Flying Squad revealed for the first time the full extent of the raid and how at least seventy boxes had been 'affected'. But the police remained extremely vague about what had actually been stolen because they didn't actually know. Detectives refused to discuss the raid in any detail, except to confirm the raiders had seemingly gone back a second time to complete the burglary.

Newspapers and TV news broadcasts not surprisingly led on the raid that morning, which was already being compared to Britain's most infamous so-called professional crimes such as the Great Train Robbery, the Brink's-Mat gold bullion heist and the Security Express raid.

The media referred to wildly differing estimates of the value of the stolen goods. One newspaper claimed it was 'upwards of £200m' while another talked about 'something in the region of £4m'.

One source, who worked in the building where the vault was housed, told reporters: 'The crooks opened 72 boxes. The ones that were opened were all at waist height, which detectives believe is because it is easier to hold heavy drilling equipment at that level.'

The same source also told the media: 'Detectives found jewellery all over the floor. The crooks couldn't carry it all. They were obviously confident because they made two trips to the vault over the weekend.'

The media seized on how the raiders had gone back to the premises a second time. This seemed to show extraordinary confidence and professionalism, as well as courage. In many ways the Hatton Garden Job sounded to many as if it harked back to the old days when professional robbers hijacked security vans and banks with impunity and were hailed as working-class heroes back in their own communities.

In Hatton Garden itself, detectives told at least three people whose safe deposit boxes had been stolen that items too heavy to carry – including some gold bars – had been left behind by the gang.

One victim, a gold dealer, told reporters that he'd heard from police there were six suspects and they must have been hunting for something specific because relatively few of the 900-plus boxes had actually been opened, even though the raiders had plenty of time to carry out the break-in over the Easter weekend.

At a press conference on the day after the burglary was discovered, the Flying Squad's Detective Chief Inspector Paul Johnson hinted at the possibility of an 'inside job' because there had been no sign of forced entry to the building. Johnson said there were indications that the thieves had a key, or that someone had let them in from the inside.

DCI Johnson kept his cards close to his chest when answering any probing questions from the assembled news pack. The police did admit, though, that they hadn't yet talked to the Sudan-based owner of the vault company. It was also revealed that the owner's son was in overall charge of the vault. But he had also not yet been interviewed.

Johnson also disclosed that the raiders had left rubbish all over the basement area and that the wrought-iron cage door into the vault had been smashed in half. Johnson said an angle grinder, concrete drills and crowbars had been found amid the battered security boxes strewn across the ground of the vault.

Johnson said he believed those items and other forensic evidence left at the scene by the raiders might well turn out to be the key to tracking down the perpetrators. Some Flying Squad detectives were openly surprised by the sloppiness of the raiders. The villains had done all the hard work of getting through the wall brilliantly but then they'd gone and left a bunch of clues in their wake.

One of Brian Reader's oldest associates later explained: 'Something happened down in that vault because leaving all that gear behind was a big mistake. Brian said it wouldn't have happened if he'd been there the second night. But none of them have ever explained why they left in such a hurry.'

Many in South London, in particular, still remembered how the Great Train Robbers were only caught because of a print left on a tomato ketchup bottle, which had been sloppily handled by one of the gang members.

DCI Johnson was duty bound to keep the public informed, although he would have much preferred to keep the details to himself because he knew how important they might turn out to be in relation to building a case against the perpetrators.

Ex-robber Billy's overview of the job in the few days following the raid summed up the underworld's view of the Hatton Garden Job. He said: 'The lads did well. They overcame a fuckin' thick concrete wall, a lot of alarms and some tricky moments by all accounts, but they seemed to have got away with it.'

The Hatton Garden Job was already having an extraordinary ongoing ripple effect in New York and the renowned diamond capital of the world, Antwerp. Gemmologists, jewellery designers and private jewellers were reeling from the news of the raid. One gemmologist explained: 'Robbery at one of the biggest safe deposits in Hatton Garden over the Easter weekend. The loss is huge. A lot of jewellers and dealers put their stock in safe deposits over holiday periods such as Easter and Pesach [Passover]. This is awful news.'

One big name in the Hatton Garden diamond trade put it rather more bluntly: 'This is catastrophic. Everyone knows someone in this business, who uses that Hatton Garden vault. It seems incredible that these robbers could just walk in, break into the vault and escape with tens of millions of pounds' worth of stones without alerting any attention.'

The following day, Thursday, 9 April – Flying Squad boss Detective Superintendent Craig Turner told the media they had no idea who'd committed the Hatton Garden Raid. He did reveal, however, that the gang had used a diamond-tipped drill bit on a Hilti DD350 drill to get through that two-foot-thick concrete wall and make a hole that was 50cm deep, 25cm high and 45cm wide. It was 89cm off the ground and police were surprised by the relatively small size of the hole bored through the concrete wall, pointing out that whoever managed to wriggle through would not have been physically large by any means.

Police said during the same press conference that they'd recovered some CCTV footage, as well as those clues left behind by the raiders. But officers did not admit that many hours of CCTV footage appeared to have been stolen by the raiders themselves.

DS Turner was adamant in his press briefing that the safety deposit boxes that were left unopened would be returned to their rightful owners. But he did concede that the police were already struggling to trace a number of the stolen boxes' owners. Turner explained: 'Of the seventy-two boxes opened during the burglary, we have only been unable to make contact with six people who we believe have been a victim of crime. We continue to make efforts to trace them.'

Then came the biggest bombshell of all, when Turner admitted for the first time that an alarm callout alert from the vault was received by the police on the evening of 2 April, the first night of the raid. The assembled journalists were stunned by the Flying Squad officer's seemingly low-key admission. He insisted the call had been allocated a grade that 'meant that no police response was deemed to be required'. Not surprisingly, the alarm 'scandal' was exposed in great detail in all the following day's newspapers and TV news reports.

Scotland Yard later issued a further statement to try and explain what had happened. A spokesman said: 'It is too early to say if the handling of the call would have had an impact on the outcome of the incident. But a call was recorded and transferred to the police's computer-aided dispatch system. A grade was applied to the call that meant that no police response was deemed to be required.' The statement added. 'An internal investigation is ongoing to identify why this grade was applied to the call in conjunction with the alarm company.'

One security company pointed out that the insurance company covering the vault would have insisted that only the police could enter and investigate after a callout *not* a private security guard.

The company said: 'Vault guard Stockwell was most probably under strict instructions to do a security sweep of the outside of the building, and if there were no signs of a break in then to continue his normal patrol. Obviously if he'd seen any signs of an actual break-in then he was supposed to call the police and then observe the building from a safe distance.'

Scotland Yard eventually apologised profusely for not following procedures after receiving that text from the intruder alert system at the Hatton Garden vault offices. But Scotland Yard's admission sparked a host of 'Keystone Cops' jibes in the press and on social media. Things seemed to be going from bad to worse for the police.

Ex-robber Billy later explained: 'The boys were knocked sideways by the huge amount of publicity the job was getting. Sure they was laughin' at the cozzers about the alarm business, but the boys didn't really want it to run and run as a story. They hoped it would die down quickly because then the police might start to ease off on the enquiry.'

THE JOB

The Metropolitan Police were undoubtedly deeply embarrassed by the revelation that they did not visit Hatton Garden after that alarm went off. And it's certainly true that the resulting 'inquest' seemed to partly divert their attention away from tracking down the actual thieves. But some believed the police were being unfairly criticized.

Another security company claimed the system in the vault had 'already suffered a significant number of false alarm activations'. The implication was that the alarm system inside the vault was always going off for no reason. But in actual fact it had never gone off in the eight years since it had been installed. Presumably, this was said to gain a competitive advantage from a rival's misfortune.

A couple of days after the Hatton Garden Job, the wife of one of the raiders was out with her daughter and grand-daughter when she spotted a headline on a newspaper while they were on a bus.

'Good luck to 'em,' muttered the daughter of the robber, who actually had no idea her own father was one of the Hatton Garden gang.

She later recalled: 'I suppose I did have this hunch when I saw the newspaper headlines. In any case I was brought up in the East End and we knew when to ask questions and when to keep our traps shut.'

That was the way it was.

CHAPTER TWENTY-FIVE

FEEDING THE PACK

The London underworld was awash with rumours about the raid. Many were saying a bunch of Eastern Europeans belonging to the infamous Pink Panther diamond gang had carried it out. I later established that a lot of these rumours were being 'helped along' by some of the real members of the Hatton Garden Mob.

The value of the haul remained of most interest to the media at this stage. If the total did turn out to be £40 million or above, then it would qualify as the biggest burglary in British criminal history.

'Some papers were talkin' about the loot being worth hundreds of millions,' explained ex-robber Billy. 'Naturally, there would be some characters on the edge of things, who'd believe they had a right to a piece of that. Then of course there were the other villains further down the food chain, who were picking up rumours and thinking that they could squeeze a few bob out of the Hatton Garden Mob in exchange for their silence. There really is no honour among thieves.'

Although there was no suggestion that the directors and staff of the safety deposit company had done anything wrong, the media and general public continually referred to the notion that the gang may well have had some 'inside help'. The lack of a forced entry and the professionalism of the raiders helped fuel that speculation. Many were saying they must have at least had access to details of the vault's security set-up.

Among some awkward moments for the police, insurance loss adjusters acting for the victims were questioning the slow progress being made by Scotland Yard in the days following the raid. One insurance man told the media: 'All the victims have given statements and some have been invited back to look at what police found on the floor of the vault. But those meetings haven't happened yet. It could hold up insurance claims, so they need to hurry up. One of my clients said that the police told him there were only half a dozen items found, another said hundreds, so the picture is unclear.'

Then the media revealed for the first time that there had been an 'aggravated burglary' back in 2013 at the North London home of Manish Bavishi, day-to-day manager of of the Hatton Garden Safe Deposit company and son of the owner. The Metropolitan Police confirmed the break-in was still 'under investigation'. Meanwhile Manish Bavishi was nowhere to be found and said to be on holiday in Sudan and not answering calls. His father – who was also over in Sudan – told reporters he thought his son was in London.

The police were growing heartily sick and tired of all the criticism being thrown their way. The Flying Squad in particular wanted to just get on with their job as 'thief takers' and bring down the Hatton Garden Mob.

Ex-robber Billy later explained: 'The coppers were getting it in the neck but I knew it wouldn't last long. The police were like wounded animals and their reputations were at stake. That's when they are at their most dangerous.'

On an official level, the police tried to distance themselves from the media because they were super sensitive following those earlier mistakes. To make matters worse for Scotland Yard, so-called experts were now speculating that the items stolen during the raid were 'probably' worth as much as £200 million.

Scotland Yard's reluctance to speak to individual reporters had been sparked by accusations of overly close relationships with journalists at the Leveson hearings in 2011 when the police's 'proximity' to the press came under extreme scrutiny during the UK phone hacking scandal. As one officer said shortly after the Hatton Garden raid: 'Not only were the Met getting it in the neck for all sorts of reasons but they had to tread extra carefully so as not to appear to be in "partnership" with any journalists. They wanted to control the outgoing of information without adding any personal comments for fear of a comeback.'

A number of former police officers even voiced their grudging admiration for the Hatton Garden gang. One Flying Squad officer told BBC Radio 4's *Today* programme: 'There's a sort of old-fashioned audacity about it. The amount of money and the goods that are taken is never fully revealed . . . and there's a good chance that not everybody would declare.'

The Met – which still refused to comment on the specific value of the items stolen from the Hatton Garden vault – insisted its investigators were still examining the crime scene in minute detail and they would not have any further developments to report for quite a few days yet.

Back in Hatton Garden, traders refused to talk to the media pack now on daily duty outside the seven-storey building where the vault was located. Journalists were barred from most shops and many local traders said the press intrusion was almost as irritating as the robbery itself. Half a dozen huge satellite trucks had been set up on Greville Street, just near to the fire exit that the raiders had used to get into the building less than a week earlier. Numerous worldwide TV news outlets were broadcasting a live stream from the scene of what was already being called 'The Crime of the Century'.

With so many unwelcome strangers in its midst, Hatton Garden saw a huge downturn in business over the days following the raid. Not surprisingly, many traders were extra careful not to let unknown faces into their premises, and there was a general climate of suspicion out on the streets around the area.

Companies in Hatton Garden were clearly shell-shocked. One local businesswoman told reporters: 'We're a very close-knit group round here. All we're thinking is, "How did they do it, and why didn't we prevent it?" This circus is just making things worse. I wish they'd all go away and leave us alone.'

Antique jewellery dealer John Jeffrey was a classic victim of the Hatton Garden burglary. His safe deposit box contained £30,000 in cash, a diamond and pearl necklace and two gold bars. It took Mr Jeffrey almost four hours to look through photograph albums created by police after they'd recovered items.

He later recalled the police had initially photographed between thirty and fifty items and another thirty pieces in photos of items grouped together. These included Georgian miniatures, a number of 'gold blobs' weighing between 100g and 300g, which had been created from melted scrap gold, and a navy blue canvas money bag full of scrap gold and other jewellery.

Meanwhile one group of retired Flying Squad detectives were so perturbed by what they saw as the police's public 'humiliation' in the aftermath of the raid that they began speaking to the media on behalf of their serving colleagues. Those officers had been effectively banned from dealing directly with the press, especially when it came to talking about the value of the items stolen during the raid and the circumstances behind it.

One such ex-Flying Squad detective said at the time: 'They've got away with a huge amount of gems and cash. You have to give them credit for a brilliant piece of work. But that was the easy bit. Now they've got to avoid being brought to justice. The aftermath of these sorts of jobs is always the trickiest for the villains involved. They always start splashing their cash around. Then one of them makes a fool of himself and gives the game away to a woman or maybe a mate when he's drunk. It only takes one friend to get jealous or notice that someone is flashing the cash around and everything will go down the pan. No matter how smoothly the heist was planned and executed – it can still go tits up afterwards.'

The same retired detective went on to explain: 'There are so many examples of this in London underworld history. The classic one was the Bank of America heist in 1975. Plain stupidity and greed got two of the robbers banged up. No doubt this mob will make the same sort of mistakes and they'll end up giving themselves away. You see, what you are seeing at this stage of the enquiry is the Flying Squad at its finest: studying every clue and gathering all the evidence together in little pieces while they start putting the whole jigsaw puzzle together.'

Back in the quiet and leafy(ish) suburbs of Dartford and Enfield, the majority of the Hatton Garden gang had gone back to their normal lives and were keeping to all the habits they'd had before the previous weekend's raid. They'd read about the ongoing police mistakes and relished seeing them on the back foot but they all knew only too well that it was still early days.

More worrying for the gang was the spectre of Basil and his crime family bosses now hanging over the job like the sword of Damocles. The gang feared that if they put a foot wrong then the family would either have them eliminated or arrested.

So while forensic scientists sifted through the hundreds of pieces of evidence left behind in the vault, the Sweeney put the word out to their informants in the London underworld that there would be 'a nice drink in it' if anyone could help point them in the right direction. The Flying Squad were looking into the possibility that some of the boxes in the vault were owned by a gang of notorious criminals, who had had past links with the area. And they wondered if these same villains might have played a role in the Hatton Garden raid.

Scotland Yard's criminal intelligence unit then began examining all the known details of every single person – past and present – who'd ever had any connections to the Hatton Garden Safe Deposit company. The Flying Squad also uncovered the exact details of the vault's insurance policy. And one hand-picked unit of officers was given the task of tracking down the latest addresses and details for more than two dozen old-school professional criminals who might have been capable of pulling off the Hatton Garden Job.

Back in Hatton Garden, anger continued to grow. It seemed to be fuelled by the police's incorrectly perceived inactivity on the enquiry. One jeweller, a 63-year-old named Michael, told one tabloid: 'As far as I'm concerned the police have got a lot to answer for. Suing anyone is a last resort but it's something I would consider.'

Meanwhile those earlier rumours about the notorious Eastern European diamond gang the Pink Panthers were now being openly discounted. One expert on the Panther gang told a newspaper: 'I think it is more likely to have been local British criminals.'

But most police officers and criminals alike initially dismissed such a notion because all the vault-type robbery gangs in London had disbanded many years earlier and, according to one ex-detective, most of those characters were either dead or in old folks' homes.

CHAPTER TWENTY-SIX

SECOND BITE OF THE CHERRY

On the Saturday following the raid – 11 April – the police took another body blow when the *Daily Mirror* newspaper announced on its front page that it had managed to get hold of 'exclusive' CCTV footage from inside and just outside the building during the raid.

The *Mirror* published a full length article and encouraged readers to download the video footage posted on their website. The footage they had obtained came from a camera that was operated on a third separate system in the 88–90 Hatton Garden building; this camera had been missed by the police, as well as Basil when he stripped out the CCTV hard-drive as he left the premises ahead of the other raiders.

The paper proudly described their exclusive as: 'The first real-time account of how the daring theft was executed' and insisted to its readers that releasing the footage so early could well help detectives track down the robbers much more quickly.

But enquiry officers were furious. They believed the tabloid should have 'done its duty' and let them have the footage before publishing it. The police didn't want such video images made public until they had had a chance to examine the footage first.

As one ex-Flying Squad detective pointed out: 'An element

of surprise is vital on an investigation like this one. The Flying Squad often prefers to sit on CCTV images because they don't want the villains to know they have them at such an early stage following a crime of this size. But the *Mirror* went and put a spanner in the works.'

Another retired Flying Squad officer later explained: 'A key element to any investigation like this one is to always be able to control the outlet of news to the media, just in case the information actually helps the crooks, rather than the other way around.'

In fairness, police experts were still trawling through hours and hours of other video footage trying to grab any clue that might help them track down the gang and they weren't yet ready to share those findings with the world.

The *Mirror* footage itself showed all the raiders in disguises but with certain recognizable features. One raider could be seen on the CCTV footage wearing a high-visibility jacket with the word 'Gas' on it. The *Mirror* speculated as to whether this might mean they were involved in that underground fire a week before the robbery, which some believed had been deliberately started.

The video on the *Mirror*'s website also showed that six men were clearly involved in the raid. The paper even nicknamed them Mr Ginger, Mr Strong, Mr Montana, The Gent, The Tall Man and The Old Man as if they were characters out of a Quentin Tarantino movie.

The paper also reported that the police feared the gang 'may have already left the country'. But of course nothing could have been further from the truth. The article speculated about the nationality of the gang but conceded that their methods did suggest a home-based crew of professional robbers.

At Scotland Yard there were suspicions that a renegade detective might have provided the newspaper with its exclusive video footage and accompanying story but this was later discounted. One recently retired Flying Squad detective later said: 'There was a right old witch hunt at the Yard after that story and video ended up in the *Mirror*. Officers helping journalists was considered as bad as consorting with criminals because the police were already in the firing line and now a tabloid newspaper had made them look even more inept.'

The video footage itself got worldwide coverage. Brian Reader's flamboyant socks, scarf and traditional brown leather shoes were there for everyone in the London underworld to see as he stood just inside the fire exit doorway on the first night of the raid. Old-time robber Billy explained: 'Seeing that video in the *Mirror* sent alarm bells ringing in some quarters. For starters, it wasn't hard to work out who at least a couple of the old fellas were, if you mixed in the right circles.'

On 11 April – the same day the *Daily Mirror* published its scoop – the Met Police responded by releasing more CCTV images of three of the suspects, showing them using the fire exit side door of the building. But instead of contacting the media, Scotland Yard simply released the images on their website describing the heist as 'highly audacious' but being extremely careful not to attach themselves to any particular news outlet.

Meanwhile, police technicians who'd examined the vault in minute detail had been able to deduce the precise sequence in which each security box was targeted. Strangely there was only one box taken from the left side of the vault and it was the first one to be completely removed.

In the suburbs of North and South London, the gang were still managing to keep a low profile and going about their business in a 'normal way', exactly as they had discussed during the planning stages. Terry Perkins had a penchant for gardening, which he found helped keep his mind off the raid. It was late April and clusters of daffodils were blooming all along the edge of his lawn, much to his delight.

Occasionally Perkins would pop down to his local DIY centre in his modest little Citroen Saxo and buy a few bits and pieces for the garden. Then it would be off to the pub for a quiet pint before returning home to his six-bedroomed bungalow in the heart of London's commuter belt. Perkins had always been on nodding terms with most of his very middle-class neighbours, many of whom were accountants, lawyers and doctors. They in turn presumed Perkins was now retired after a career none of them were quite sure about.

Brian Reader – despite being almost ten years older than Perkins – was much more active when it came to trying to earn a living.

A couple of years earlier, Reader had started building two small houses in the large back garden of his house in Dartford Road, much to the irritation of some of his neighbours. The two properties were supposed to have been Reader's 'pension plan' until he had to abandon them when he ran out of money. A few months before the raid, Reader managed to borrow some cash off an associate after assuring him he would be 'in the money' by the summer because of a 'big deal' he'd pulled off.

It was certainly true that following the death of his beloved Lyn from cancer six years earlier, Reader had taken his eye off the ball when it came to his second-hand car business. He'd also long regretted not contributing a single penny to any pension schemes, leaving him with nothing but the equity on his large house in a very unfashionable area.

THE JOB

Brian Reader tried to keep himself active because he was genuinely worried he might just 'give up and keel over'. Not an unusual train of thought for someone of his age whose wife had died after a seemingly long and happy marriage.

So now Reader was back home in Dartford all alone once again, and not even guaranteed he would get any of the loot from the raid because of his decision to pull out on the second night. Reader had received a second-hand message via two associates that he would get something. But he wasn't sure what to believe and he knew he mustn't contact Perkins directly. He didn't want to jeopardize the others, but at the same time he wanted to know if he really was going to be looked after.

Reader, like all the gang, was astounded by the huge amount of publicity sparked by the Hatton Garden raid. When journalists referred to the loot being worth anything between £10 million and £40 million it made Reader feel even more irritated with his decision. He also knew very well what Basil's crime family bosses were like, and he had no doubt they'd be planning something devious in the light of all this 'megabucks' publicity about the value of the loot. Of course Reader had no idea that Basil had already been 'given' all the most valuable gems from the raid.

Then there was the eccentric egomaniacal Danny Jones. He lapped up all the column inches of publicity and avidly read every single word in the newspapers, watching the TV news channels virtually round the clock. Jones's friends and family later said he walked around his home in Enfield whistling merrily whenever he read a story or saw something on the news about the raid.

Ex-robber Billy explained: 'Danny was a bleedin' news junkie. He couldn't get enough of it. It was going to his head. Most villains hate this sort of publicity but Danny wasn't like most villains, was he?'

As the gang's so-called resident computer expert, Jones considered that it was his duty to collate all the articles and TV reports on his laptop. Jones had boasted to the others before the raid about how he read true crime books at the rate of one a week. The other old boys in the gang hadn't read more than a couple of books in their entire lives.

Jones hero-worshipped the older legendary London 'faces' from the 1960s, including the Krays and the Richardsons. In his world knowledge was power and he'd always believed that by learning about such gangsters' exploits he could pick up valuable tips about committing crimes, as well as covering all exits when it came to the aftermath of the Hatton Garden Job.

Jones had even read in one true crime book that it was best to spread your own share of the loot around in different locations. His smaller stashes would be there simply to offer the police something, just in case he ever got arrested. Naturally Jones hadn't mentioned to the others that the largest portion of his share of the loot was hidden under a memorial stone to his own children's grandfather, just a few yards from where he'd stashed two other bags, which contained less valuable items. As one of the raiders later told an associate: 'If we'd known where Danny had put it we would have told him to find somewhere a little less obvious. But none of us wanted to tell each other that sort of stuff for obvious reasons.'

Five days after the raid, Terry Perkins broke his own 'no contact with anyone' rule and got a message to Reader via his son Paul's mobile phone, explaining how Basil had taken all of the valuable gems. Reader wasn't surprised. And they both feared that it was only a matter of time before Basil's bosses came knocking once again.

Brian Reader was welcomed back into the fold by Perkins, despite pulling out of the second night of the Hatton Garden raid. Reader was thankful to Terry Perkins for contacting him and it seemed to help energize Reader to a certain degree, or so his associates later said.

Perkins and Reader soon began regularly exchanging texts and mobile phone calls. They seemed almost relieved to be in touch with each other once again. But neither of these stubborn old men could bring themselves to throw away the dirt cheap pay-as-you go mobile phones they were using, after each call. It seemed such a waste of money to them.

As ex-robber Billy later explained: 'These fellas came from an era when leaving a light on was deemed to be a waste of money. They should have just left the job, gone their own separate ways and kept away from each other for months. But things were already going a bit strange on them, so I guess they wanted to get their stories straight and they needed each other's support.'

During their initial calls, Reader and Perkins were careful not to mention Basil's actual name directly on the phone, or indeed any mention of the crime family directly, just in case someone was listening. But they completely failed to appreciate that it wasn't just their conversations that could be monitored. Their movements could be tracked through those mobile phones and in many ways that could provide just as damning evidence of what they were up to.

Perkins told Reader he was convinced he'd be called into a meeting with Basil's bosses within days and he needed Reader's advice because he had had many more dealings with the family in the past. One or two decisions needed to be made, otherwise the entire job could cost them their liberty or even their lives.

And in the middle of all this, gang member Kenny Collins began having a 'major meltdown'. He was terrified that Basil's bosses would come after them all. Collins told Perkins and Jones he was prepared to hand every bit of his share of the loot to the crime family to get them off his back. Perkins and Jones were not very impressed with Collins, to say the least. They'd always recognized that Collins wasn't the 'smartest tool in the box' – later they described him as 'wombat-thick' – but they still needed to tread carefully, otherwise he might land them all in the shit.

CHAPTER TWENTY-SEVEN

TROUBLE ON THE HORIZON

Throughout this period, the London tabloids continued feeding their readers with stories that seemed extremely sympathetic towards the gang. A whimsical, almost romantic vision of the men was emerging. Many even spouted away on social media about how they hoped the villains would get away with their crime. One newspaper columnist summed it up:

> *Even the most law-abiding, 'hang 'em and flog 'em' sort of person seemingly can't help but feel a little thrill when reading about crimes like the Easter jewellery theft in London's Hatton Garden. Otherwise sensible news reporters find themselves gleefully sounding like extras from a film noir – talking about 'blags' and 'heists' and 'villains'.*
>
> *If there's one feeling that regular people of all political persuasions have in 2015, it's the sense that the rich are getting filthier than ever, and that there is a club at the top of the country that is acting with impunity.*
>
> *Maybe we like the idea of a jewel heist because it feels that the victims are part of this wealthy elite who a) can afford it anyway, and b) had it coming.*
>
> *It feels like most of Britain is happy to imagine how much*

fun it would be to knock off a few priceless gems belonging to the super-rich.

A retired robber from South London added to this upbeat theme by telling one newspaper: 'It's gone back to the old days, hasn't it? No one's been injured. No one's been shot. Everybody's happy because everybody's skint at the moment and they reckon – rightly or wrongly – that whoever's lost something can afford it.'

In Hatton Garden itself, increasingly nervous traders feared they could be targeted by other criminals, especially since they'd all stopped using the boxes inside the vault since the raid. Some diamond dealers hired burly Russian and Eastern European security guards to protect them against any street robberies. Their musclemen stood at either end of Hatton Garden like overweight guardsmen in tight fitting black suits, white shirts and black ties constantly whispering conspiratorially into chunky mobile phone headsets.

Meanwhile Flying Squad detectives were running out of patience with some of the less 'responsive' owners of the boxes that had been ripped open or stolen during the raid. One ex-Flying Squad officer explained on behalf of his serving colleagues: 'Some of the box owners were playing silly buggers and refusing to even admit what was in them, let alone put a value on their items. Everyone knew a lot of this stuff was stolen, so it was all a bit of stand-off. But detectives needed to know the actual contents because their value would have a big bearing on the level of charges the raiders would eventually face if arrested.'

When one detective threatened to arrest a box owner for obstruction, he was warned by the man's lawyer that he would sue the police. The officer knew only too well that would hold everything up, so he and his colleagues stepped back from this line of enquiry for the moment.

It must have seemed to the police at this stage that all the odds remained very much stacked against them. And the lack of a response from some of those box owners further convinced investigators that there could be 'other motives' behind the burglary.

Danny Jones was particularly unhappy about the way his old friend Carl Wood had pulled out of the raid. Jones even wondered if Wood might inform on the rest of the gang. Perkins insisted this wouldn't happen. But Wood's 'disappearance' since the raid was certainly doing all their heads in.

In fairness, Carl Wood had a lot of other things on his mind. He was trying to keep multiple debt collectors at bay and every time he saw a newspaper, he wished he'd not walked off the job.

Wood must have realized he was considered *persona non grata* by the others. But he would never consider going to the police although the other gang members weren't to know this, necessarily. They feared that if Wood spoke to anyone about the job then Basil and his crime family bosses might come after all of them.

Ex-robber Billy explained: 'The boys had hoped that by keeping a very tight ship there wouldn't be a split in the ranks. But no one was to know that two of them would refuse to go back on that second night. Now one of those lads [Wood] was considered a 'security risk'. Trouble is – as all professional villains will tell you – there's nearly always someone out there prepared to stitch up his mates. That makes others feel very paranoid and can lead to unnecessary disagreements during and after a job. And once the rot sets in, it's fuckin' difficult to stop.'

The elusive Basil and his bosses continued to loom large over the gang. Brian Reader and Terry Perkins had both seen at first-hand how nasty it could get when other criminals put their mind to trying to get hold of the proceeds of a big crime. In Reader's case, he still lived in fear of the type of fallout that dominated the aftermath of the Brink's-Mat heist. It had so far cost at least twenty people their lives as the tentacles of revenge spread through the London and Kent underworld. Ironically, Basil's crime family bosses were rumoured to have been at the centre of that bloodbath as well.

On top of all this pressure from 'exterior forces', one of the gang members further down the 'food chain' informed Perkins and Reader he needed an urgent cash injection immediately, rather than waiting three to six months as had been their original agreement. Perkins batted off the request by pointing out it would be madness to start trying to flog the loot so soon after the raid. But he knew others were sure to come back and make similar requests again in the near future.

At Scotland Yard, detectives received a call from one of the Flying Squad's most successful ever 'thief catchers', who'd retired back in the late 1980s. He'd been reading all about the Hatton Garden Job at his retirement home on a Mediterranean island. He said he believed one of the men in the CCTV images of the raiders might be Security Express robber Terry Perkins.

The same retired officer also mentioned notorious South London villain Brian Reader, who had close connections in Hatton Garden. But since Reader would be almost 80 years of age by now, it was highly unlikely he was directly involved, said the detective. The officer who took the phone call from the retired

Flying Squad man listened patiently to what the former detective had to say. Then he logged the names and promised to pass them on to his superiors.

But detectives concluded that it was highly unlikely that North London-based Perkins would ever join forces with Reader, who came from south of the river. In any case, once this type of villain got beyond a certain age, he'd give up the big energetic crimes and retire somewhere to soak up the sun.

However, the same retired Flying Squad officer later told this author: 'These people don't just retire. They need to keep committing crimes to stay afloat. It's a drug to them but it's also a means to earn money and I can tell you these characters never switch off. They're always planning something, even if it's only in their senile old heads.'

Back in Hatton Garden, police continued to face criticism from all quarters. Twenty-five people belonging to the trade association London Diamond Bourse (LDB) – some of whom had lost their livelihoods thanks to the robbery – gathered in Hatton Garden to discuss what action they could take in the wake of the raid. People were annoyed it had taken so long for Scotland Yard to allow them to visit the crime scene and to give them a definitive account of what happened. There was even talk of suing the police.

The victims of the raid who did come forward to police had heartbreaking stories to tell. Batcha Hussein, a 45-year-old small gold dealer who'd worked in Hatton Garden for more than two decades, had stored around £15,000 worth of gold coins in the vault, having run out of space in the small safe in his shop. 'We really thought it was the safest place in Hatton Garden,' he told reporters. Mr Hussein didn't even realize the vault had been previously robbed. Many smaller traders said if they'd known about the previous raids they might not have stored their items there in the first place.

There was also widespread criticism of the lack of surveillance cameras inside the seven-storey building that housed the vault. Hatton Garden traders pointed out it was because many of the box owners didn't want to be identified. Rumours also continued to swirl around Hatton Garden about how the raiders had used an actual set of keys to access the main building. One retired London robber told reporters: 'They must have got a copy of those keys. Maybe one of them knocked a key out of someone's hand and then gave it back after taking an impression on wax in his palm?' The Hatton Garden raid might have been perceived by the general public as an audacious, even ballsy and extremely successful crime, but in the pubs and clubs of the London underworld, the raid provoked a completely different response. Ex-robber Billy explained: 'A lot of people were getting jealous. No doubt about it. They couldn't bring themselves to talk about it much. Then there were the good old boys who wanted the raiders to get away with it, so they fed the police with a load of duff leads. Others simply went out of their way to dismiss all the pub talk to also help protect whoever carried out the raid.'

Many people viewed the raid as the equivalent of a win on the lottery, something everyone wants to have but very few ever actually get. There were also comparisons to other heists from the past, including the Knightsbridge Safe Deposit Centre job in 1987, when Italian gangster Valerio Viccei found the perfect inside man and ended up with tens of millions of pounds worth of loot.

And then there was the Brink's-Mat heist at Heathrow airport in 1983. It didn't have a similar MO to the Hatton Garden Job but there was a rumour going round the London underworld that some of those involved with Hatton Garden had 'worked' on Brink's-Mat.

Obviously the main objective of the police in the aftermath of the Hatton Garden Job was to identify the men behind it. The perpetrators had been dubbed 'diamond geezers' in the press, and that grated with the Flying Squad in particular. They resented the way the raiders were being granted almost super-hero status. One retired Flying Squad officer explained: 'It was outrageous. These men had committed a major crime and every-one was talking about them as if they were Robin Hood and his Merry Men. Yet many officers believed the gang were probably carrying weapons and wouldn't have hesitated to use them if anyone had confronted them.'

Meanwhile, every day that passed without an arrest piled more pressure on the police, especially the Flying Squad. It looked to many as if the gang had disappeared off the face of the earth, and were probably sunning themselves on a beach in Rio.

Detectives believed that the two characters whom they knew had pulled out of the second night of the raid would be the gang's 'weakest link'. But with no clue as to their identity so far, the Yard's examination of all available CCTV footage – much of which came via their automatic number plate recognition system (ANPR) – continued to get immediate priority.

The ANPR system recorded an image of all vehicles' registra-tion numbers as they travelled in and out of the area and if any of those vehicles were seen on a regular basis then they were flagged up for closer examination. But this was a mammoth task as there were thousands of vehicle registration numbers recorded every day.

SEXY BEASTS

It was clear that Scotland Yard's elite Flying Squad had not been so severely tested since the £53 million Securitas cash robbery at Tonbridge, in Kent, in 2006.

And for the moment, the police investigation still seemed to be going at a snail's pace.

CHAPTER TWENTY-EIGHT

UNDER THE COSH

Even more pressure was piled on Scotland Yard following a phone call made on Sunday, 12 April, by Prime Minister David Cameron to Metropolitan Police Commissioner Sir Bernard Hogan-Howe.

The two men had enjoyed a reasonable relationship, despite hefty spending cuts being enforced on the police by the austerity-obsessed Tories and their Chancellor of the Exchequer, George Osborne.

A Scotland Yard source later told me: 'Cameron had seen all the "Keystone Cops" stuff in the press and told Hogan-Howe that the world was watching and waiting for results on the Hatton Garden raid. It was a very subtle way of putting him under immense pressure.'

Met Commissioner Hogan-Howe came away from his phone conversation with David Cameron very rattled. He had never known this level of interference in a case involving what was basically an 'everyday crime' as opposed to terrorism, which was top priority for the police at this time.

The following day – Monday, 13 April – Hogan-Howe told senior officers at Scotland Yard that all non-essential leave would be cancelled until the Hatton Garden Mob were apprehended.

Hogan-Howe made it clear they had a month to turn the situation round. It was time, he said, to step up to the plate.

Scotland Yard immediately poured even more resources into the case and pledged to work around the clock until all the raiders were brought to justice. Investigators were assured they would be allowed to use any surveillance methods deemed necessary to nail the gang. But the problem was that at the moment they had no suspects to target.

Some Flying Squad detectives believed the actual items that were stolen – as well as the security boxes ignored by the gang – might well provide the best leads. Detectives privately remained convinced that approximately half of the items found in those security boxes had themselves been stolen or purchased with black money from the proceeds of crime.

One ex-Flying Squad officer told me: 'I once dealt with a drugs gang who admitted to me they hid millions of pounds worth of stuff in safe deposit boxes in that very same Hatton Garden vault. One box I saw was so crammed with £50 notes, Rolex watches and deeds to houses that it was impossible to close.'

One of the Flying Squad's most legendary detectives had been led by an informant to a cash-filled safe deposit box, also in the same Hatton Garden vault. It belonged to one of the robbers convicted of involvement in the Bank of America raid nearly forty years earlier, in London's Mayfair.

So a team of detectives began specifically focusing on tracking the whereabouts of the loot. One retired Flying Squad detective explained: 'Find the loot and you find the bad guys. It sounds simple, doesn't it? But of course it wasn't. No one knew what that stuff was really worth and that was undoubtedly helping the raiders, which was also not good. But there was no point in the police beating themselves up about earlier mistakes. They needed to get cracking before all the loot got smuggled out of London.'

Detectives knew that once everything had been dispersed it would make their job much more difficult. Some detectives were even sent out in pairs to try and trace where the power tools used by the raiders had been bought or hired from. This would prove an uphill task because most of the serial numbers had been scratched off.

On Saturday, 18 April, detectives analysing car registration numbers from the Yard's ANPR system spotted that a white top-of-the-range Mercedes had driven in and out of the Hatton Garden area on each of the two nights of the raid, as well as on many other occasions. But it was the grainy image of at least three passengers wearing high-visibility jackets in the vehicle on the second night of the raid, which made detectives especially suspicious.

The Flying Squad quickly established that the registered owner of the car was 74-year-old John 'Kenny' Collins. And when they investigated further they discovered that Collins had a long record as a professional criminal. Flying Squad detectives went straight to their Scotland Yard bosses and were given approval to launch a full-scale surveillance operation, starting with a twenty-four-hour shadow on Collins.

Specialist surveillance officers immediately placed an electronic tracking device on Collins' Mercedes. Detectives would also use cameras with long range microphones capable of picking up dialogue from up to 50 feet away, and even lip readers if necessary. They could also keep tabs on Collins' movements through the GPS coordinates of his mobile phone.

Scotland Yard's surveillance techniques had been nurtured on the streets of London in recent years during dozens of mainly anti-terror operations. Now officers had been given permission to use those same highly specialized skills to try and bring down an old-fashioned team of professional criminals from a bygone era.

The Met surveillance teams' modern targets tended to be mainly fanatical Jihadis, most of whom were very 'tuned in' to using computers and a wide range of technical equipment. These terrorists always used safe email addresses, threw away their phones and computers on a regular basis to avoid detection and were constantly looking over their shoulders to see if they were under surveillance.

But the Hatton Garden gang had taken no such precautions. Even Danny Jones – who'd boasted to the others he was a master technician – had completely ignored the electronic 'trail' the raiders had left in their wake.

The older gang members Terry Perkins, 68, Kenny Collins, 74, and Brian Reader, 76, had never taken to the computer world in the first place. They preferred good old-fashioned face-to-face meetings at motorway service stations and on A-road laybys. After all, that had been the way of the world back in the 1970s and 1980s, when they ruled the streets of London and mobile phones hadn't even existed.

Full surveillance coverage of Kenny Collins began on the morning of Sunday, 19 April, just two weeks after the raid. Initially, Collins did relatively little of interest, except drive around a lot in his slick Mercedes saloon with his Staffordshire bull terrier Dempsey for company. The two looked an incongruous sight whenever bald, overweight Collins took the dog out for a walk in a park or stopped to let Dempsey relieve himself on a lamppost.

Detectives would, in any case, have been surprised if Collins was in touch with any other potential suspects, since they were all supposed to be professional criminals and so were highly unlikely to be speaking directly to each other after such a big money job. So this was deemed by police to be the ultimate 'wait and see' operation.

Scotland Yard then announced a £20,000 reward for information leading to the arrest of the gang. The offer was derided from all directions because it seemed such a small amount of money compared with the alleged value of the items stolen from the vault. But the Yard hoped that it would make the gang believe the police still lacked any decent leads.

Ex-robber Billy later described his reaction when he heard about the police reward: 'Twenty thousand quid was a drop in the ocean compared to what the boys had managed to nick. I was stunned because I couldn't quite believe the police would be so naïve. Then it dawned on me that maybe they already had their eyes on somebody and just wanted to give the impression they were struggling.'

The police were battling against the ultimate ticking clock in regard to many aspects of the investigation, though. They knew that the jewels would be easier to get rid of than even banknotes. And they also knew that after their earlier mistakes and the pressure from Downing Street they needed to ensure they had concrete evidence and not just vague hunches, otherwise the public might turn completely against them.

While a surveillance team followed cumbersome Kenny Collins around north London in his white 'pimpmobile' – as some detectives had christened it – other investigators began uncovering more information about previous similar crimes committed in Hatton Garden itself. It now seemed that the vault had been a potential target for at least three different gangs of professional criminals over the previous forty years, as well as being robbed on at least three occasions during that same period.

Looking back at those past crimes, and the villains behind them, took on a new significance to the Flying Squad in the light of the possible involvement of Kenny Collins. During their enquiries, officers picked up further whispers about specific old 'faces', who'd taken quite an interest in that same vault in recent years. Two of them were connected to the same notorious crime family who – unbeknown to the police – had muscled their way on to the Hatton Garden raid.

Over in Islington, North London, Kenny Collins' mundane life was virtually sending his police surveillance team to sleep. One detective involved with the operation later told a colleague that Collins had 'one of the most boring fucking lives I'd ever come across for a major criminal'. Collins also struck his police shadows as being 'a bit on the thick side', thanks to his tendency not to look both ways whenever he was crossing the road. Also rather oddly, his canine friend Dempsey seemed to spend more time with his master Kenny Collins in his souped-up Merc than any friends or family members.

Collins' habit of taking his Mercedes out for a drive at least four times a day had initially led detectives to presume he was up to no good. But it was now becoming clear that he liked his flashy 'motor' so much he just enjoyed cruising around his manor, showing off to any locals he came across.

But Collins' criminal inactivity pushed the surveillance team's skills to the limit. One ex-Flying Squad officer explained: 'This is where the real art of surveillance comes into play. You see, the officers did not want their target to get even a sniff of the police interest. But it's much harder to hide from a target if they're doing the same old thing day after day.'

The police team had to start using multiple vehicles to shadow Collins in case he spotted them. Back at the Yard, a full analysis of Collins' phone and computer records was under way in the hope that would throw up more clues as to what he was really up to.

So while the surveillance team monitored Kenny Collins and his dog Dempsey's toilet habits, two detectives from the Flying Squad took a two-hour flight from London to interview one of the officers involved in the original Brink's-Mat investigation, who'd had dealings with the crime family now vaguely rumoured to be linked to the Hatton Garden Job. The ex-detective had been retired for more than twenty years and was surprised to get a visit. He later recalled: 'I wasn't able to help them much but I have to admit I was astonished to see them. We talked about a couple of old villains I'd dealt with back in the day but they didn't seem to have any specific leads and soon flew back to London.'

The police desperately needed a breakthrough before all the loot disappeared.

CHAPTER TWENTY-NINE

THREE OLD MEN IN A PUB

At Scotland Yard, another team of detectives was working round the clock trying to identify the raiders from the CCTV footage of the gang at work on both nights of the raid. A couple of officers noticed one of the raiders resembled the so-called 'King of Diamonds', whose image had also been captured on CCTV cameras during the highly publicized armed robbery on the Graff jewellery store in Baker Street, back in 2007.

This character was considered the mastermind of that particular job. The gang that day had scooped watches, stones and gold worth tens of millions of pounds. Detectives who examined the grainy Hatton Garden CCTV footage reckoned one of the men in the corridor had a similar build and walked in the same way as the robber who'd worn a Panama hat in the first raid.

Meanwhile, all detectives were urged to keep quiet about the robbery, unless there was a tactical reason for speaking in public. Individual officers were warned again that they could face disciplinary action or even the sack if they talked to the media without their superiors' permission.

'Everyone was bloody paranoid but with good reason,' said one ex-Flying Squad officer. 'Officers were told to report any approach by the press to ensure that no one was accused of speaking out of turn. It wasn't a pleasant time, I can tell you. There was this overriding feeling of mistrust between the ranks and that is never good for morale. But the Flying Squad had a job to do and they were prepared to put up with just about anything to catch those villains.'

The Flying Squad naturally assumed the gang would be monitoring newspapers and TV to see how the police were progressing. So they continued to give the impression they were on the back foot because this in turn would lull the raiders into a false sense of security while they continued to shadow Kenny Collins.

Unfortunately, Collins wasn't up to much. Officers watched him regularly walking Dempsey, whom they reckoned greatly resembled Collins whenever he snarled at anyone who came too near to them. Some officers began wondering if this breath-less, roly-poly, dim-witted character usually dressed in a dirty grey flannel tracksuit could possibly be part of a gang of highly skilled professional criminals, who'd just pulled off the biggest burglary ever seen in London.

Kenny Collins certainly didn't look as if he had the energy or fitness levels to leap down lift shafts. He seemed at least five years older than his 74 years as he shuffled awkwardly round North London getting his car washed every other day by Alba-nians at a nearby petrol station and shopping at his local Aldi supermarket.

When – five days into the surveillance operation – Collins visited The Castle pub in Islington, the police surveillance team cheered up just because he'd never been out for a pint at his local before. They followed Collins from a safe distance as he met with two elderly associates, who both looked well over 65 years of age. One of the men kept going outside to use his mobile phone to make calls. The conversations seemed quite intense, judging from the expression on the man's face each time he walked out of the pub.

A video camera secretly perched at the end of the bar that day captured the three men at a corner table sipping drinks and indulging in some fairly tense looking conversations.

The blackboard above them advertised the gastropub's upcoming summer party – and the gang should have been basking in the successful afterglow of a job apparently well done. But the expressions on their faces were far from happy.

As Collins repeatedly looked nervously around the bar, a police lip reader transcribed the conversation taking place between one elderly man, who was explaining to another how they'd bought and then used the brand new hydraulic pump to ram through into the vault on the second night.

'. . . yeah, but he went down . . . to find a pump . . . boom . . . okay, a big one . . . and so you wind everything around . . . the whole, the whole thing becomes smaller.'

Detectives were astonished because these unhealthy looking old codgers were talking in vivid terms about the Hatton Garden raid as if they had participated in it.

Before that first meeting of the main gang members had even finished, detectives had emailed surveillance photos of the two other men to Scotland Yard for immediate identification. When the results came back, the surveillance team were astonished.

One of the men was Terry Perkins, aged 67, a notorious armed robber whose profile as a Hatton Garden gang member fitted much better than Collins. Perkins, it seemed, had been one of the gang who carried out the legendary 1983 Security Express heist.

The other man was 76-year-old Brian Reader, who'd been

present when his criminal associate the notorious Kenneth Noye killed an undercover police officer in the garden of Noye's Kent home during the investigation into the Brink's-Mat robbery, back in November 1983.

'Coppers never forget a case, especially if it involves someone who hurt or killed one of their brother officers. And here was Kenny Collins with one of the characters from such a notorious case,' said one ex-Flying Squad officer. The news of Reader's link to the raid was, in the words of the same detective, 'like putting an Exocet missile up all our arses'.

Most serving officers were too young to have been around when Reader found underworld infamy in the bloody aftermath of the Brink's-Mat robbery. But inside Scotland Yard there was a collective feeling of disgust towards him. If Brian Reader really was one of the Hatton Garden gang, then police had caught themselves a mighty big fish, even if he was pushing 80 years of age.

Initially, detectives couldn't trace any mobile phones registered in Reader's name in order to monitor the calls he'd made during the course of that first meeting with Perkins and Collins. It was only later that detectives established Reader regularly used his son Paul's mobile.

Some officers were highly sceptical at first that these three doddery old pensioners from opposite sides of the London underworld would have the energy and skill to pull off the Hatton Garden Job. Just watching them meet together in a pub and talking about it wasn't enough evidence to prove they really were the raiders, so surveillance teams were immediately put on Perkins and Reader.

The police attached a monitoring device to the outside of Perkins's blue Citroen Saxo. It was the same sophisticated bug as the one used on Collins's white Mercedes. But it seemed that Reader travelled everywhere by public transport so he would be a lot harder to monitor.

The following day, police watched as Collins called in at The Moon Under Water pub in Enfield, where he met an emergency plumber called Hughie Doyle. Doyle had no criminal record so the police presumed he was unlikely to be a member of the Hatton Garden gang.

In the middle of all this, Scotland Yard bosses were pressurizing the Flying Squad for immediate results because Hatton Garden continued to be used by politicians and journalists to hammer away at the overworked and underpaid police. Behind the scenes, there was also concern that some of the surveillance methods being used by police might have repercussions as it might be classified as 'entrapment' in the eyes of the law.

But Flying Squad detectives were adamant they had to get proper, concrete evidence which would stand up in a court of law. Older officers even warned their colleagues that this breed of old-school professional gangsters had been extremely adept at avoiding prosecution in the past, so they needed to nail down a lot of irrefutable evidence. No stone would be left unturned.

One ex-Flying Squad officer explained to me: 'It's always a risky strategy to step up surveillance because if any of the villains got a sniff they are being watched then they'd be off on their toes and we'd probably never see them again. But catching and then successfully prosecuting thieves is all about patience and the best way to bring these characters to justice was to turn those conversations with other gang members into usable evidence.'

The Flying Squad were still surprised Collins, Reader and Perkins had even got together so soon after the raid. What they didn't know was that the gang had come out in the open because they were terrified that the crime family who'd 'introduced' them to Basil was on the verge of taking over their entire job. It was predictable in many ways and typical of how this crime family had bullied and intimidated their way into positions of power over the previous forty years.

A couple of days after Collins' first meeting with Perkins and Reader, the three men met again at The Castle. But with them this time was Danny Jones. Detectives soon confirmed his criminal background through photo identification. Watching detectives surmised that the gang must have been having some problems because elderly Reader had now twice ventured out of his manor in Kent and travelled north of the river in the space of just a few days. And for an old man it was no easy journey by public transport, either.

Another thing that surprised officers was the mix of the gang. As one ex-Flying Squad detective explained: 'London villains usually work with other villains from their own patch. That's the main reason why they got away with so many blaggings [robberies] back in the 1970s and 1980s. These guys went to school together. Their wives knew each other. They moved in very tight circles and that meant few people knew what they'd been up to, so the chances of them being grassed up were slim.'

But the police's surveillance operation clearly showed that the Hatton Garden suspects consisted of North Londoners (Jones and Collins), East Londoners (Perkins) and one South Londoner (Reader). As ex-robber Billy later explained: 'You can take the robber out of North London but you can't take North London out of the robber. Same with an Eastender. I'm South London through and through and I've never liked that lot up there. They're a right nasty lot. They never helped old ladies cross the street like we did back in South London when the Richardsons

ruled. Us in South London like to think of ourselves as gentlemen thieves. We're above all that murder and mayhem stuff. We
just like to get the job done and then get home to our families,
put our feet up and watch the telly.'

During the meeting in The Castle that day, Danny Jones told
the others that one of his relatives' police contacts believed
officers were treating the raid as an 'inside job', which would
work to their advantage.

Perkins agreed and said: 'They will not put 100 per cent into
it, 'cos they'll think, "You mugging us off you cunt, you want
us running all around London when its fuckin' from inside."'

As police sirens could be heard in the distance, the men then
talked self-confidently about a gadget – '900 quid to fit it in
your motor' – that would let them know when a police vehicle
was within half a mile. Jones insisted the device was linked to
police radio frequencies and could supposedly alert criminals
when officers were near to them.

'Fit it in your car, you can hide it, hide the aerial,' said Jones
excitedly. 'It's a little black box like that and it will go "bip bip
bip bip bip" if the old bill is twenty feet away from you, plain
clothes, anything.'

Kenny Collins said little as the others talked. He wasn't the
type to say much in any case. As usual his eyes panned around
the bar, nervously looking in all directions just in case someone
was watching them.

After monitoring that meeting between the main gang members, the Flying Squad asked for a further time extension for the
operation plus additional funds to pay for more sophisticated
surveillance techniques. One ex-detective explained: 'A pledge
had been made to the top brass that we'd get the evidence if they
allowed us longer on the operation. We knew these characters

were tough old birds, who'd seen off more police interrogations than hot dinners over the previous half century. We needed everything in triplicate.'

Meanwhile some officers were still questioning how this huffing, puffing band of old codgers could really have pulled off such a headline-hitting raid. One surveillance team found themselves watching Terry Perkins' house in Enfield, while the 68-year-old spent hours mowing his lawn and snipping the dead heads off his roses. It was difficult to believe this wheezing, white-haired old man was one of the ringleaders of London's most notorious team of burglars.

Detectives also found it hard imagining this mob of old-timers lugging all that heavy equipment down to the basement of 88–90 Hatton Garden and then struggling to aim that super-powerful diamond-tipped drill into a two-foot thick concrete wall. An ex-Flying Squad officer explained: 'One young detective said to me he couldn't believe this mob could even manage to tie their own boot laces, let alone commit a multi-million-pound crime. But these fellas had served long stretches in jail and maybe they'd always kept fit and healthy in prison gyms. Prison inmates don't tend to age as much as the general population. They keep themselves trim and fit and that probably also helps them get through all those years inside.'

Flying Squad detectives later said they were surprised that the gang were hiding in plain sight, which clearly implied they had no idea they were under surveillance. But then again Edgar Allan Poe once pointed out: 'The best place to hide anything is in plain view.'

The police presumed the gang must have decided to sit tight and wait for the dust to settle. It made sense, but some detectives couldn't understand why the gang hadn't simply left the country for sunnier climes. And why had they started meeting up together in London so soon after the raid?

Meanwhile the media reported that detectives investigating the Hatton Garden raid were 'still waiting for the results of a battery of forensic tests, hoping that the gang left DNA traces, fingerprints and even footprints in the dust and rubble created as they drilled through the reinforced concrete wall'. No one in the media had any inkling that the police were already trailing the main suspects.

The press did, however, try to jump on a statement from the City of London police insisting that they'd passed information to Scotland Yard about the theft in December 2014 of the Hilti drill. But the story did not spark much interest, much to the relief of the police no doubt.

Out on the streets of North London, the main gang members were coming out into the open even more. The pressure and confusion sparked by the crime family's involvement had convinced them they might be on the verge of losing their share of the loot that they'd each taken away on the first day after the raid.

Ex-robber Billy spoke to someone in touch with the gang two weeks after the raid. He recalled: 'Everyone was getting twitchy by this stage. That's why they broke cover. Brian and Terry were getting sick of it all and starting to question why they did the job in the first place. They told Danny Jones to stop banging on about all the news coverage because it was driving them all potty.'

Rumours then began circulating that there might have been a deadly fallout between the gang. The police compared it to the legendary aftermath of the Brink's-Mat robbery, which had led to the death of at least twenty people. The police obviously hoped these stories might cause a split in the gang. That in turn could lead to one of them breaking ranks and turning informant.

None of this speculation helped Kenny Collins' mental state, which was going from bad to worse. When he heard the stories about the supposed 'deadly fallout' he repeated his pledge to the others that he wanted to hand back his loot and 'get his life back'. The others warned him that that would be tantamount to professional suicide and Collins was told in no uncertain terms to stop complaining.

Then – in the middle of all this – another sensational story hit the tabloids. This one claimed that the 'tall man' seen in the CCTV footage (Basil) had travelled to Britain from Spain, specifically to carry out the job. He was said to now be 'on the run' with a large quantity of loot belonging to the other gang members.

The odd thing was that this story was almost entirely true, suggesting that someone involved with either Basil or the gang themselves was blabbing to the newspapers. Reader and Perkins warned the others not to talk to anyone else about the article. They also began putting the word out to see if anyone had seen Basil. It was a risky strategy because Basil's bosses would go ballistic if they thought Reader and Perkins were chasing after their man.

Ex-robber Billy explained: 'All these sensational stories in the press had a negative effect on the lads. They'd already had enough problems with that crime family leaning on them, who'd offered help with one hand while at the same time planning to take whatever they wanted with the other.'

No wonder Reader and Perkins found themselves watching each other's backs. It must have felt like the crime family would take them out at any moment. Originally they'd planned to turn the loot into cash a minimum of three months after the raid. But now they were seriously considering getting rid of it more quickly before the crime family stole it all from them.

Dividing up the loot this way was known in the trade as 'slaughtering'. Once everything had been converted into cash it was untraceable and only then could the gang truly say 'job done'.

Elsewhere it seemed that other criminals were unashamedly cashing in on the Hatton Garden Job. A gang of phone fraudsters in Tayside, Scotland, used the raid to scam vulnerable people out of their personal details.

One victim, a pensioner from Newport in Fife, told how she was tricked by a man claiming to be a senior Scotland Yard police officer, who even offered his name and badge number. The 'policeman' urged his elderly victim to call the number on the back of her bankcard as a matter of urgency. Criminals had hijacked the phone line and intercepted the call in order to secure bank details and financial information.

On Thursday, 23 April, Detective Superintendent Craig Turner, Head of the Flying Squad, appeared on BBC TV's *Crimewatch* to appeal to the programme's millions of viewers for new information about the raid and its perpetrators. A small selection of CCTV images of the suspects wearing masks in the vault building were screened. But police were careful not to use any of the footage that showed Kenny Collins' Mercedes circling round Hatton Garden.

Turner then asked the TV audience: 'Were you in the area of Hatton Garden? Did you see anyone acting suspiciously around Hatton Garden Safety Deposit Ltd? Did you see anyone in a vehicle loading or unloading heavy equipment nearby?'

THE JOB

The £3,500 Hilti DD350 drill used by the gang to get through the concrete wall was elevated to superstar status on that same episode of *Crimewatch*. Photos showed the large, cumbersome contraption that looked like some kind of modern handheld weapons system. It was revealed that only a few hundred people in the UK had been trained to operate this highly specialized piece of equipment.

An appeal was made on *Crimewatch* asking for the 'wives and girlfriends' of anyone who had the knowhow to use such heavy-duty drills to come forward if their partner had been behaving suspiciously. Again, it appeared to the outside world that the police were desperate and still lacking any decent leads. The Flying Squad hoped that if any of the gang were watching the programme they'd presume exactly the same thing.

Shortly after the programme aired, an informant contacted the police to say that one of the men shown on the CCTV camera footage was a well-known South London 'face'. The source didn't know the man's name, but jokingly mentioned that his stripy socks and traditional brown leather lace-ups were 'the big giveaway'.

CHAPTER THIRTY

THE WIRE

The Hatton Garden gang's inability to cover their own tracks in the run-up to the raid and its aftermath was mainly down to their complete lack of understanding of electronic devices. And the Scotland Yard specialists monitoring them round the clock were gathering evidence at such a pace that it made even the detectives featured in TV series *The Wire* look like amateurs.

Experts were accessing billing data for the suspects' phones that showed the date and time of incoming and outgoing calls, as well as geographical locations of where the calls were made. They were also able to outline specific mobile phone and cell-site data collected by the police surveillance teams. The handsets themselves showed contact numbers and the content of texts. It was fully comprehensive surveillance coverage on a massive scale.

On 1 May 2015, Kenny Collins, Terry Perkins, Danny Jones and Brian Reader had a drink again at The Castle in Islington. Detectives suspected by this time that much of the raid had been planned there and in a small lock-up building rented by plumber Hughie Doyle behind another pub, a few miles away in Enfield.

During the latest meeting at The Castle, Perkins and Jones

had discussed with Reader why they'd opted for going back a second time to complete the job without him. Jones said it had been 'common sense' to insist they went back but none of them mentioned the threats from Basil's crime family bosses.

At one stage during the conversation, the ever twitchy Kenny Collins looked across at a couple sitting near by who seemed to be watching them. They immediately looked away and he lost interest in them.

In The Castle that day, Perkins and Jones proudly boasted about how they'd carried out the bulk of the work themselves before describing the moment the vault was finally breached.

Danny Jones excitedly deferred to Perkins as he said: 'And you said, "Smash that up. Smash that up now, put that down." Its fuckin' working 'cos you're egging one another on, going "It's working, it's working, you got to take it off."'

Jones – hardly able to contain his excitement – continued in animated fashion, waving his arms around as he spoke: 'Remember me saying that it ain't fuckin' coming back – we're in, we're in! And you started pumping again, "Get some more, get some more."'

During another meeting between Perkins, Jones and Reader, the men talked about how Reader had pushed the others to recruit Kenny Collins. Jones said to Reader: 'Your bit of fuckin' work and you pulled out.'

Perkins then described Collins as a 'wombat thick old cunt' while Jones complained about Collins' skills as the lookout. 'I'd say: "Kenny, let's get things right, you got money for nothing, mate. You sat up there and fell asleep,"' said Jones.

On another occasion, when Reader was not present, Jones and Perkins discussed Reader's decision to quit on the second night. Jones described him as once a 'full-on thief' but now an 'old ponce'.

Sarcastically referring to Reader as 'The Master', Perkins described their previous escapades together, adding that he 'fucked every one of them'.

Talking about the first night of the heist, Perkins said of Reader: 'Fuck, he carried one thing in there. He diddley'd and doddley'd about and then it was all in. He's not a thief.'

Then Perkins laid into his old friend's personality, saying: 'He's a fuckin' know-it-all, that's what he is, and anything he knows he's got wrong.'

Jones later observed: 'All them months and fuckin' years' work he's put in to go "Look, I won't be here tomorrow." 'Cos he's thought you'll never get in there and the simplest fuckin' thing, common sense thing, got you in.'

Jones and Perkins even discussed how Reader had joined a 'Monday Club' and now spent all his time with other pensioners 'talking about all their yesterdays'.

Jones then lowered his voice and said that Reader 'ain't getting a dollar' and that 'he will never work again'. He continued: 'I really want to have a go at him, but I've got to stop myself. Really want to hit him and say: "Toughen up you fuckin' prick. That's what you are, you lost all the fuckin' work, you bottled out at the last minute."'

Jones also called Reader a 'liability' who is 'jealous of the youth', adding: 'He was a thief forty years ago. They never took no chances, had it all their own way. Like all them thieves then.'

When Jones referred in a derogatory way to Reader's old age, Perkins shrugged his shoulders and begrudgingly admitted his own ill health and how he'd taken insulin injections for diabetes while on the raid.

Yet despite all Perkins' two-faced criticism of Reader, he still fully intended to make sure Reader got a share of the loot. But Perkins didn't want any problems with Jones, so he didn't mention it during that meeting. However, it was certainly true that Perkins had for some reason changed his tune about Reader over the previous few days.

During another meeting – this time in a café in Clerkenwell – Perkins talked to his partner-in-crime Jones about his ambition to buy a second property in Portugal for 'sixty grand' to rent out for the holiday season.

'Mate, yeah, in the season you get [a] monkey [£500] a week for it,' Perkins said. 'You'd make say five or six grand a year, it pays all your exes and all your holiday and that.'

In another conversation between Kenny Collins, Terry Perkins and Danny Jones it became clear that the huge publicity about the raid had turned their heads to a certain degree. Jones and even Perkins couldn't resist bragging about the job again, which provided yet more evidence to the listening police surveillance team.

Perkins summed it up when he said to Jones: 'That is the biggest robbery that could have ever been. That will never happen again. The biggest robbery in the fucking world, Dan — and we was on that cunt.'

Jones, with admirable foresight, then observed: 'If we get nicked, at least we can hold our heads up that we had a last go.'

Jones then used Cockney rhyming slang as he spoke further to Perkins, whom he clearly looked up to: 'The biggest cash robbery in history [Security Express] at the time and now the biggest tom [foolery = jewellery] in history in the fuckin' world, that's what they are saying ... And what a book you could write. Fuckin' hell.'

Perkins rolled his eyes at mention of a book. No way was he going to put pen to paper. But it was clear that Jones was a different kettle of fish when it came to self-promotion. He seemed to have aspirations to be the next John McVicar, a man who'd once been notorious in London criminal circles for swapping bank robbery for a career as a best-selling writer in the 1970s.

Terry Perkins came from an old fashioned 'school of villainy' where you never talked about your crimes to anyone outside of your immediate circle, let alone write about them in books and newspaper articles. Perkins had always known Jones was a bit of a wannabe but he was going to have to watch him like a hawk in case he landed them all in it.

By this time the police were steadily gathering countless snippets of conversation linking all the men to the Hatton Garden raid. But it still wasn't enough to really nail them. A clever defence barrister could have shot most of the conversations down in flames by claiming the men were simply boasting and making everything up.

So the police surveillance operation was cranked up another notch, which meant officers began following and monitoring family members and friends of the main men. It was a gamble because with more targets came more risks that the entire police operation might be discovered. But the need for watertight evidence continued to be paramount.

Then, a few days before the UK General Election on 7 May 2015, the police's 'nightmare scenario' occurred. The gang completely stopped meeting and talking to each other. The Flying Squad initially feared that they'd been tipped off that they were being watched. Back at Scotland Yard, the top brass were warning detectives that the Flying Squad's entire future was at risk if this operation failed.

THE JOB

Departments and specialist units inside Scotland Yard were accusing each other of 'giving the game away'. Jobs were on the line but, even worse than that, the Yard believed that they would face humiliation in the eyes of the general public and politicians if it was known they'd had surveillance teams on the gang and then lost them. As one ex-Flying Squad officer later said: 'It was squeaky bum time at the Yard. Maybe they'd missed their golden opportunity and the gang had sussed them out? If the villains had dispersed then the whole operation would collapse. The surveillance boys had no choice but to keep monitoring them.'

It wasn't until a couple of days after David Cameron's resounding general election victory on 8 May that the gang suddenly began talking to each other again. More threats from Basil and the crime family may well have once again forced the men out into the open. Reader and Perkins started talking about their fears in relation to the other men connected to the gang such as Billy Lincoln, Hugh Doyle and the elusive Carl Wood. They might give the game away, either to the police or, worse still, to the crime family. All it needed was for one of them to blab and the entire job would go up in smoke.

As state prosecutor Philip Evans later told a court hearing: 'The circle, by now, had widened beyond the original circle of trust . . . This widening made its original members increasingly nervous.'

Detectives quickly established from the latest conversations who these other characters were. 'Carl', was Carl Wood, 58, while 'Billy' was William Lincoln, 60, and the 'taxi driver' Jon Harbinson, 42 (he was later cleared of all involvement). They already knew that the man called 'Hughie' was Hugh Doyle, 48.

Perkins, Reader, Collins and Jones had known all along that

the 'second tier' members of the gang were the ones who might prove the biggest risk to their liberty. After all, these were the men basically recruited at their local pub. They were the ones who fancied a bit of adventure in their lives but didn't perhaps appreciate the cold, hard reality of the situation.

Detectives were surprised but delighted when they heard Jones, Perkins and Collins discuss specific items stolen during the raid. It seemed as if the gang had 'broken cover' this time because they'd decided to start selling off some of the items taken from the Hatton Garden vault. This could provide the secure evidence needed by the police to ensure successful convictions in a court of law.

In one conversation recorded on Friday, 15 May, in Terry Perkins' Citroen, Perkins was heard talking to Jones about the loot: 'Sellable yes, necklaces – all stone ones, few of them. Few of those bracelet ones, then you got the necklace with the fuckin' big emeralds in it with the matching earrings. Another one there, they look nice . . . Put stones in them, the necklace. Must be a couple hundred rings there, but he's got a wrap like that, two of them, full of rings and . . . Big diamonds, rings there.'

Terry Perkins then told his fellow gang members what he intended to do with some of the stolen gold jewellery. 'I'm going to melt my good gold down . . . The Indian, the 18 [carat], that could be my pension if I could get half an idea of what's there, you know what I mean . . .'

Still in Perkins' Citroen on the same occasion – on 15 May – Perkins mentioned once again that it was good that the police thought the raid was an inside job. This clearly implied the gang had indeed succeeded without any inside help.

Perkins said: 'No, they can't work that out. That is the biggest robbery that could have ever been.'

'Yeah,' replied Jones, sounding as ever like an overexcited schoolboy.

Then Perkins and Jones changed tone as they began talking about Carl Wood, who'd walked off the job on the second night of the raid.

Jones said Wood was 'screaming like a fuckin' pig' when he'd left Hatton Garden that second night.

Terry Perkins pointed out to Jones and Collins that Carl Wood must have been 'cursing himself and considering committing suicide' after pulling out of the raid. Perkins went on: 'I'm trying to put myself in his mind . . . I bet he is boozing now . . . Unless he has seen the light.'

Jones told Perkins that having Wood in the gang was his fault. The older man responded: 'Yeah, well that's my fault with him anyway. I said to him to stay there.'

Jones shook his head from side to side before continuing.

'And he goes fuckin' right, and what's he do? [Blows a raspberry.]'

'. . . and that cunt [meaning Wood],' said Perkins. 'The whole fuckin' twelve years I've been with him, three, four bits of work, fuckin' every one of them.'

Just then Kenny Collins chipped in: 'Never give up. The old saying comes round, never give up.'

The gang's deep unhappiness with Wood for quitting the Hatton Garden Job was clear to listening detectives. It would provide yet more evidence of *all* their involvement with the raid.

Back at Scotland Yard, the police surveillance team were amazed that this supposed gang of professional criminals were continuing to incriminate themselves left, right and centre.

In another conversation recorded a few days later by the police, Jones, Collins and Perkins couldn't resist another trip back down memory lane to the 'good old days'. Danny Jones once again showed just how in awe he was of Terry Perkins and his role in the Security Express heist.

Jones described how Perkins had 'seen enough money in his life' (referring to the Security Express job).

Then he even blabbed about another of Perkins' robberies 'at the airport'. He said: 'A million pound out of the airport ... Fuckin' hell.'

Perkins ignored him and responded by boasting about the £6 million haul from the Security Express robbery: '£6 million out of there, fuck me.'

The raiders even discussed the prospect of being arrested. Perkins – a man who'd needed insulin and twenty pills to get him through the burglary – knew what he would tell officers if they ever accused him of taking part: 'I'll say, "What, you dopey cunt? I can't even fucking walk."'

Danny Jones then unashamedly switched the conversation back to himself by telling the other gang members he wished he'd taken a selfie outside the vault.

Surprisingly, Terry Perkins agreed with Jones, despite all his old-fashioned disdain for 'blowing his own trumpet'.

He said: 'I wish I had a photo to show me sat outside all on my own, right, doing what I had to do, to say to him [Reader], "That's where you left me Brian, look, all okay on my own."'

Perkins added: 'I wish I had a photo, Dan. I know you and Basil was inside [at the time].'

This was the first reference heard by the police surveillance team to 'Basil'. They knew there was a member of the main gang missing from all the meetings they'd monitored. But it seemed unlikely that Basil was his real name. It just didn't sound right.

During another meeting, Perkins and Jones implied they

thought Basil had been overpaid for his role in the raid; Jones called it 'money for old rope'.

Flying Squad detectives started to wonder if perhaps Basil had been on the job for some other reason. Maybe Perkins and Jones were planting false information about Basil? Officers once again started to wonder if the men knew they were being monitored.

At another meeting, Jones deliberately tried to 'diss' Basil by saying to Perkins: 'Basil learnt in fucking two months what he [veteran robber Reader] had to learn in forty years.' And later Jones added: 'Basil never done his job right, Tel.'

Perkins then replied: 'No, he fucking didn't.'

Jones responded: 'He got money for old rope there, Terry.'

Then there was a rare outburst by the extremely worried Kenny Collins: 'I still don't know why Basil let that fuckin' alarm go off,' he said, referring to the mistake that almost led to the gang being caught red-handed.

Terry Perkins replied: 'No, well I think he made a rick [mistake] there.'

Perkins then went on: 'I still don't know how he [Basil] let that alarm go off. It wasn't one that they confirm. Basil would . . . make some shit up. I don't know enough to challenge him, you know what I mean? He can baffle me with bullshit.'

There were a few hints on the police transcripts from these bugged conversations that Basil lived overseas, perhaps on the Spanish Costas, or in a country such as Thailand.

Throughout the numerous conversations between gang members bugged by the police, amounting to nearly seventy pages of transcripts, there is not even a hint of Basil's real identity.

In his Citroen a few days later, Terry Perkins began the conversation by talking to the other gang members about how he'd paid for his daughter's holiday out of the proceeds from the raid 'and made sure she was all right'.

Then he said to Collins and Jones: 'Let's see what we got once we chop it up. We will have half a clue. You can't plan on doing anything until you know what you got, can you?'

Detectives monitoring the conversation immediately seized on Perkins' reference to 'chopping it up' as it confirmed that the gang were indeed planning to move the loot on imminently. That meant they'd bring all the items together, hopefully in one place. This could provide the police with plenty of evidence when they finally rounded up the gang.

Police surveillance teams then picked up clear signals from the gang that they were going to take everything to a house in Sterling Road, Enfield, which belonged to Perkins' daughter. The only problem was that officers did not yet know when that meeting would take place, although it sounded as if it was going to happen very soon.

A police surveillance team was 'put on' the house in Sterling Road while other teams continued watching and listening to the gang as they planned for what Terry Perkins had called 'the big chop up' but what most villains call 'The Slaughter'.

On 16 May, Danny Jones was seen by a police surveillance team pulling a large plastic bucket into the Sterling Road address. This was later found to be full of jewels.

Two days later, Billy Lincoln was seen placing three bags in a seven-seater Mercedes taxi belonging to his nephew, Jon Harbinson, who had no idea what was in them. The bags remained in Harbinson's vehicle overnight, even though they contained gems said to be worth £3–4 million from the Hatton Garden vault.

That same afternoon of 18 May, plumber Hugh Doyle met

Kenny Collins near his Enfield workshop, just before items stolen during the raid were to be handed over. Doyle leaned into Collins' white Mercedes moments after the older man had pulled up next to a park. Doyle was heard saying to Collins: 'Can you tell me what you need, 'cos we have options.'

Ten minutes later Doyle was seen on CCTV footage getting out of his work van, walking up to Collins' white Mercedes again. This time the electric window came down and Doyle said to Collins: 'Give me two minutes, I'll try and get rid of Dave. I'll tell him to go get a coffee or something.'

Then Doyle walked off towards the car park at the back of The Old Wheatsheaf pub, where he had his workshop.

Moments later Collins got out of his car with his Staffordshire bull terrier, Dempsey, and took him for a walk in nearby Chase Gardens.

Doyle then came back out of his workshop and walked towards the same park. After a few minutes he was filmed coming back to his premises. Later Doyle's van was seen driving away towards Enfield town centre.

Less than an hour later, detectives heard via their electronic listening device in Kenny Collins' Mercedes that the 'chop up' was going to happen the following day, Tuesday, 19 May. It was time for the police to round up the troops and put a watertight plan in place.

PART
THREE

THE
JUSTICE

It's like one of them silent, deadly farts. No clue, and then pow, you go cross-eyed.

London mobster Harold Shand in *The Long Good Friday*

CHAPTER THIRTY-ONE

LAMBS TO THE SLAUGHTER

The Flying Squad knew their jobs were on the line if the Hatton Garden gang slipped through their fingers, so they were determined there would be no cock-ups this time. Detectives had been working round the clock for almost a month, steadily and effectively gathering intelligence information as they shadowed the elderly suspects. It had been a complex, well-organized operation known only to a select band of senior officers.

On the evening of Monday, 18 May, more than two hundred police officers were briefed in preparation for a complex operation to round up all the gang members the following day. Carefully synchronized swoops on at least nine different locations were in the pipeline and detectives were told it was essential that some of the items stolen from the Hatton Garden vault were also recovered as they could be used as crucial evidence for any upcoming criminal trials.

Early next morning, innocent taxi driver Jon Harbinson – who just happened to be Billy Lincoln's nephew – drove those three bags containing Hatton Garden items from his home in Essex to the car park of The Old Wheatsheaf pub in Enfield, where he then waited in his vehicle. This was where plumbing engineer 'Hughie' Doyle had his workshop, which had featured extensively during the recent days of surveillance.

Harbinson later said that although he had no idea what the bags contained, he knew 'it wasn't right'.

Within minutes Kenny Collins, Terry Perkins and Danny Jones turned up around the corner from The Old Wheatsheaf, just in front of Doyle's workshop. Jones was wearing shorts despite the cold weather and looked as if he was going on holiday. He greeted Doyle briefly. The three bags were then transferred from Harbinson's taxi into Collins' car and Harbinson drove off. Detectives didn't consider him a 'big fish' (later he would be found completely innocent of all charges) so they held back and continued watching activities at the location. They already knew where the three other men were going. Jones and Perkins then departed in Perkins' Citroen. Collins drove away in his Mercedes.

A few minutes later, Kenny Collins arrived at Terry Perkins' daughter's home in Sterling Road, Enfield. Collins got out of his Mercedes and lugged the three bags into the property. Shortly after this Jones and Perkins arrived and also entered the house.

Moments later, six police vehicles screeched to a halt in front of the bungalow and more than a dozen officers broke down the front door and detained all three suspects. Shortly afterwards, officers were seen removing items in at least a dozen bags, including one containing a box for a Hilti drill.

At the same time, police officers swooped in the car park of The Old Wheatsheaf and arrested Hughie Doyle. He did not put up any resistance.

Just up the road from there, more plain clothes officers surrounded Billy Lincoln's black Audi A3. The front passenger side window of the car was smashed in by Detective Constable

Matthew Benedict using a truncheon. He looked into the vehicle to see Lincoln sprawled on the floor like a beached whale, leaning over the centre console, close to where some torn-up pieces of a handwritten note lay scattered in the passenger side footwell. The note gave the address of the pub, which would have helped incriminate Lincoln.

Lincoln claimed he was unable to move following a double-hip replacement. He also said he had a 'weak bladder' and seconds after being helped from the car he was allowed by detectives to relieve himself on the side of the road. Then he was taken off to nearby Wood Green police station.

At the same time as these swoops, police raided Terry Perkins' £700,000 five-bedroom bungalow in Heene Road, Enfield and recovered what they believed was some of the Hatton Garden loot being prepared for the 'slaughter'. This consisted of three large black holdalls on the living room floor of the house, all filled with jewels and watches from the Hatton Garden vault. These included diamonds and sapphires, rings, necklaces and brooches worth many thousands of pounds each, as well as Rolex, Omega and Breitling watches.

There was also a brown leather holdall containing tools and a pot full of Asian necklaces, bangles and pendants. Police then found cash, blue overalls, five pairs of white fabric gloves and a quantity of Euros. Assorted yellow metal rings, chains and gold sovereigns were discovered inside bank change bags kept in a clear Tupperware box hidden behind the wooden plinth at the base of the kitchen units. Crucibles and tongs used for smelting gold were also discovered in a washing machine at Perkins' house. There were also two magnifying glasses, which had been used to examine the gems, plus a set of electronic scales and numerous small white cardboard folders containing more precious stones.

At Danny Jones's house, also in Enfield, police took away various items, including a computer and a number of mobile phones plus a book called *Forensics for Dummies* along with masks, a walkie-talkie and a magnifying glass.

In Cheshunt, Hertfordshire, police didn't bother knocking on Carl Wood's front door, either. Instead, officers smashed their way into his house and detained him on the spot. They didn't find any items from the Hatton Garden raid, but that wasn't a surprise since Wood hadn't been present on the second night when the gang finally got into the vault.

When interviewed by police later that day Wood, following the advice of his solicitor, refused to comment, adding that he had not wanted to 'put [Danny] in a position'. But he did not offer any alibi in relation to his movements on the two nights of the Hatton Garden raid.

At Kenny Collins' home in Bletsoe Road, Islington, detectives found items including a large amount of cash, wristwatches, coins, jewellery and a money counter. It was a similar story at Billy Lincoln's home in Bethnal Green. Six officers removed bags of property from the house. One neighbour told reporters: 'William is a big stocky bloke, East End through and through and a bit of a geezer, but I didn't think he'd be involved in something like this.'

More than forty miles south, three police vans containing twenty officers swooped on Brian Reader's house in Dartford, Kent, coordinated with the arrests elsewhere. Reader's 50-year-old son Paul was brought out of the house in handcuffs. His father followed fifteen minutes later. A police helicopter monitored the scene overhead and guaranteed maximum press and public attention in the neighbourhood. Paul worked with his father in the used car business and had been living with him since the break-up of a relationship. That night was Paul Reader's first ever behind bars.

Inside Reader's house, police found a book on the diamond underworld, a diamond tester, a diamond gauge, diamond magazines, and the same distinctive scarf Reader could clearly be seen wearing on CCTV footage from the first night of the Hatton Garden raid. Officers also began examining the two half-constructed houses in the garden of Reader's home, ripping open cavity walls and lifting floorboards.

In all that day, nine men had been detained on suspicion of conspiracy to burgle after a total of twelve addresses were raided in London and across the Home Counties.

The Enfield connection to the Hatton Garden Job was soon the talk of this leafy, mainly middle-class community. After all, it was a quintessentially respectable neighbourhood, where a round of golf or a game of tennis preoccupied the majority of male residents when they were not working nine to five. Each of the Enfield houses raided by police had uniformed officers positioned outside them overnight. Residents who knew the occupiers of the raided properties described them as 'normal friendly people' with no hint of their connection to the Hatton Garden Job.

Some detectives still privately wondered if Perkins and the others had deliberately set themselves up to be arrested. It had all seemed so easy to the police. No one put up any resistance and the police surveillance teams had been virtually spoonfed vast amounts of verbal evidence, culminating in the gang's decision to 'slaughter up' the loot.

At Scotland Yard, police computer specialists analysed the

contents of Danny Jones' laptop seized from his house earlier that afternoon. They uncovered evidence that as long ago as August 2012, Jones had been searching on the internet for drills. By mid-2014, those searches had escalated to 'more meaningful searches' for the specific drill that was to be used by the gang. There was also evidence on the computer that Jones had accessed YouTube for demonstrations of how to use this drill.

That evening at a north London police station, Jones sat down in the interview room with two detectives. He was asked if he was the man who held the drill that pierced the concrete wall of the Hatton Garden vault.

Jones replied: 'No comment.'

One of the officers then said: 'Did you mess up?'

Jones: 'No comment.'

Officer: 'Your role was to get through that hole, right?'

Jones: 'No comment.'

The detectives then played recordings from Perkins and Collins' cars to Jones, who then realized they had substantial evidence against him and his fellow gang members. But Jones still refused to cooperate with the police and demanded the right to call his lawyer.

At Wood Green police station's custody suite that same evening, Detective Constable Matthew Benedict of the Flying Squad informed other officers that 60-year-old Billy Lincoln needed to be regularly allowed to use the toilet.

Not long afterwards, Lincoln was refused permission to go to the toilet by the station's custody officer and wet himself in front of two policemen. Police later learned that Lincoln also suffered from sleep apnoea. He also repeatedly asked for the walking stick from his car but his requests were refused.

*

The following morning, Scotland Yard publicly confirmed all the arrests and stated the ages, but not names, of the suspects. A police spokesman told the media how detectives had 'done their utmost to bring justice to the victims of this callous crime'. Not surprisingly, there was a certain 'spring in the step' of the officers involved with rounding up the Hatton Garden gang. After many weeks of humiliation in the eyes of the public, London's police had cracked the Hatton Garden raid in style.

Flying Squad commander Peter Spindler told the media: 'At times we have been portrayed as if we've acted like "Keystone Cops". But I want to reassure you that in the finest traditions of Scotland Yard these detectives have done their utmost to bring justice for the victims of this callous crime. They have worked tirelessly and relentlessly. They have put their lives on hold over the last six or seven weeks to make sure that justice is served and they have exemplified the finest attributes of Scotland Yard detectives.'

As word of the Hatton Garden suspects' arrests spread through the country, there was utter amazement at the ages of the alleged gang members. The oldest of the eight was said to be 76. Some of the other alleged conspirators were 74, 67 and 60; the youngest was 48, the rest in their fifties. The police said they all came from London and the Home Counties.

With a combined age of 533, the tabloids were intrigued by how a bunch of 'old boys' could have pulled off such an energetic, high-intensity job. The papers had a field day next morning; describing the gang as 'Dad's Army' and that Flying Squad favourite, 'Diamond Wheezers'. They also got wind of Brian Reader's name as well as Hughie Doyle's, although the police were still refusing to officially confirm the identity of any of the suspects picked up during the raids.

All the earlier talk of smooth young 'Pink Panther' gangsters from Eastern Europe had turned out to be rubbish. But some in the London underworld immediately claimed the police had 'fitted up' a bunch of harmless old boys because they had to arrest someone. Other villains claimed it was obvious they'd been framed because they were easy targets.

Elsewhere, the arrests were greeted with disdain and anger by Basil's crime family bosses. This was not part of their plan. They'd intended to bleed the gang dry of all their loot but the arrests effectively prevented that from happening. So the crime family stepped back into the shadows, safe in the knowledge that the gang wouldn't dare tell the police about their involvement.

Almost thirty-six hours after the dramatic police swoops, Scotland Yard let it be known that their '76-year-old suspect from Kent' was the so-called 'mastermind' of the raid. Police even suggested that the man had been arrested after they received help from a 'supergrass' – an underworld informant. But detectives still refused to officially name 'mastermind' Reader or any of the other suspects, even though Reader's name was already well known in the press and had been given extensive publicity.

Ex-robber Billy has since labelled the police 'supergrass' claims as 'bollocks'. He said: 'There ain't no grasses involved in this case. The lads may have made some mistakes on the technical side of things, but no one grassed them up. I can assure you of that.'

'The mastermind' (Brian Reader) was described by Scotland Yard as a 'great strategist' with 'a brilliant mind'. The tabloids lapped up Scotland Yard's 'Mister Big' angle, much to the irritation of the London underworld. Those who knew Brian Reader saw him in a different way: as a stooping old age pensioner suffering from all sorts of ailments, and prone to bouts of breathlessness at the best of times.

Not surprisingly, Reader was soon being projected as the ultimate genius 'baddie'. One paper wrote: 'The architect of the raid is believed to have had substantial criminal knowledge and was able to draw on a team with sophisticated skills, able to overcome the alarm and penetrate the vault's wall.'

Details of the police surveillance operation that led to the arrests also began to emerge publicly for the first time. Detectives were said to have watched a number of addresses including that of a seemingly respectable 48-year-old plumber (Hughie Doyle) with no previous criminal record.

This particular suspect – again not officially named but still referred to in the media as Hughie Doyle – was described in the newspapers by those who knew him as 'a perfect gentleman' with a penchant for planes, yachts and powerful motorbikes. It was even claimed that the suspect had given up an unspecified but well-paid job in the City to follow his dream of running a heating and plumbing business in Enfield.

Doyle's neighbours told reporters that a family of four, including two children, resided in his large suburban semi-detached house. One woman – who'd employed the suspect on plumbing jobs in her nearby home – said that Doyle's neighbours couldn't believe that this charming man with a friendly Irish accent was one of those involved in such an outrageous criminal enterprise.

Back in Hatton Garden, traders sounded relieved, although still deeply sceptical about the news of the arrests because few could believe that a bunch of frail old age pensioners were responsible for a crime on such an immense scale. Another Bank Holiday was about to occur at the end of that week. But at least nobody was now worried about a repeat performance of the raid on the Hatton Garden vault.

'I cannot believe they didn't get it all out of the country,' said one woman who worked in Hatton Garden. 'My boss was laughing — he thought they must have been sitting on piles of the stuff. They should have had cutters ready to go, make it all look different, get it on the black market. Once it's out of the country, it's gone.'

At 9.40 a.m. on 21 May – two days after the main series of arrests – detectives detained 42-year-old taxi driver Jon Harbinson at his home in Essex. He was the tenth person to be arrested in connection with the Hatton Garden Job and was taken into custody at an undisclosed London police station. He applied for bail but this was refused.

When police searched Harbinson's home they uncovered a book called *Killer* written by former armed robber and safe-blower Charlie Seiga, now a successful author. Detectives found a page in the memoir detailing a theft using high-powered drills and other equipment. It was, they later claimed, marked with a piece of grey card.

Harbinson told officers: 'I am not a thief – I have worked hard all my life. I presently work six days a week as a taxi driver to provide for my family. The first I knew of any family member being involved in this burglary was on Wednesday morning when my aunt told me my uncle [Bill Lincoln] had been arrested for this high-profile burglary.'

Harbinson added: 'I am unable to help police in this matter in any way. I have morals and I would not nick anything.'

CHAPTER THIRTY-TWO

FAIR COP, GUV

On the afternoon of 21 May, the streets of central London were blocked by units of armed police as the Hatton Garden suspects were driven in police vans across the capital to make their first court appearance. They arrived at Westminster Magistrates Court escorted by armed officers with a police helicopter hovering overhead.

As the men stepped into the court, some supporters in the packed public gallery waved towards the dock, before they sat and listened to the brief hearing. The men appeared side by side in two rows in the dock, dressed in a variety of grey, black and brown jumpers, while a number of them wore glasses. Terry Perkins' spectacles hung around his neck by a cord.

Each of the suspects then told the court their names, addresses and dates of birth. Two of the men had to ask for the questions to be repeated because they were so hard of hearing.

The charge stated that together, between 1 April and 19 May, they conspired to enter as a trespasser a building, namely The Hatton Garden Safe Deposit Ltd at 88–90 Hatton Gardens EC1 with intent to steal.

The court appearance meant that for the first time all the main suspects (in alphabetical order) could be publicly identified.

They were: John Collins, aged 74, from Islington; Hugh Doyle, 48, from Enfield; Jon Harbinson, 42, from Benfleet, Essex; Daniel Jones, 58, from Enfield; William Lincoln, 59, from Bethnal Green; Terry Perkins, 67, from Enfield; Brian Reader, 76, from Dartford; his son Brian aka Paul Reader, 50, from Dartford, and Carl Wood, 58, from Cheshunt, in Hertfordshire.

All the suspects were remanded in custody by district judge Tan Ikram and told their next appearance would be at Southwark Crown Court on 4 June. Afterwards police closed more roads to allow their convoy to make its way south of the river to Belmarsh Prison where the suspects would be held.

The gang's first court appearance had turned out to be the one and only time that Terry Perkins and Brian Reader really felt like they'd travelled back in time. The vans carrying the men had been escorted by police motorcycle outriders just like in the old days. Armed officers in high-powered police cruisers guarded the front and rear of the convoy to and from the court. As ex-robber Billy later said: 'They stopped more traffic to get those vans through London than they would have for the bleedin' Queen. It was so over the top. A bunch of old codgers who hadn't harmed a fly and they was being treated like evil mass murderers.'

Reader and Perkins were well used to all these theatrics from when they'd once been top of the most-wanted lists. But Danny Jones, as ever, seemed to have a different attitude to it all. He was photographed by paparazzi cameramen looking out through the window of one of the police vans on the way out of the court beaming proudly. At last fame had arrived at his doorstep and he was determined to make the most of it.

The website for Hugh Doyle's plumbing business got more hits on the day he was identified than it had the entire previous year. And when Doyle's mother in Ireland was asked by his uncle if she had 'heard about Hughie' she assumed he'd had a heart attack from overwork. When told of his arrest for involvement in the Hatton Garden burglary, her response was, 'How would he have the time?'

There was initially some confusion in the press after the names were announced because Brian Reader's son was also called Brian, except he was known as Paul. The media reported that the pair lived in a detached 1930s house that could have been worth £750,000, £800,000 or £850,000 depending on which newspaper you read.

In the middle of all this, the press also continued to make wild guesses about the real value of the contents of the deposit boxes raided by the gang. The loot was now being variously valued at £10m, £35m, £60m, or £200m. Ultimately, Scotland Yard knew only too well that, when it came to estimating the value of the loot, charges against all the men would have to relate to the lowest amount.

The police no doubt hoped that now the gang's names had been officially disclosed it might kill off the public's perception that they were nothing more than a bunch of penniless old boys forced into committing a crime by a cruel and uncaring state. This impression had infuriated the police, especially when it came to Brian Reader and Terry Perkins.

All of the main suspects' previous records and crimes were soon being accessed by the public through Google searches, and those feelings of sympathy began to fade – with some justification.

One media outlet was keen to 'put the record straight':

Brian Reader, the grandfather of the gang. A second-hand car dealer living in an £800,000 house in Kent. Is this the same

Brian Reader who as a 45-year-old was charged alongside the notorious Kenny Noye with the murder of detective constable John Fordham in 1985? The same Brian Reader who was seen by detective Neil Murphy kicking John as he lay on the ground after being stabbed by Noye 11 times? The same Brian Reader who was sentenced to nine years' imprisonment for his role in laundering proceeds of the £26 million Brinks-Mat robbery of 1983?'

Even though the first court appearance of the main suspects had taken place, the police still had a lot of loose ends to tie up. A few days after the arrests, they went back to The Old Wheatsheaf pub in North London where they had detained Hughie Doyle and gained entry to the small outhouse that had been regularly used by the gang before the Hatton Garden raid as a meeting place.

The tabloids eventually got hold of the story and it was claimed that the outhouse had close links to the same crime family who employed Basil. The tabloids splashed photos of the pub lock-up on their front pages, describing it as 'the hideaway the Hatton Gardens thieves are believed to have used to plan the crime that gripped a nation'.

But the police's well-publicized success in rounding up the alleged Hatton Garden suspects conveniently camouflaged an issue that had become a big problem for Scotland Yard. The police had claimed they'd recovered much of the loot on those highly publicized swoops, which led to the arrest of all the suspects. But had they really got most of it? Some were claiming the police had been too fast to announce such a claim. Traders in Hatton Garden reckoned probably only about 15–20 per cent of the stolen items had been recovered. And it wasn't helped by the fact that no one yet knew exactly what was in many of the boxes.

One Hatton Garden source told reporters shortly after the arrests: 'We're talking about thousands of diamonds and other jewels mixed up together and much of that was already stolen when it was stolen. There is no inventory of what was in the vault and not all the owners of the boxes have come forward, so working out who owns what will never be achieved. Some will undoubtedly remain unclaimed.'

Another Hatton Garden dealer informed the media: 'I understood why the police felt so elated after the arrests but they were wrong to say they'd got most of the loot. It dawned on me at the time that if I had been the gang I would have made sure the police only got their hands on a few bits and pieces, while hiding all the rest to await their release from prison.'

The gang appeared to have been well and truly stitched up by Basil and his crime family bosses. Just staying alive would be a half decent result for the Hatton Garden mob now. They'd already conceded to themselves that the valuable gems Basil had taken were in all likelihood gone for ever. Reader and Perkins even implied to some associates before their arrests they might be safer in prison rather than in the outside world.

Soon after the arrests, it became clear that the prospect of criminal trials over the coming months and years meant there would be no insurance payouts to any of the Hatton Garden victims. All recovered property would be required by the prosecution as evidence. Police could only begin a proper financial investigation at the conclusion of any trial.

Meanwhile behind the scenes, a Flying Squad unit was now prioritizing tracking down and identifying mystery man 'Basil' of whom they'd heard brief mention during the surveillance operation. That enquiry was run separately from every other aspect of the Hatton Garden Job because prosecutors did not want to hold up the legal process in relation to the suspects already in custody. Detectives suspected Basil might have a link to a notorious crime family but for the moment he seemed to have disappeared into thin air.

None of the other gang members in custody would say a word about Basil. They insisted they didn't know his real name and claimed they'd never even seen his full facial features thanks to an omnipresent red wig, baseball cap and sometimes even huge oversized 1970s-style dark glasses. Detectives were frustrated because Basil definitely represented the final piece of the jigsaw, so until they had him under lock and key the Hatton Garden Job would not be done and dusted.

Despite the obviously hardcore criminal background of the four main men – Reader, Perkins, Jones and Collins – the public still seemed to feel some sympathy for this gang of old-timers. Many pointed out once again that no one was hurt during the course of the raid. One journalist even made a heartfelt plea on their behalf: 'These old boys hadn't harmed a fly so maybe they could be dealt with swiftly and with a bit of mercy. After all, no one wants any of them to die in prison. They were just professional villains doing their jobs.'

But being professional criminals meant that any attempt by the police to get them to tell all continued to fall on deaf ears. Reader, Perkins, Jones and Collins all refused to comment when grilled by the police. But as detectives drip fed them more details from their surveillance operation, all four realized they were, in the words of their friend Billy, 'completely fucked'.

The gang's main priority now was to make sure they didn't

say anything that could incriminate anyone else involved in the raid. Not only did 'grassing up' go against the grain for these old-school villains, but they wanted to make sure that Basil and his bosses had no excuse to hit back at them.

'Talk about being stuck between a rock and a hard place,' said Billy. 'The fellas didn't dare say anything in case it incriminated Basil and his bosses because they'd have ended up dead if they did that.'

One ex-Flying Squad detective later said: 'The Sweeney were surprised at how mellow those four were being. These guys seemed pragmatic about their situation. Some detectives actually formed quite good relationships with them. Everything was on first-name terms and there was this old-fashioned sense of respect between both sides. It was almost as if the villains were saying, "Fair cop, guv."'

The ex-detective continued: 'They were on the whole given decent treatment because they were old, apart from that little mishap with Billy Lincoln after his arrest. We didn't want any of them dying on our watch. That would have gone down very badly. After all, their criminal pedigree was impressive, especially in the case of Reader and Perkins.' But what about their use of violence in committing crimes in the past? 'I know, I know. Reader had been with Noye that night he killed the undercover officer,' he agreed. 'But we still had to give him a measure of respect because of his career as a professional criminal.'

Media coverage of the case began fading after the arrests because of the UK's strict laws of sub judice, which prohibited any prejudicial publicity between a suspect's arrest and trial. The police also didn't want any of the gang wriggling out of the charges on the basis that a jury had been tainted by what they had read in a newspaper or seen on TV.

CHAPTER THIRTY-THREE

THE ANIMAL FACTORY

All the suspects were now incarcerated at Belmarsh Prison, renowned as the most secure jail in Britain. It had been specially built to house inmates considered a security risk. And despite – or maybe because of – their ages, the Hatton Garden Mob were considered such a risk. To many people, Belmarsh seemed like a ludicrous overreaction to a bunch of mainly old age pensioners, suspected of carrying out a burglary.

When it was opened in 1991, the Belmarsh Prison complex had been the first new prison to be built in London since 1885. Life inside the top security unit could be so grim and relentless that it was better known to many inmates as 'Hellmarsh'. The Hatton Garden gang found themselves sharing prison landings with terrorists, murderers and even serial killers. But they considered themselves above such riff-raff, so tended not to talk to many of their fellow inmates. They were also convinced that the police might try and gather more evidence via their conversations inside prison.

Belmarsh's so-called 'celebrity inmates' included the Muslim Boys, a gang of Islamic converts with links to al-Qaeda. There were also the jihadists who murdered soldier Lee Rigby outside Woolwich Barracks, as well as notorious Soham killer Ian

Huntley, who'd killed two young girls in one of Britain's most shocking double murder cases.

Anyone visiting the Hatton Garden suspects faced the prison equivalent of Fort Knox to gain access to Belmarsh Prison. Two air-lock doors had to be negotiated just to get to the security area. This was followed by a thorough search, which included taking off belts, watches and emptying pockets. Next came an X-ray machine and a metal-detector test followed by a full-blown pat-down. Then visitors were taken through solid doors and gates just to reach the prison's visiting area.

The cells on wing three where the Hatton Garden gang were incarcerated were about 6ft wide by 10ft long. A small window covered by wire mesh provided a dour view of a wall outside. A small TV on a plastic desk in one corner and a metal toilet in the other were the only 'amenities'.

Each morning, breakfast for the Hatton Garden suspects con-sisted of cereal, milk, a teabag, sugar and jam, which they'd collected the night before. Incredibly they also even had a ket-tle in their cell, despite troublesome inmates sometimes adding sugar so the hot water would stick to their least favourite prison officers' skin.

At 8 a.m., inmates were allowed out of their cells for legal vis-its, education workshops and employment. The Hatton Garden gang members all got on well with the prison staff. But then all of them – except Hughie Doyle and Paul Reader – had been inside before. They knew that any bad behaviour would result in their power being turned off, as well as the water supply to their cell.

All Belmarsh prisoners were allowed just an hour every day in the exercise yard, where they'd walk around in a circle chatting to each other about the case. Sometimes other inmates would gather round to hear all about the gang's adventures but mostly they kept to themselves.

One of the worst things about Belmarsh as far as the Hatton Garden gang were concerned was that the prison had its own underground tunnel linking it directly to Woolwich Crown Court, just 500 yards away. That meant they'd be trapped inside the confines of two buildings round the clock until after any subsequent trials.

The tunnel at Belmarsh had been constructed to provide a secure route for bringing high-profile, potentially dangerous defendants before the court. Armed police were often deployed to provide additional security in the corridors of Woolwich Crown Court once the prisoners had emerged from the tunnel exit in the basement of the building.

On 4 June, all ten suspects appeared before another preliminary hearing, this time at Southwark Crown Court via a video link live from Belmarsh. They all faced charges of conspiracy to burgle between 1 April and 7 April 2015, and conspiracy to conceal, disguise, convert or transfer criminal property, namely a quantity of jewellery and other items, between 1 April and 19 May.

Ex-robber Billy pointed out: 'No more rides in a prison van with motorcycle outriders to court. They just hooked them up to a camera and Bob's yer uncle.'

As the men waited more than fifteen minutes for the video-link to connect properly, Terry Perkins asked the clerk: 'Can you ask the judge and yourselves to come down to Belmarsh so we can have tea together?'

Perkins' tongue-in-cheek remark got a few laughs in the public gallery and press area at Southwark Crown Court. One reporter later said the gang looked and behaved like characters out of the

Lavender Hill Mob, a 1950s British film starring Alec Guinness as the mastermind of a bunch of ageing villains. Others remarked that the defendants seemed extremely relaxed and jovial as they each nodded into the videolink camera to confirm their names and other details.

Brian Reader's son Paul was the exception. By his own admission he was 'a complete fish out of water' when it came to the Hatton Garden charges. He'd found himself cast in the role of a master criminal and yet all he'd done was lend his mobile phone to his father. And like his father, Paul Reader had major health problems. In 2013, he'd suffered an aneurysm, and he had polycystic kidney disease. He spent his time in prison reading David Jason's autobiography and keeping his head down.

Paul had been so naïve when he was first arrested he hadn't even asked for a lawyer. He later said he had no idea whatsoever about his father's role in the Hatton Garden Job. Paul Reader's health deteriorated in Belmarsh and he had to be taken to hospital, handcuffed and accompanied by ten armed officers with a helicopter hovering above as the ambulance travelled through the streets of South East London. Armed officers had even wanted to be present for Paul Reader's CAT scan, but the nurse was adamant that they couldn't be.

Brian Reader was distraught about his son's predicament and pledged to get him released as quickly as possible, but for the moment both father and son remained under lock and key.

Within days of that second court appearance it became clear to detectives and prosecutors that the gang was splitting into 'two camps' when it came to the charges they were facing. Significantly, the four alleged ringleaders – Reader, Collins, Perkins and Jones – were seriously contemplating pleading guilty to a charge of conspiracy to burgle. Their lawyers advised that they might avoid heavy sentences if they admitted their roles and that would save the justice system a lot of time and money, which would also be taken into consideration when it came to sentencing.

In any case, the four main gang members didn't really have much choice in the matter. If they did fight the charges then Basil's crime family bosses would presume they'd helped the police, especially if they then got found not guilty. That would then spark the sort of bloodbath all four desperately wanted to avoid. It was a chilling, inescapable Catch 22 scenario.

Presumably, the police had no inkling at this stage about the additional pressures on the main gang members. But many detectives were still trying to work out why the raiders had already clearly implied they were strongly considering putting their hands up and pleading guilty. It just wasn't in the DNA of these old-school professional criminals to cough up to everything without a fight.

Two of the other suspects, Billy Lincoln and Hughie Doyle, had already made it clear through their lawyers that they were not prepared 'to roll over' and they would be pleading not guilty to all charges. But then it's highly likely they knew little or nothing about Basil and his crime family bosses, so they were under less pressure than the others. Brian Reader's son Paul, and taxi driver Jon Harbinson, had not yet confirmed their responses to the charges. Carl Wood was undecided at this stage. The case against Paul Reader was not strong because it was based mainly around the use of his mobile phone, which of course he regularly lent to his father. Harbinson continued to insist he had nothing whatsoever to do with the gang, apart from being Billy Lincoln's nephew.

If all five did fight the charges then that would mean the

police and prosecutors would have to get the 'big guns' out in expectation of a long and costly criminal trial.

Meanwhile the four so-called ringleaders were told that if they went ahead and pleaded guilty as had been suggested, then any sentencing would be delayed until after the trials of the other alleged gang members. This news dismayed Reader, Perkins, Jones and Collins because it effectively left them in limbo for many months. Also, a delay in sentencing would give detectives time to try and negotiate for more inside information – including clues as to the identity of Basil – in exchange for lighter sentences.

Inevitably, there were rumours in the London underworld that the four main gang members had already grassed up others involved in the raid after being promised lighter sentences. But the opposite was the case. By admitting their crimes, all four men had been able to avoid difficult probing by detectives, as well as the risk of evidence from others, which might have put them in potential danger.

Brian Reader also had another ulterior motive: he wanted to ensure that his son Paul had all the charges against him dropped. Reader knew the police case against Paul revolved around his use of his son's mobile phone in the aftermath of the raid. Eventually, the police accepted Reader's claims and the charges against Paul were completely dropped.

In Belmarsh Prison, the four main gang members received 'messages' from Basil's crime family bosses through other inmates 'thanking' them for keeping quiet about their involvement. Ex-robber Billy later explained: 'They was basically saying, "We know everything that's going on, so don't be tempted to grass us up." The lads must have still been bricking themselves but at least they was a bit safer inside nick than out on the streets.'

Also in Belmarsh, Hughie Doyle – who'd never been in a prison before in his life – was spending much of his time exercising in his cell in order to relieve the boredom of being locked up. He soon lost two stone in weight and was even able to do handstands against a wall. Typically, Doyle had also got hold of a copy of Christopher Hitchens' book *God is not Great*, so he was better equipped to discuss religion with extremists on his wing.

In July 2015, it was reported that a movie was being made from an autobiographical book being written by none other than gang member Danny Jones. It was the first anyone had heard about Jones actually writing a book. Other members of the gang were irritated to say the least. A report in one tabloid said the alleged 'movie' – called *Thief* – was being rushed into production and would star almost every silver surfing actor still working in 2015 from Michael Caine to Bill Nighy.

The movie's producers insisted the rights to the story had been purchased by their production company from Danny Jones and that film bosses were also seeking Oscar nominated actor Tom Hardy to play a lead role in the movie. He'd just starred in a Krays biopic, playing both Ronnie and Reggie.

Danny Jones didn't care what the others thought. He was delighted that the book he planned to write was going to form the basis of a film, even though he hadn't actually put pen to paper yet. He ignored protests from Perkins and Reader, who accused Jones of being disloyal. They also warned him to avoid any references to Basil and his crime family bosses for obvious reasons.

Danny Jones prided himself on always 'looking at the bigger picture' and genuinely saw himself as a future media star after he'd completed what he hoped would be a relatively short sentence, now he'd decided to plead guilty.

In fact, Jones had alerted the film company's interest in the first place by writing letters to journalists from Belmarsh telling them all about his plans for a book. One of those he wrote to was Sky TV's veteran crime correspondent Martin Brunt.

Brunt later recalled to me: 'Danny is a larger than life character. He seems to see everything as some kind of game. I was happy to correspond with him because obviously he was going to get a lot of publicity when then trials came up. But I could never really work out whether the crime he'd committed was as important to him as the possibility of being famous.'

At the end of August 2015, Hatton Garden Safe Deposit Limited closed down after going into voluntary liquidation. The robbery and its highly publicized aftermath had obliterated its entire customer base, leaving the company with no choice but to close. The firm itself issued a brief statement: 'Unfortunately, as a result of the extensive damage and losses, the company has now gone into liquidation to protect the clients' and creditors' interests.'

On 3 September, police investigating the Hatton Garden Job raided a millionaire's luxury apartment overlooking the Thames. Scotland Yard forensics teams conducted a fingertip search of the flat, which was housed in a 52-storey tower block with its own infinity pool. Neighbours allegedly included Premier League footballers, Russian and Saudi businessmen, as well as millionaire City bankers. Gleaming sports cars and 4x4s were parked in the buildings high-security underground car park. The block's concierge service even offered delivery of items from Harrods. The police later admitted no one was charged despite their dramatic, high-profile raid.

On Friday, September 4, during a hearing at Woolwich Crown

Court the four main so-called 'ringleaders' of the gang Reader, Perkins, Jones and Collins, as expected, all entered guilty pleas to conspiracy to commit burglary with intent to steal jewellery. The remaining defendants, Wood, Doyle, Lincoln and Harbinson, all pleaded not guilty and were given a provisional trial date of 16 November at the same court. One of Brian Reader's old school friends was in the public gallery that day. It was a measure of the 'other side' of Reader that he still retained friendships from almost seventy years ago.

On 6 October, at a further preliminary hearing at Woolwich Crown Court for the four alleged gang members who had pleaded not guilty, police confirmed for the first time that they'd not recovered a 'significant amount' of the items from the safety boxes, as had been previously claimed. Prosecutor Philip Evans told the court: 'It's fair to say the amount which has been recovered is very significantly less than the amount taken. The process of identifying those figures is long and complex but the Crown states a significant amount of jewellery is still outstanding.'

There were, it seemed, tens of millions of pounds worth of loot still missing, which must have been music to the ears of certain members of the London underworld.

A few days later, gang member Danny Jones offered to show detectives where his share of the loot was hidden. He claimed to be worried in case someone else found it. Jones said he'd buried the items in a memorial plot at Edmonton Cemetery, North London, that belonged to a male relative of his partner, and said if he was taken from prison he would show police exactly where it was hidden.

Jones' initial offer was rejected by suspicious Flying Squad officers. Jones then accused the police of not wanting the loot back. He said in a letter to his new penpal, TV journalist Martin Brunt: 'As I'm the only person in the world to no [know] where it is, deep down. I want to do the right thing and give it back.' He added: 'They better hurry up, we don't want anyone finding it, do we?'

It was typical of 'showman' Jones to try and grab the limelight by telling all in a letter to a well-known TV news journalist.

Jones described himself in the same letter to Martin Brunt as a 'burnt-out burglar' and insisted the police were trying to make him look bad.

His letter went on: 'I'm trying my best to put things right and for some reason they don't want me to give it back. If I don't get the chance to go out under armed escort, I hope some poor sod who's having it hard out there with his or her family finds the lot and have a nice life, as you never know, Martin, people do find things, don't they? Maybe they think I'm going to get [a] hit squad to get me out, my God how stupid.'

A Scotland Yard spokesman reacted to the offer from Jones by saying: 'We are not prepared to discuss an ongoing investigation.'

Suspicious Flying Squad officers searched the cemetery themselves and found a larger stash hidden under the memorial stone of Jones's father-in-law just a few yards from the smaller stashes originally mentioned by Jones in his letter. They didn't tell Jones about their discovery.

One week later, on 15 October, the police took Jones up on his offer and escorted him to the cemetery. Jones directed the police – perhaps unsurprisingly – to where the smaller bags of stash were hidden.

He then insisted to the police he was the only person who

knew the stash was there, and, importantly, he said 'There's no other outstanding property. That is all I had.'

Jones was then specifically asked again whether there was anywhere else the police needed to go in order to recover property, and he replied, 'That's all I had. The rest of it you got on the day.' Jones was then returned to the prison.

It was later said in court that Jones had not told police about the existence of the larger stash because he wanted to keep it for his 'future use'.

Jones's widely reported activities at this time worried Reader and Perkins immensely because Jones was winding up the police, which could lead to longer sentences for all of them. Also, they didn't want Jones upsetting Basil's crime family bosses.

Other villains close to the Hatton Garden gang were also far from impressed with Jones's 'kind offer' to Scotland Yard. Ex-robber Billy said: 'Danny Jones was proving a bloody liability. He had no right to start making that sort of offer and then winding up the coppers. Fuckin' idiot.'

When police once again tried to suggest to Jones and the other gang members who'd already pleaded guilty that they might get more lenient sentences if they helped detectives to find mystery man 'Basil', they were greeted with a mute response.

Billy explained: 'The lads had coughed up to what they'd done and were prepared to serve their bird [time]. But grassing up Basil was non-negotiable. The fellas knew they'd live a much longer life if they let him get away with everything he'd done.'

Many newspapers, however, were trying hard to follow the trail of mystery raider Basil. One tabloid claimed the elusive gang member was now known in the underworld as 'The Ghost' and lived less than a mile from Hatton Garden. He was also described as the 'brains' of the outfit.

The same newspaper claimed that Brian Reader was the only gang member who knew Basil's true identity but he didn't even have his phone number. Reader was outraged when he was told about the claim because knowing Basil's real identity was of no interest to him.

But then the tabloid revealed its own naivety by asserting that 'Basil is not believed to be his real name and he carefully hid his greying brown hair under a ginger wig during the raid.'

As Billy said when he read the article: 'What a load of cobblers.'

In the London underworld itself there were surprisingly few rumours about the real identity of Basil. In many ways it was true that he was a 'ghost'. No one seemed to know him and even fewer were willing to speculate as to his real identity. But the ominous shadow of that crime family probably played a big role in quelling all the gossip.

CHAPTER THIRTY-FOUR

TROUBLE BREWING

Even from the relative safety of their cells inside Belmarsh, Brian Reader and Terry Perkins worried that they could still be targeted by Basil's crime family bosses. As the full-length trial of the other four alleged gang members approached, Reader and Perkins received another 'communication' from the crime family asking if they could tell them about the four men's intended defence 'strategy'.

It was made clear that if any of the not-guilty four mentioned Basil and his bosses in open court, then they would be 'dealt with appropriately'.

As a result, Reader, Perkins, Jones and Collins pulled back from talking about the case to the other four whenever they met up in the Belmarsh yard for the their daily one-hour exercise routine. They didn't want to be accused of trying to influence the trial in any way. Reader and Perkins also suspected that the police might still try to monitor their conversations because they were determined as ever to bring the mysterious Basil to justice.

The police once again dropped hints that the sentences for Reader, Perkins, Collins and Jones could be reduced if they helped detectives track down Basil.

Ex-robber Billy later explained: 'Someone I know went to see one of the lads during this period and he was in pieces. He was exhausted and stressed by it all and voiced regret about having carried out the job in the first place. I think they was annoyed with themselves 'cos they should have known better when it came to that crime family.'

On Thursday, 12 November 2015, defendant Hughie Doyle's counsel Paul Keleher QC was told by His Honour Judge Kinch at Woolwich Crown Court that Doyle would no longer face a charge of conspiracy to burgle the Hatton Garden Safety Deposit company. But Doyle still faced charges alongside Carl Wood, Billy Lincoln and taxi driver Jon Harbinson at the upcoming trial, due to start the following week.

Later that same day, Doyle was present in court when his lawyer applied for him to be granted bail after almost five months in custody. Doyle claimed he'd not been allowed visits from his family since his original arrest following the police raids. On the basis that he had no previous criminal record, Doyle was granted bail, while the other defendants remained in custody at Belmarsh. Doyle's bail conditions included that he resided only at his home in Enfield, kept to a curfew between 9 p.m. and 6 a.m. and surrendered his passport to police.

On Friday, 13 November – the day after Doyle's release on bail – a gang of Islamic terrorists murdered more than one hundred innocent people in Paris and the story of the Hatton Garden gang took a back seat in the media. Reader and Perkins were particularly relieved because whenever the case appeared prominently in the press it risked sparking a response from Basil's crime family bosses.

If ever there was a place that was built to put people off committing crimes it was Woolwich Crown Court. It is nestled on a bleak, windswept industrial wasteland in what locals called 'the armpit of Plumstead', a drab South East London suburb. There was none of the glamour, intrigue and history of the world famous Old Bailey here. This was a multifaceted building connected to Belmarsh Prison by that 500-yard underground walkway. No more dramatic high-speed police convoys through the heart of London for the Hatton Garden suspects.

Even the weather in the Woolwich Crown Court area seemed to be permanently grey, which perfectly summed up the atmosphere for most cases heard in Court Number Two. Yet there was a feeling that the alleged Hatton Garden raiders might provide some welcome light relief.

Presiding over the trial would be His Honour Judge Christopher Anthony Kinch QC, aged 63. Judge Kinch's upbringing in Bromley, Kent – near to Brian Reader's old manor of Dartford – seemed to bely his hesitant, squeaky Oxbridge accent. With his red face and puffy cheeks peering out from under his traditional wig and robes, he could have been presiding over any British criminal trial held during the past 250 years.

On Monday, 16 November, the much anticipated trial finally got under way when Judge Kinch walked into Court Number Two to the customary 'all rise' order from his clerk. Six men and six women were then sworn in on the jury. Eleven of them took the oath on the Bible, one on the Qur'an. The jury consisted of a predictable mixture of young and old, black and white, men and women, most of whom would remain admirably expressionless throughout the majority of the trial.

Before being empanelled, the potential jurors were asked by His Honour Judge Kinch: 'Do you have any close personal connection with the jewellery trade in general, or the Hatton Garden area in particular, or with any person or business that lost property in the Hatton Garden burglary earlier this year?' None of them were disqualified. The jury were then informed by the judge that the trial was expected to last around four weeks, but that the 'worst case scenario' was that it would not finish until 15 January 2016.

Initially, no details of the case were referred to in open court while learned counsel and the judge discussed between themselves the legal ramifications of how many of the police's secret surveillance conversations would be admissible in court. There were many behind-the-scenes discussions over the following days and none of it directly involved anyone else in the court. It wasn't until the following Monday, 23 November, that the trial 'proper' would actually get started.

On that grey and misty morning three of the defendants – Wood, Lincoln and Harbinson – were herded like cattle along the neon-lit tunnel that led directly from Belmarsh Prison to the basement of the court building. From there they were escorted by assorted prison staff and armed police officers into a long dock area separated from the main courtroom by bulletproof glass.

Meanwhile Hughie Doyle – now out on bail – bounded energetically into Woolwich Crown Court's waiting room, smiling at assorted journalists and legal staff. He wore a black T-shirt advertising his plumbing business. A TV news cameraman stationed outside the court every morning throughout the trial later said that Doyle made a point of beaming in his direction every time he arrived at the entrance to the main court building. Doyle entered the dock just after the others had taken their places. All of them nodded at each other.

Even the prison staff – three men and three women – seemed impressed by the four defendants as they took their seats directly behind the suspects in the dock. Every now and again there was a smile and a jokey slap on the knee between the uniformed officers and their prisoners.

None of the defendants – apart from possibly Harbinson – seemed particularly anxious or dejected about their predicament as they waited for the trial to get under way that morning. There was a chirpy 'buoyancy' to 58-year-old Carl Wood, with his trim beard and crisp white shirt, always tucked neatly into his designer jeans. Wood spent much of his time glancing across at the jury and then back at the rest of the court, sometimes smiling upwards in the direction of the overhanging public gallery.

Next to him was Billy Lincoln with his round, flushed face, whose health problems made him seem much older than his 60 years. Lincoln resembled a huge, round, bad-tempered red balloon at bursting point; a character whose mood could switch in an instant if something bothered him. Lincoln's small, beady eyes constantly panned around the court.

Then came Lincoln's nephew, taxi driver Jon Harbinson. His face hardly ever changed expression. Dour. Empty perhaps. Struggling to raise a smile and often looking down at his feet rather than the proceedings in front of him. He seemed the only one of the quartet who was genuinely bemused to find himself on trial.

Harbinson occasionally talked in heavily guarded whispers to co-defendant Hughie Doyle, sitting directly next to him at the end of the row of four accused men. Doyle smiled warmly at anyone who looked in his direction. Doyle stuck out for many reasons; he was quite a bit younger and more boyish looking than the others. Doyle's casual clothes contributed to the overall impression that he was just passing through on his way to mend someone's faulty central heating system. Apparently he even went for a run near the court before the trial started most mornings.

As they continued waiting for the judge to appear, there were numerous grins and polite good mornings between the four defendants and their well-spoken legal counsels, which seemed to contradict the seriousness of the charges. One journalist later said the atmosphere was so light hearted it was hard to believe that these rather jovial looking old boys were accused of a major criminal enterprise.

Billy 'The Fish' Lincoln's counsel asked him if he'd had a good weekend. Lincoln looked slightly bemused considering he'd just spent the weekend in Belmarsh Prison. 'I slept a lot,' he said, with a wry smile.

Still waiting for proceedings to begin, all four defendants then stood up and held more closely guarded conversations about tactics with their barristers, who leaned against the narrow slits in the bulletproof glass screen that separated the dock from the main courtroom in order to hear their clients.

Above the main courtroom, a large group of spectators looked down from their places in the public gallery through yet more bulletproof glass. Throughout most of the proceedings, many of those in the public gallery appeared to be family or friends of the defendants. Every now and again, each of the accused would look up and smile in their direction.

After the judge walked in to the familiar daily chorus of 'all rise', the four men – Wood, Lincoln, Harbinson and Doyle – spoke briefly to each deny the charges and confirm their names and details. Bespectacled Lincoln once or twice asked the clerk to speak up because of his poor hearing. But there was no sign of Lincoln's walking stick, which he'd had in his car when he was arrested by police more than four months earlier.

Prosecution counsel Philip Evans QC was soon on his feet outlining his case against the four defendants. He intended focusing much of the case on those technical aspects, such as phone data, electronic monitoring equipment and testimony from the police surveillance officers who'd shadowed the suspects after the raid. Evans's glasses and wig made it difficult to put an age on him but he seemed around the mid-forties mark. And once he got going he barely paused for breath.

The packed courtroom heard Evans describe how the gang consisted of pensioners who were serious criminals and how they'd had spent months if not years planning to carry out the raid.

The defendants looked on expressionless as Evans ran through the four main ringleaders Reader, Perkins, Jones and Collins using mugshots and photographs of their homes and cars shown on screens for the jury and the rest of the court to see.

Evans referred to Kenny Collins as 'the lookout', Danny Jones as 'the technician' and Perkins as 'the transport man'. Brian Reader was dubbed 'the master' because he had planned the entire raid. Prosecutor Evans said: 'These four ringleaders and organisers of this conspiracy, although senior in years, brought with them a great deal of experience in planning and executing sophisticated and serious acquisitive crime not dissimilar to this.'

Prosecutor Evans then told the court that £9 million of the stolen valuables had not been recovered. He said the best estimate was that the gang stole a total of £14 million in valuables. This had the unfortunate effect of confusing the whole question of the real value of the stolen items yet again. Evans went on to give the court final confirmation that the gang had opened 73 safety deposit boxes, 29 of which were empty. Evans said the vault held a total of 996 boxes, of which more than 500 contained valuables.

The prosecutor revealed police had identified forty people whose valuables were stolen, and that the vault was predominantly used by local jewellery businesses as their 'company safe'. Evans said lower value goods had been recovered but many loose precious stones were still missing, as were 'gold, platinum and other precious metal bars, ingots and coins'.

The court heard that the contents of one defendant's computer showed the raid had been planned since at least August 2012. He mentioned that one gang member had made searches on the internet for drills, and by May 2014 those searches had escalated to 'more meaningful' searches for the specific drill which was used. The gang had, said Evans, even studied YouTube clips featuring demonstrations of how to use the drill.

There were sniggers in the court when Evans told how Brian Reader was caught out after using a Freedom travel pass for old people to catch two buses and trains to get to 88–90 Hatton Garden on the first night of the raid.

On a screen to the right of the judge the jury were shown clips of CCTV footage taken at the scene of the crime. Prosecutor Evans said: 'This is the moment work began on what was to become the largest burglary in English history.'

Images taken outside 88–90 Hatton Garden showed the raiders' white Transit van being parked on the street by the fire exit. Members of the public could be seen walking past, oblivious to what was happening. In further video evidence showed to the jury the men could be seen entering the building, after they were let in through the fire escape by the ninth suspect, known only as Basil, whom Evans told the court had never been identified. More CCTV footage then clearly showed Basil inside the building, where he appeared to unlock the fire escape before the others entered through the door 'ferrying' tools and equipment from the white van.

Prosecutor Evans said the gang had set out to hide the loot until the resulting publicity had died down. 'When they were confident that had happened,' he explained, 'they could split it up, melt it down, sell it or hide for a rainy day.'

Under questioning by prosecutor Philip Evans, a young police detective outlined to the court how officers had examined more than 6,000 phone calls during the investigation. The court was told the suspects didn't dump their pay-as-you-go mobile phones and had left the police a perfect electronic trail, which had eventually helped lead to their arrests and subsequent charges.

The four men in the dock showed no reaction as the young detective delivered his damning evidence, which clearly flagged up some of their most stupid mistakes.

The jury was also told how some of the CCTV footage from 88–90 Hatton Garden appeared to have been stolen by the gang, leaving only recordings from a camera owned by a nearby jewellery shop called Braganza, plus footage from a camera belonging to an independent company called Premises 21, based on the second floor of the building that housed the vault.

The court then heard from vault security guard Kelvin Stockwell, who told the jury he thought the raid 'must have been an inside job'. Stockwell said the gang would have needed detailed knowledge of the alarm to avoid detection. In his evidence Stockwell stated that the alarm was triggered on the first night of the raid and that he'd then inspected the premises and found the outside doors were secure at around 1.15 a.m. He said: 'I don't know if it was a false alarm. I turned up, the building was secure and that's it.'

Stockwell then agreed with prosecutor Evans' assessment that the gang seemed to know to target boxes on the right of the vault. However he denied under cross examination – by Carl Wood's counsel Nick Corsellis – that he ever gave anyone details about the vault. Corsellis stressed that he did not seek to criticize or cast aspersions on Stockwell.

CHAPTER THIRTY-FIVE

FISHY TALES

On 12 December, prosecutor Philip Evans disclosed for the first time to the court the full criminal history of Reader, Perkins, Jones and Collins, which provoked a flurry of headlines in the following day's newspapers, particularly in relation to Reader because of his role in the Brink's-Mat gold bullion robbery, which had led to the death of an undercover policeman.

Then it was the turn of the defendants to try and convince the jury of their innocence.

Billy Lincoln took the stand and his barrister, Mark Tomassi, immediately asked him: 'Were you involved in the burglary at Hatton Garden Safe Deposit?'

Lincoln replied: 'No, sir.'

When asked if he was able to understand the charges against him, he said: 'I am not a divvo, but I am not the sharpest knife in the drawer.'

Lincoln's old fashioned phraseology made him sound like a character from a 1950s Ealing comedy, and provoked a few sniggers from the press box and public gallery.

Asked where he was in the early hours of Good Friday, Lincoln told the court he'd been buying fish at Billingsgate fish market – as he did every Friday. Lincoln claimed that he remembered being at the market at around 5 a.m. on 3 April – the first night of the burglary – because data from his mobile phone showed he made a call to his good friend Jimmy Two Baths.

Lincoln told the court he introduced Jimmy Two Baths to the fishmongers at the market that night, so his friend could buy his own seafood. Explaining who this character was, Lincoln told jurors he met Jimmy at Porchester Hall Steam Baths in Westminster, where visitors would give each other baths. Lincoln said: '[He's called] Jimmy Two Baths because he goes down twice.'

More sniggers in the court followed that last comment.

Prosecutors, however, insisted Lincoln was well aware of where the raiders had all been that night. It was alleged he'd agreed to be the getaway driver for all the stolen loot many months earlier, contrary to Lincoln's own claims to police of complete innocence.

Next it was defendant Carl Wood's turn to convince the jury of his innocence. He was soon wiping tears from his eyes with a handkerchief as his wife of nineteen years, Paula, told the jury that Wood was with her in bed on the first night of the raid.

Dressed in a pastel-green woollen sweater, Paula Wood said she went to bed between 11 and 11.30 p.m. and slept next to her husband. Asked when Wood had last pulled an all-nighter away from home, she said: 'Not for years, not since he was young, in his twenties.'

She added: 'He would have been at home with me. I would remember more if he hadn't been at home, but he would have been at home with me.'

Paula Wood told the court that she and her husband had hosted a barbecue at their home in Cheshunt, Hertfordshire, the following day – 4 April – but it was a 'flop' after her daughter and Wood's friend Danny Jones had both pulled out.

Carl Wood told the court he'd invited Jones to join them but Jones changed his mind at the last minute, with Jones telling him: 'That thing I was talking about before is happening . . . just keep watching the telly and you'll see it.'

Wood described to the court his close friendship with Danny Jones, saying that they liked to go on walks where they would talk about 'man things: boxing, keep fit, animals, hobbies'.

Prosecutor Philip Evans then accused Wood of implicating his wife and daughter in the 'lie' about the alleged barbecue. He also challenged the jury to decide if the man seen in one clip of CCTV footage was Carl Wood or not. In court, Wood was asked why he did not use his phone – a 'cheap Tesco' mobile – again after the raid. Wood said he thought it had been stolen.

Prosecutor Evans said that Wood was 'living on the breadline' and had missed out on a massive payday from the raid after pulling out partway through when the gang ran into trouble. He then suggested to Wood that his debts were his motive for joining the gang in the first place.

Wood replied: 'No, it wasn't.'

During the same cross-examination, Evans told Wood: 'He [Jones] knew that you were a man who didn't have two pennies to rub together. You knew that Mr Jones was busy stashing his jewellery in a cemetery. One or two of those rings, if you had sold those, could have paid off your debt.'

But Evans told the court Jones didn't give Wood any of the proceeds from the heist because Wood had 'lost his bottle and bailed out half way through'.

Evans went on: 'That's why Mr Jones didn't give you a single penny. He wouldn't give you a single ring to help you with your debts, would he? That is why police didn't find anything at your house – because they didn't give anything to you.'

Referring to secretly recorded conversations between the other gang members in which the name Carl was mentioned, prosecutor Evans then asked Wood: 'That "Carl" – that is you, isn't it? They are talking about you being in debt and you walking away from the Hatton Garden burglary?'

Wood didn't respond.

When asked by Evans why, when he was arrested, Carl Wood did not tell police of his alibi that he'd been at home with his wife on the evening of the heist, Wood said he 'wasn't well' and 'wasn't thinking straight'.

Throughout his evidence Wood was repeatedly evasive, saying he could not remember dates, the details of conversations, where he had been on particular days or why he had been at certain places at particular times. At one point Wood claimed to have such a poor memory that he could not remember when he had got married – only that it was 'when they stopped giving the yearly renewable passport out' – or his daughter's birthday.

Cut to more sniggers in the press gallery.

Prosecutor Mr Evans put it to Wood that he was simply trying to hoodwink the jury. 'You are making your evidence up as you go along, you are lying to this jury, aren't you?'

Next it was taxi driver Jon Harbinson's turn to try and convince the jury of his innocence.

The court heard how a book by a former Liverpool criminal called Charlie Seiga outlining a heist 'exactly like Hatton Garden' was found at Harbinson's home by police after he'd been arrested.

Prosecutor Philip Evans asked him: 'He [Seiga] is talking about his criminal life and heists he had been involved in. Is that something you had an interest in?'

Harbinson replied: 'Many years ago, possibly.'

Evans went on: 'There was a bookmark in this page.'

Harbinson replied: 'That's what you say but I don't know, I wasn't there.'

Evans: 'Were you interested in the plan [Hatton Garden] you were engaged in?'

Harbinson: 'I wasn't engaged in it. If this book is so relevant in evidence against me why wasn't it forensically examined?'

Mr Evans: 'It was bookmarked on a page that is exactly what took place in Hatton Garden.'

Harbinson: 'I had no knowledge of what happened in Hatton Garden.'

Evans then showed Harbinson the grey card, which Harbinson agreed was probably the back of a book of taxi receipts.

Evans said: 'This was your book and you were reading it, weren't you?'

Harbinson replied: 'No sir.'

Cherie Wright – Harbinson's partner and the mother of their three children – then took the witness stand and told the jury that jewellery found stashed in their house by police at the time of his arrest was more than fifteen years old. Police had discovered designer watches, gold chains, rings and other valuables hidden behind kitchen cupboards at the property in Essex.

Cherie Wright told the court Harbinson could be seen wearing the items in family photographs that were taken more than a decade earlier. She insisted she was '100 per cent sure' that a ring seized in the search belonged to her partner and added that he hid valuables around the house because he was 'a little bit security conscious'.

Harbinson himself then told the court he had no reason to suspect that three bags he picked up from the hall corridor at his uncle Billy Lincoln's Bethnal Green house were stuffed with jewellery from the raid.

Harbinson told jurors he'd gone there to talk about his ill grandmother, who was Lincoln's mother, on the evening of Monday, 6 April.

Asked what he was told was in the bags, Harbinson replied: 'He [Lincoln] just said it was a load of old shit.'

Harbinson said he did not think anything of it until 18 May, when Lincoln arranged a meeting in The Old Wheatsheaf pub car park, in Enfield, North London, for the following day.

Harbinson said he became suspicious when the bags were taken out of the side door of his people-carrier taxi and put into the boot of someone else's car.

Philip Sinclair, defending, then asked Harbinson: 'What did you think was going on?'

Harbinson replied: 'I didn't have a clue to be honest, but it wasn't right.'

Next up was chirpy Irishman Hughie Doyle. He described Kenny Collins as an 'Arthur Daley' type character and said he used to drink with him at The Harlequin pub near Sadler's Wells about fifteen or twenty years earlier. He also told the court he had met Brian Reader and Terry Perkins at the same pub.

Prosecutor Philip Evans suggested Doyle was 'part of their circle'. But Doyle denied any knowledge of Reader's involvement in the Brink's-Mat robbery or Perkins' connection to the Security Express robbery.

'I don't think people involved in that kind of work would have been quick to divulge,' he said.

Doyle insisted to the jury he had no idea about any of the Hatton Garden plans. He said: 'It's something I was not paid for and I had not agreed it.'

He also told the court the car park at the back of The Old Wheatsheaf pub off Windmill Hill (which featured in video footage and was the location where Doyle was arrested) was not a suitable place for a criminal act. He told the jury: 'This car park has CCTV all over it. No way in a million years was this a good place to do something like that.'

Prosecutor Evans pressed Doyle about CCTV footage of the meeting behind the pub, which clearly showed him tapping another ringleader, Daniel Jones, on the arm.

Evans said: 'That morning, on the 19th of May, was the first time you'd met Daniel Jones?'

Doyle replied: 'First time ever.'

Doyle denied making up an excuse to get a colleague and his wife, Jenny, out of his office so the men could use the premises that day.

Doyle said: 'There was no agreement entered into, I had no knowledge of what was taking place. The car park is a public space.'

Doyle told the court he gave a key to his work premises to Kenny Collins because Collins was looking for somewhere to store items connected with his business and his late father's home.

Prosecutor Philip Evans accused Doyle of lying to the jury and pointed out it was the first time the court had heard anything about an alleged arrangement with Collins to have a key for the office.

Doyle's wife Jenny Fraser recalled to the jury plans to pick up her mother at 10 a.m. on the day of Doyle's arrest on 19 May. She said Doyle played no part in telling her to leave.

After Mrs Fraser's evidence, Judge Kinch QC announced to the jurors the evidence in the Crown's case had now been brought to a conclusion. The prosecution, he said, would begin a closing speech later that week, followed by counsel for each of the accused men.

In his closing speech to the jury, prosecutor Philip Evans again branded the four defendants as 'liars' and said that despite their denials they were indeed members of the Hatton Garden gang. He said: 'I imagine many of us would be extremely excited if we were to win the lottery to the tune of £14 million. The property belonged to people who have no doubt worked hard to run their businesses, to get that property together and keep their businesses going.'

Evans asked the jury of six men and six women to consider whether the men who'd already pleaded guilty – the ringleaders – would have trusted those on trial to look after their jewel-laden bags and not take a 'peek' inside.

Evans added that the raid had been carefully planned and, while there had been mention of it being an 'inside job' earlier in the trial, it was clear that those involved knew what they were doing, knew where the safe deposit boxes were, knew where the alarms were, and knew where the CCTV cameras were.

Referring to the defendants' evidence, Evans said: 'In this case, lies have come from the defendants from that [witness] box. On each of the four occasions that you have heard the defendants give evidence, each of them has told you lies. Some of them might have been half-truths. But in the end, the evidence which you have heard is not true.'

In his closing speech, Carl Wood's counsel Nick Corsellis said that his client could not have been involved in the raid because the gang must have used an inside man. Wood had also insisted he was not the man referred to as 'Man F' in a CCTV video clip shown to the jury.

Jurors then heard Corsellis describe his client Wood as a 'general dogsbody' who had nothing to offer the gang, and that Man F could not simply have been an extra pair of hands (EPH). He added: 'And what would they have said about Mr Wood on such an analysis? We need someone to touch up the paint when we leave?'

Corsellis also said that Wood would have been an unlikely choice because there could be no guarantees he would not be in hospital receiving treatment for Crohn's disease.

Corsellis then summed up: 'This case has given you a glimpse of the inside track to serious organised crime. This is an important aspect of Mr Wood's defence. The reason is, that the way that this crime was planned and effected demonstrates Mr Wood's innocence. Criminals who are going to take part in this exercise do so for one reason only. Money, and hopefully lots of it. It's not about improving your reputation, publicity or Instagram following. It's not about doing a person down on his luck a favour. It's all about the money.'

Mark Tomassi, defending Billy Lincoln, argued that there was no proof his client even knew what was inside the bags taken from taxi driver Harbinson's vehicle on the morning of 19 May, just before all of them were arrested.

Mr Tomassi told the court: 'There is no evidence that he opened the bags, inspected the contents or physically touched anything inside.'

Hughie Doyle's defence counsel Paul Keleher QC told the jury the events of 19 May, when the prosecution alleged some items from the Hatton Garden jewel heist were transferred in the car park near Doyle's office, were 'absolutely nothing to do with him'. He added: 'They were actually momentarily put off their stroke by the fact that Mr Doyle was there. They did not expect him to be there. But once they ascertained he was leaving they carried on.'

Jon Harbinson's defence counsel Philip Sinclair told the jury that his client was completely innocent of all charges and referred back to much of the evidence Harbinson had given when he'd earlier been in the witness box.

Judge Christopher Kinch then summed up the case to the jury. He reminded them that Doyle claimed he 'had been kept in the dark' over plans to hand over items from the raid in the car park near his office behind The Old Wheatsheaf pub.

There was also no suggestion Doyle was involved in the Easter Bank holiday raid, the jury was reminded by the judge.

However the judge did point out to the jury that Doyle could be clearly seen on CCTV meeting Collins at the car park on 18 May, the day before the handover.

Judge Kinch then went through the cases against the other three defendants with similar emphasis, repeating well worn evidence and trying to be as balanced as possible with his words. Finally on Wednesday, 13 January 2016, Judge Kinch sent out the jury to consider a verdict. He told them: 'You thought it would be a couple of weeks of your life, but it has turned out to be a very much longer saga than that.'

CHAPTER THIRTY-SIX

FUTURE SHOCK

Just after lunchtime the following day, the jury returned with their verdicts; Wood, 58, and Lincoln, 60, were both found guilty of conspiracy to commit burglary and conspiracy to conceal, convert or transfer criminal property. Hugh Doyle, 48, was convicted of concealing, converting or transferring criminal property. The fourth man Harbinson, 42, was cleared of all charges.

The guilty three were told by the judge that sentencing would be on 7 March 2016. The decision to delay sentencing had partly been motived by the police's determination to try and nail down the identity of mystery raider Basil. Behind the scenes, detectives continued to make it clear that if any of the gang helped them find the so-called 'ghost', then they might be rewarded with a reduced prison sentence.

Ex-robber Billy insisted none of the seven convicted men would ever consider informing on Basil. He said: 'There is no way any of the lads would give Basil away. For starters, none of them know his real name. But even more importantly, they all know that if Basil gets nicked they'll face the full wrath of his crime family bosses. Nah, they're all better off doing their time . . .'

THE JUSTICE

In theory, the four main gang members Reader, Perkins, Jones and Collins could be out of prison within possibly as little as three and a half years, if the sentences turn out to be in the six to seven-year range, which was predicted by some legal experts because they saved the court time and money by pleading guilty.

If they did receive these relatively short sentences then it would be in part a testament to the will and determination of Brian Reader. He'd insisted they should only do the job if they avoided all contact with people. He knew only too well that the maximum sentence for robbery – which meant threats with weapons – was life.

As ex-robber Billy later said: 'Brian deserves some praise for sticking to his pledge about not carrying weapons. Three and half years is not a bad result if that's what they end up serving. But of course it may be longer if the coppers push for repossession of some of that loot. I feel sorry for them, though, 'cos Basil and the crime family will probably try and nick what's left while this lot are inside. If that happens then the whole thing would have been a complete waste of time.'

In many ways, so-called mystery man Basil effectively held the key to the entire issue of sentencing because he had the most valuable gems and it was likely the police would push for longer sentences for the gang members if the gems were not returned.

'It's a bad situation for the lads,' explained Billy. 'Basil has all the best gems but if they're not returned then in all likelihood the lads will get longer sentences. That seems very unfair but it could well turn out that way.'

Billy also believes that the gang should never have held onto the items they stole for so long. He said: 'They was inviting problems because as long as the loot was around someone was gonna come after them. And of course the loot itself provided a direct physical link to their involvement. The moment the police got their hands on some of it they were able to prove it was connected to the lads through forensic tests.'

With the main trial now over, the media was legally safe to report that Perkins' daughter Terri Robinson, 35, of Sterling Road, Enfield, had pleaded guilty earlier that same week to concealing, converting or transferring criminal property. Her brother-in-law Brenn Walters, 44, of Manor Court, Enfield also admitted the same offence. They were both also due to be sentenced in March.

The end of the trial dominated the newspapers and was the lead item on most TV news programmes. One tabloid claimed the gang had been 'grassed up' by the mistress of one of the raiders. Others talked about a whole range of far-fetched theories as to the real identity of mystery man Basil.

Police then released for the first time video footage and dozens of photographs of the inside of the vault taken shortly after the raid. It showed how the safe deposit boxes had been ripped from cabinets as the gang hastily went through the contents for valuables. There was a ghostly, almost surreal aspect to the photos. Everything was discarded as if the gang had had to flee the premises at high speed.

The day after his client Jon Harbinson's acquittal, lawyer Philip Sinclair surprised many by publicly describing the raid as 'very well planned, very well executed, if in the end flawed'. He told BBC's Radio 4 *Today* programme he could appreciate the gang's audacity, especially because nobody was hurt. Sinclair said: 'Like a lot of people, I think, I do have a grudging admiration for the way they did it and when they did it, at their time of life. I know some of them have got very shady pasts indeed.

But this particular heist, no one was hurt in it, no one was even scared. They did not confront anybody within the building.'

Danny Jones continued writing numerous letters from his cell at Belmarsh Prison. He'd changed tactics from earlier and now insisted his main priority was to get publicity through the case to help expose the poor living conditions in Britain's prisons. Jones even wrote to the Archbishop of Canterbury and was delighted to get a reply, although it amounted to little more than an impersonal, standard response.

Jones's associates on the outside told me that Jones is now in the middle of writing that autobiographical book about his life, including the Hatton Garden Job. The earlier much publicized 'movie deal' never actually materialized. But Jones believed he would one day sell his story to Hollywood and could look forward to a legitimate 'payday' when he eventually gets out of prison. One very well-known movie producer told me: 'Good luck to him but Jones needs to realize there are more sharks in Hollywood than Belmarsh Prison. He might be promised millions but the reality is that he'll probably end up being eaten alive.'

Danny Jones is in many ways reminiscent of one of the team of disgruntled ex-servicemen who carried out a robbery in the 1960 movie *The League Of Gentlemen*, starring Jack Hawkins. At one stage one of those criminals says to another: 'Give them their money's worth at the trial and then flog your memoirs to the Sunday papers.'

Meanwhile, Hatton Garden's Sexy Beasts will further swell the ever-increasing pensioner population in Britain's prisons. In 2014, the numbers of over-sixties passed 4,000 for the first time, twice the number of a decade earlier. One sickly elderly ex-inmate summed up the attraction of prison in old people's lives. 'I miss prison so much,' he said. 'You know where you stand in there. In care homes, it's a different proposition altogether. It's not so personal and everyone's so bloody doddery. At night in prison you say goodnight to your friends and know that you'll be seeing them again the next morning. In care homes, there's a much smaller pool of people to get to know and you don't have a clue if they'll still be around the next morning. Then there's the food. It's a lot better in jail than an old folks' home.'

And there is no doubt that geriatric crime poses all sorts of special challenges. During the recent trial of a gang in Germany known as the 'Grandpa Gang', the accused described how their 74-year-old co-defendant almost botched a bank heist by slipping on a patch of ice, forcing them to take extra time to help him into the getaway car. And the same 74-year-old had another problem, one co-defendant told the court: 'We had to stop constantly so he could pee.'

Meanwhile Scotland Yard admitted that two-thirds of the original haul from the Hatton Garden Raid was still 'out there'.

One well-placed underworld source told me that also still missing is a man's diamond ring worth £50 million. If that is true, then the original police estimates of the value of the items stolen is at least ten times lower than the true figure.

CHAPTER THIRTY-SEVEN

WHAT COMES AROUND

In mid-January 2016, just a few days after the end of the trial, a tall, slim man aged about 60 could be seen sipping a black Americano at a table outside a café just twenty-five yards from the entrance to 88–90 Hatton Garden. The man had three large henchmen sitting with him.

Before they'd arrived at the café, the atmosphere had been relaxed. But the moment this imposing character with a poker face and clad entirely in black – from his expensive overcoat to his mirror-polished shoes – strolled in, the tension ratcheted up. Other customers looked away, trying to avoid being noticed by the man and his heavyweight entourage.

Later, the same character sauntered across the road to another of his haunts – a stall at an indoor 'jewellery emporium' which offered instant cash loans, cheque clearance and pawn broking facilities, in addition to trading rings, brooches, bracelets and other assorted bling. The stall was inside the same building entered by Kenny Collins on the evenings of April 3 and April 5, where he kept watch from its first-floor window (at least, until he dozed off) during the raid on the Hatton Garden vault.

CHAPTER THIRTY-EIGHT

DEAD MAN WALKING

In some ways, Basil has turned into a real-life version of the infamous Keyser Söze, who provided film buffs with one of the best ever movie twists at the end of *The Usual Suspects*, thanks in part to actor Kevin Spacey's superb acting skills as Söze.

Word on the London underworld grapevine is that Basil has 'gone missing' since the Hatton Garden Job. He was last heard of back in Spain in late April 2015, and many believe he double-crossed the crime family as well as the gang by making off with all the most valuable gems with no intention of ever coming back to the UK with the proceeds.

Ex-robber Billy says that if that is the case, Basil is a dead man walking. 'I've heard the same rumours and I can believe them. The guy thinks he's a law unto himself but he won't last long if he doesn't come back with the takings from those gems.'

Not surprisingly, 'ghost' Basil continues to be the subject of more London underworld gossip than anyone since the Kray twins. In all likelihood, he is indeed abroad soaking up the sunshine, confident that no one will ever dare give him away to the police. Scotland Yard's much-heralded £20,000 reward for information leading to the arrest of Basil continues to stand despite being derided in the London underworld. As ex-robber Billy – who has made such a significant contribution to this book – said: 'Twenty grand? That's what Basil's crime family bosses would pay for a few bottles of bubbly on a big night out. If the coppers are going to stand any chance of finding Basil, they need to up their game considerably.'

And what of the contents of that mystery safe deposit box which Basil took on behalf of the crime family in the first place? Ex-robber Billy explained: 'It's connected to another case and the box itself belonged to a villain who was holding it over the crime family because there was evidence in that box linking them to two murders.'

Billy continued: 'The moment they got the box off Basil, they went after the bloke who owned it because he'd been using that evidence as a lever to keep the family away from him.'

There is no direct evidence to connect the Hatton Garden raid with the murder of a notorious London criminal two months later. But Scotland Yard continue to examine both cases and say they have an 'open mind' about a connection between the two crimes.

Billy is convinced the murder of the criminal and the Hatton Garden raid are connected: 'I only sussed it all out after this villain was shot dead by a hitman not long after the robbery. He was notorious. Suddenly it all made sense. That means my mates were nothing more than sitting ducks.'

Sources who have heard all seventy pages of transcripts of the conversations of the suspects recorded by police insist there are no mentions of Basil's crime family bosses. But as Billy pointed out: 'The police could easily have edited those references out because they don't want the family to know that the gang spoke about them. Maybe they intend to use those tapes later and they don't want the family trying to lean on the lads any more than they already have done.'

On 8 February 2016, Danny Jones tried to plant a red herring about Basil by writing once again to his 'new best friend', Sky News crime reporter Martin Brunt. In his letter, Jones claimed he'd been recruited by Basil and even implied Basil might be an ex-policeman. But most looked on his claims with nothing more than mild amusement since Jones had already tried to trick the police about his main stash of stolen items from the raid and was a proven liar.

One retired Scotland Yard detectives told me: 'It's hard to believe a word Jones says because of his "previous". It feels to me as if he is playing silly games and these claims about Basil are nothing more than a load of old bollocks.'

And so the rumours about Basil went round and round. But one thing is for sure; he continues to evade capture and seems to be laughing all the way to paradise.

As ex-robber Billy said: 'That Basil has certainly got some bottle. He's taken off with the best gear and no one even has a fuckin' clue who he really is. You couldn't make it up, could you?'

CHAPTER THIRTY-NINE

AFTERMATH

So have the missing tens of millions of pounds worth of jewellery, gold and cash from the Hatton Garden Job already sparked a bloody war in the London underworld? When a bodybuilder confessed some years back to being the resident 'dismemberer' for the same crime family who employed ghost raider Basil, it provided an ominous insight into what the future may hold for the Hatton Garden gang.

This criminal family has been regularly investigated by police in connection with numerous murders, as well as having built up an estimated fortune of £200 million through their vast racketeering and drug trafficking empire, not to mention the money they allegedly made laundering Brink's-Mat gold. It's no big surprise that potential witnesses have always been too terrified to testify against them.

The family's resident 'dismemberer' kept different knives for jobs, as well as a cleaver, chainsaw and hacksaw. He later recalled: 'We were in a club. One of the brothers nodded in a geezer's direction. "That one. He's got to go." Later that night the bloke was taken on a detour on his way home ... and stabbed to death.'

As one senior detective who worked on and off on the Brink's-

Mat investigation for more than twenty years commented: 'Nothing really surprises us any more when it comes to these sorts of criminal enterprises. There are villains out there who are completely out of control, many of them off their heads on drugs, often bought with their newfound riches. The trouble is that when that money either runs out, or in the case of some of them, never materializes, then there is only one way to respond and that's to kill people to show others that if they dare to cross the gang they will pay for it with their life.'

So it seems highly likely that a so-called Curse of Hatton Garden will emerge as it casts a shadow over the lives of many people. By the early part of 2016, I was hearing stories relating to the case and its aftermath with alarming regularity, even though the crime itself had only just been dealt with in a court of law. No doubt the newly dubbed Curse of Hatton Garden will build and build over the coming years, leaving death and destruction in its path as well as good and bad men haunted by the horror of its power and influence over so many people's lives.

Meanwhile police and villains alike believe that there is unlikely ever to be another crime on the scale of the Hatton Garden Job. As the old-timers discovered for themselves, security systems are far more sophisticated today, and few criminals would see the sense in such a high-risk operation. In the end it was mobile phones, laptops and CCTV footage that was to prove their biggest downfall. None of these things existed when the Hatton Garden Mob were at the top of their game back in the seventies and eighties.

But it's also certainly true that many of these old codgers would rather take the secrets of their biggest crime to their graves. One or two might try to cash in through films and books about their lives but the really powerful characters will never give much away. It's all part of a deeply rooted criminal ethos developed while many of them were youths on the streets of Britain's big cities: 'Never tell anyone a thing. Never give an inch.'

Whatever the full extent of their power and influence over London life, these veteran criminals revelled in their image as the romantic villains. They wanted to prove that crime really does pay, even though, as previously mentioned, most don't believe it does.

The old-timers used to love pitting their wits against Scotland Yard and its worldwide reputation for skill and dogged determination. They nearly always considered they had one big advantage over the long arm of the law: the police had to work within certain rules and regulations. They, on the other hand, could do whatever they want.

For these legendary characters, robbery was their raison d'être. They'd grown up in gangs where a fight was the natural means to settle a dispute and they could never truly understand the middle class's abhorrence of violence. Many had a selfish drive to escape from the slums of their childhood.

But there is an intriguing core of loyalty from many of the Hatton Garden Mob's associates. Virtual strangers come to them with information, often not even wanting money or a drink, but because they enjoyed helping their battle against the police.

The men behind the Hatton Garden Raid were part of a bygone era of London crime. Yet they saw all the young upstarts cruising to millions in other heists and decided it was time to pull off the Big One they'd been talking about for decades.

They were a ragtag bunch of grizzled men in late middle age and older. Theirs was not a world of white tie and glamour, but of white vans and grit. They were ruthless gangsters for whom thieving was a profession. They considered themselves old school and were mightily proud of their working-class roots but that didn't stop them dreaming of one last job which would set them and their families up for ever . . .

So crime continues to boom. There will always be characters out there happy enough to bust open a bank and pull triggers for money or grudges. It's as flash as playing for Chelsea or being a big-time fighter. It's showbiz. And as Legs Diamond says in the musical named after him: 'I'm in showbiz, only a critic can kill me.'

So where does all this leave the Old Geezers of the British underworld in 2016? Sure, there will always be a Gangland; the police know that and merely wonder how to stop its boundaries spreading. But these days they are more reluctant to get in among the criminals than they were in the heyday of the characters you've just read about in this book. The chances of planting an undercover cop in the most potent gangs are very slim. Budgets, politics and so-called ethics have all played their role in changing the rules of the game.

Yet for the last hundred years the emphasis had always been on trying to read the soul of the criminal and that is what, to a certain extent, I've tried to do with the story of the Hatton Garden robbery. Were these guys really obliged to carry out one last big job, or did they simply reignite those instincts because they were bored with their lives and knew they didn't have long left? Many have attempted to prove that criminal characteristics are inherited. Others will argue, on almost Marxist terms, that 'society has the criminals it deserves'. In other words, society causes crime. In the case of the Hatton Garden crew, there do seem to have been a few clues that point in that direction. Many of them had difficult relationships with their families; uncontrolled juvenile lives on the streets; a brutal fight for survival from a young age.

As we now know, these men were very much criminals in the traditional sense. In simple terms, they refused to accept life as they found it. They didn't just want to steal an apple from a tree, they wanted to burn the orchard down as well. The gang were in effect the archetypal scavengers, on the lookout for an opportunity. No doubt they all suffered badly from long bouts of boredom and depression that could often be conquered only by committing crime.

Friends and relatives say that these men often felt stifled and trapped, viewing crime and sometimes occasional violence as the only means of escaping from the straitjacket. Many of these gangsters were complete criminals, their very existence a chain reaction, which could only end in their death or imprisonment.

Men like these didn't need to stub their toe to react. They were constantly on tenterhooks prepared to hit back at society because they didn't feel they owed it anything. Like many criminals, they also never saw themselves as being in the wrong and if they did say sorry, it was an unnatural response in a moment of weakness, which they would undoubtedly later regret.

For these old-school villains truly were the strangers among us, never one of us, despite the seemingly normal lives they often led back home. Many labels have been hung on these characters but no description can tell even half the story. Yes, they are rebels and some may even be psychopaths; but these are nothing more than two shorthand symbols for a state of mind, which is hate. Freud said that if a baby had power, it would destroy the world from the frustration of its infantile desires. In some ways, these men were each that baby, who quite simply never grew up. That's why they felt so superior to everyone around them and confident enough to try and pull off the Crime of the Century.

At the height of their criminal prowess in the sixties and seventies, the rules of the game were being constantly challenged. Yet young criminals even back then needed rules to ensure their lives had some meaning. The gang's aggressive instincts were undoubtedly born out of sheer frustration with the world. It all seemed so meaningless to many of them. There was that feeling of hopeless drifting. As their crimes started to bring in previously unimagined wealth, they also committed some offences like stealing cars purely for the thrill. But even in this environment there was a structure emerging. Codes and ranks within a gang were to be obeyed to the letter. This was a classic example of men seeking a purposeful group identity.

So, when these old pros were youngsters, like so many before and since they reacted partly against their own feelings of inadequacy. Many of their contemporaries say that if the Hatton Garden Mob had had more self-knowledge when they were younger then maybe they would not have struck out for a life of crime with such determination. These characters are basically self-destructive because their lives had little or no real purpose – and yet they loved their families deeply and in some cases remained married to one woman for their entire adult life.

Throwing men like the Hatton Garden robbers into prison will do nothing to stem the problem. They were classic examples of professional criminals intrinsically lacking in the normal psychological vitamins. Their whole life was an act of hunger. To treat them properly would have required an examination of their psyche and that is rarely achieved in anyone's actual lifetime. You see, punishment is very much wasted on these guys. It's no better than caging an animal demented by hunger and expecting it to simply reform. The kind of hunger these characters suffered from bred a terrible hatred that fed on itself.

There was undoubtedly something seductive about the life Brian Reader and Terry Perkins and some of these old villains had led in the past. They appeared to the general public to be the last of a dying breed who, despite their crimes, still relied on those old-fashioned virtues of courage and loyalty. Their lives seemed to stand and fall on the strength of friendships. They'd all taken to crime in the first place to escape dire poverty and the tedious, repetitive wages their families and friends had slaved for over such a long period of time.

These guys clearly saw obedience to the law and collaboration with the police as a betrayal of their own people, which would mean losing all self-respect. But it was their all-consuming love of gambling that was probably the most pertinent facet of their personalities. There seems little doubt that even if they'd known before the raid that there was, at best, a one in five chance they'd escape with the loot, they'd still have taken a punt on the Crime of the Century.

Richard Hobbs, a sociologist at the University of Essex who studies crime in Britain, says the country's criminal underworld has changed dramatically in recent years. Rather than congregating in pubs or on street corners, many criminals now live seemingly ordinary lives, raising families and running legitimate businesses. They still participate in crime, but only with trusted associates. 'They don't see themselves as criminals, they see themselves as businessmen,' Hobbs says.

In many ways the Hatton Garden Mob tried to work like a business syndicate. They saw themselves as the old executives of crime trying to make one more big bonus before retiring for good.

POSTSCRIPT

Shortly after completing this book, I got a call from two gangsters called Ray and Terry, who'd helped me when I was on a research trip to their 'manor', just near Brian Reader's home town of Dartford, in Kent. They'd both moved back to the UK in recent years because there was no 'work' for them out in Spain. Their 'speciality' had been smuggling cocaine and cannabis on small yachts across the Mediterranean. Both men had spent ten years on the Costa del Crime but, in their words, 'there's nothing left there. The place is like a desert. It had become impossible to make any money, straight or crooked.'

Ray and Terry both know two of the main ringleaders of the Hatton Garden raid but their opinion of that particular crime will surprise many. They said: 'Why did they bother? It just wasn't worth it. The times have gone when you could pull off a stunt like that one. The police have got the equipment to trace every part of your life these days. They can even tell you when you last shagged yer old woman. I'm not kiddin'. Stealing is yesterday's game and those old boys shoulda realized it from the start.'

BILLY

I tried to contact Billy – my primary source – at his old folks' home just after finishing the writing of this book in late January 2016. But he was feeling a bit poorly so I decided to leave it for a couple of weeks.

Then I remembered something Billy told me at the end of our series of meetings during the summer of 2015.

'Crime really doesn't pay,' he said. 'If I had my time again, I'd opt for a happy, safe, law abiding life anytime. The Hatton Garden lads are a living testimony to that.'

ACKNOWLEDGEMENTS

The Hatton Garden Job was a quintessentially English crime. A throwback to the days when gangs of 'blaggers' ruled the streets of London. During that so-called golden era of crime – between 1960 and 1990 – robbery was as profitable as the drugs trade later became. Fortunes were made and lost with alarming regularity. Some villains paid for their mistakes with their lives, others spent long periods in prison.

I have delved inside this criminal netherworld to reveal a unique story that is much more than just a book about one headline-hitting event. It's about a *way of life*; a mentality that was shaped by the bomb sites alongside the Thames and the dodgy characters who dominated south-east England during the chaotic post-war period.

As an author, I try to occupy the 'middle ground' when I write about such criminals. It's not my job to take sides and hopefully that enabled me to produce an accurate, balanced account of the Hatton Garden Job. My intention was to reveal what drove these men to commit such an outrageous crime. Did their chosen 'career path' come from a need to provide for their families or just a deep-seated determination to break the law at all costs? Either way it doesn't give them a licence to commit crime. But it's important mention here because many presume such people would not

ACKNOWLEDGEMENTS

hesitate to pull out a gun and shoot anyone who got in their way. But that simply isn't how it works in the *real* underworld, where the leaders of the Hatton Garden Mob all hail from.

In *Sexy Beasts* I've charted the work and domestic lives of the main characters leading up to and including the Hatton Garden Job. It's inevitable that I've missed out a few 'faces' and maybe even a few of the facts. So, to those individuals I say sorry, although I'm not sure if any of them will mind!

Then there were the retired police officers – some of them ex-Flying Squad – who helped me on behalf of their serving colleagues, following a short-sighted Scotland Yard clampdown on officers talking frankly and openly to journalists. Again, I can't name them for obvious reasons but their contribution to this book has been immeasurable.

Some of the dialogue represented here was constructed from available documents and court records, some was drawn from tape-recorded testimony and some was reconstituted from the memory of participants. Historic references were carefully researched from archive material.

One villain I *can* thank for his help is Billy. I wove his story into this book because of his unique perspective about the Hatton Garden Job and its eventual conclusion. Billy's contribution helped make this the *real* story behind the headlines. And with the help of Billy and others I have made some informed deductions for dramatic purposes. But the actual facts remain as they occurred.

I just hope you enjoyed reading *Sexy Beasts* as much as I have enjoyed writing and researching it.

Wensley Clarkson
London, 2016

APPENDIX

THE SEXY BEASTS

BRIAN READER – *pleaded guilty, Conspiracy to Burgle, and sentenced to six years and three months*

His continuing ill-health has meant numerous hospital visits from Belmarsh Prison that culminated in Reader having a stroke and missing the sentencing hearing at Woolwich Crown Court between March 7 and 9, 2016. Relatives and friends regularly visit him, possibly even a couple of members of the Monday Club in Dartford. Until his stroke, Reader had tried to exercise a lot in the prison gym but that's now a thing of the past. He appreciated the comradeship of prison life and admitted to feeling less lonely these days, although he still misses Lyn desperately.

TERRY PERKINS – *pleaded guilty, Conspiracy to Burgle, and sentenced to seven years*

He struggles with heart problems and diabetes but at least he gets full health cover inside prison. Perkins is a much more gregarious character than Reader and enjoys playing chess and entertaining other inmates with stories about his legendary 'work' in the underworld.

APPENDIX: THE SEXY BEASTS

DANNY JONES – *pleaded guilty, Conspiracy to Burgle, and sentenced to seven years*

He adores being one of Belmarsh's biggest celebrities and plays his part to perfection. Jones keeps super trim in the gym and has adjusted well to prison life, thanks in part to his regimented lifestyle back home where he always insisted on a lockdown every day at 5 p.m.

KENNY COLLINS – *pleaded guilty, Conspiracy to Burgle, and sentenced to seven years*

He sleeps a lot in his cell and doesn't join in with many of the prison activities. Collins finds it hard talking to the 'foreigners' on his wing and he openly tells anyone who will listen that he wishes he'd handed all the gems back within a couple of days of the raid.

CARL WOOD – *Conspiracy to Burgle – Guilty; Conspiracy to Money Launder – Guilty and sentenced to six years*

He's still the loner in the pack. Hardly talks to the others and continues trying to juggle his huge domestic debts from inside his own prison cell. Wood no doubt feels he should have trusted his own instincts and never got involved with Jones and the others in the first place.

BILLY LINCOLN – *Conspiracy to Burgle – Guilty; Conspiracy to Money Launder – Guilty and sentenced to seven years*

Avoids the prison gym like the plague due to his own lack of fitness. Lincoln finds prison life difficult and, like Collins, he spends much of his time asleep in his cell trying to forget about what might have been.

HUGHIE DOYLE – *Conspiracy to Money Launder – Guilty and given a suspended sentence. Money Laundering (alternative charge) – No Verdict Taken*

Remained chirpy despite the prison sentence that hung over him while he was out on bail until sentencing, Doyle then avoided any further jail time. He was back to work as a plumber within hours of the end of the trial/sentencing and still claims he's innocent. One friend described him as 'the most unlikely criminal you will ever meet'.

JON HARBINSON – *Conspiracy to Burgle – Not Guilty; Conspiracy to Money Launder – Not Guilty*

Innocent of all involvement, he still finds it hard to work out how he got dragged into the criminal world of his uncle Billy Lincoln and all the other members of the Hatton Garden gang. Tells friends he hasn't recovered from the pain and anguish caused by many months in custody before his trial.

It's the biggest job that could have ever been. It will never happen again. The biggest job in the fuckin' world – and we was on that cunt.

Terry Perkins, Hatton Garden gang member

THE LAST WORD

'Now it's all over, I suppose I may dare say it's been a most remarkable coup'

Pendlebury, *The Lavender Hill Mob*, 1951